Citizen Engagement: Lessons in Participation from Local Government

**Katherine A. Graham
Susan D. Phillips
Editors**

Monographs on Canadian Public Administration – No. 22
Monographies sur l'administration publique canadienne – No. 22

© L'Institut d'administration publique du Canada, 1998
The Institute of Public Administration of Canada, 1998

ALL RIGHTS RESERVED / TOUS DROITS RÉSERVÉS

Canadian Cataloguing in Publication Data

Main entry under title:

Citizen engagement : lessons in participation from local government

(Monographs on Canadian public administration ; 22)

Includes some text in French.
ISBN 0-920715-78-8

1. Municipal government – Canada – Citizen participation. I. Phillips, Susan S. II. Graham, Katherine A., 1947– . III. Institute of Public Administration of Canada. IV. Series.

JS1708.C46 1998   320.8'5'0971   C98-931110-4

PUBLISHED BY / PUBLIÉ PAR

L'INSTITUT D'ADMINISTRATION PUBLIQUE DU CANADA
THE INSTITUTE OF PUBLIC ADMINISTRATION OF CANADA
1075, rue Bay St., Suite/Bureau 401
Toronto, Ontario, CANADA M5S 2B1
Tel./Tél.: (416) 924-8787   Fax/Bél.: (416) 924-4992
e-mail/courrier élect.: ntl@ipaciapc.ca

Table of Contents

Foreword v

Acknowledgements vii

Chapter 1
Making Public Participation More Effective: Issues for Local
    Government 1
Katherine A. Graham and Susan D. Phillips

Chapter 2
Economic Development: The Public's Role in Shaping
    Winnipeg's Economic Future 25
Jeff Fielding and Gerry Couture

Chapter 3
More Than One Way Towards Economic Development: Public
    Participation and Policy-making in the Vancouver Region 49
Patrick J. Smith

Chapter 4
Helping the Public to Participate in Planning 78
John Sewell

Chapter 5
Les conseils de quartier à Québec 94
Jean Dionne, Céline Faucher and André Martel

CONTENTS

Chapter 6
Expanding the Frontiers of Public Participation:
    Public Involvement in Municipal Budgeting and Finance 113
W. Michael Fenn

Chapter 7
Public Participation in the Budgeting Process:
    Edmonton's Ongoing Experiment 137
Edward C. LeSage Jr.

Chapter 8
Negotiating, Arbitrating, Legislating: Where was the Public
    in London's Boundary Adjustment? 163
Andrew Sancton

Chapter 9
Public Participation in Restructuring Local Government to
    Create the City of Miramichi 188
John C. Robison

Chapter 10
Local Governments On-Line: How are They Doing it and
    What Does it Mean? 200
Monica Gattinger

Chapter 11
Conclusion: From Public Participation to Citizen Engagement .. 223
Susan D. Phillips and Katherine A. Graham

Contributors 241

Foreword

One of the core functions of the Intergovernmental Committee on Urban and Regional Research (ICURR) is to provide Canadian local governments with the latest information on the how-to of problem-solving and on the trends and developments that arise in the planning and management of communities.

In keeping with this valued function, we are pleased to be associated with this new study on how to make public participation in local government more effective. Not only are the nine case studies Canadian in context, they also represent four areas of key interest to ICURR's funders and clients: economic development; land-use planning; municipal finance; and local government restructuring.

We are pleased to endorse a work that is not only practical in approach (each chapter can easily stand on its own, as can each subject area) but that also investigates public participation in local government in its many incarnations. The authors document both unqualified successes in public participation (as in the case of Winnipeg's economic-development strategy) and those initiatives that could benefit from improvements (as set out in the discussion of public involvement in Edmonton's budget preparation). Nor is the future neglected. "Electronic democracy," as applied in Ottawa and Ottawa-Carleton, is accorded its due place among the changing ways in which local governments seek to involve their citizens. This fine and new contribution to the literature on public involvement in municipal decision-making is particularly welcome, as much of the country reconsiders the structure and powers of local governments.

In my capacity as executive director of the Intergovernmental Committee on Urban and Regional Research, and on behalf of the board that steers our organization, I would like to thank the Institute of Public

FOREWORD

Administration of Canada for giving us the opportunity to participate in the development of this timely and practical study.

André Lanteigne
Executive Director
Intergovernmental Committee on Urban and Regional Research

Acknowledgements

This volume is very much the result of a collaborative effort. When we were first approached to lead the IPAC Study Team on Public Participation in Local Government, we knew that the project would require the enthusiastic participation of people who work in local government, as well as those engaged in more academic study of the subject. We have benefited from the enthusiasm and energy of our colleagues on the team. They showed wonderful commitment to their own chapters. Equally, if not more important, they quickly engaged each other in discussions about what we were trying to accomplish and what we might conclude from our study.

We had other help, as well. Maurice Demers, then of IPAC, made the initial call to ask us to undertake this project. Subsequently, Don Lenihan provided excellent support and encouragement. He was very much a member of the team. His IPAC colleague, Geoff McIlroy, was responsible for shepherding the manuscript through the review and production phases. We would also like to thank the IPAC research committee for its enthusiasm and support. We are particularly indebted to professors Iain Gow and Paul Pross for their attentive work in managing the review process and to the two anonymous reviewers for their constructive comments. The Intergovernmental Committee on Urban and Regional Research (ICURR) provided financial assistance and, through its executive director, assistance on substantive matters.

Colleagues within the School of Public Administration at Carleton University also played a key role in coordinating the work of the study team and in producing this volume. We thank particularly Jacqueline Carberry, Martha Clark and Iris Taylor. Barbara Rose, now a graduate of the School of Public Administration, served as a research assistant in the early stages of the project.

ACKNOWLEDGEMENTS

We could not have produced this volume without our collaborators and the others who helped. Responsibility for the final product, however, rests with us.

Katherine A. Graham
Susan D. Phillips

School of Public Administration,
Carleton University

June 1998

1

Making Public Participation More Effective: Issues for Local Government

Katherine A. Graham and Susan D. Phillips

Instead of dismissing demands for "no new taxes" by taxpayer groups as a lack of understanding of the complexity of the budgeting process, the City of Burlington turns its concerns into constructive reform by establishing a citizens' jury that consists of a cross-section of residents, including some of the city's most prominent critics. After several months of informed deliberation, the jury recommends significant changes to both the city's budget and its budgeting process that exceed everyone's expectations.[1] A "virtual" conference on homelessness organized by the City of Santa Monica, California, (and later emulated by other cities) using the Internet connects homeless people with city officials and with more affluent citizens.[2] Increased awareness of the difficulties faced by homeless people leads directly to the creation of new facilities for the homeless in the community. In formulating official land-use plans in both Toronto and Vancouver, city planners invite elementary and secondary school children to share their views about their city's future.[3] The kids say it was "fun," and they learned how hard it is for the city to come up with new ideas to improve things. As Winnipeg tries to create a new economic-development strategy, the city struggles to include participation by the aboriginal, transient and poor residents of downtown, people who seldom come to public meetings.[4] Cleverly, city officials reach these marginal populations through their primary, and trusted, points of contact with the administration: public-health nurses are thus recruited as agents of social change.

Local governments have played long-standing roles in the institutionalization of public participation and in the development of innovative ways to engage citizens in policy-making. The opening vignettes raise a number of important questions, however, regarding the contemporary and future practice of public participation in local governments in Canada. Although local governments have been conducting public participation as a routine part of land-use planning for over twenty-five years, they increasingly are being confronted with the need to undertake citizen engagement in new areas such as budgeting, economic development, and political restructuring. The methods that had been tailored to dealing with development issues must now be modified or replaced by new approaches that can appropriately engage citizens in other policy areas.

Citizens no longer see public participation as an "opportunity," graciously granted by the council and administration; it is regarded as a basic service and an integral part of local governance. As municipalities move towards models of "citizen-centred" government – where citizens expect to take part in the planning of services that will be designed around them – and as governments struggle to re-build bonds with citizens after periods of severe financial stringency and cutbacks, citizens have greater expectations than ever for public participation as a tool of governance. On the other hand, an emerging philosophy of governance that focuses on citizen and community responsibility has created new expectations *of* the public. Rather than simply offering personal opinions, regardless of whether these opinions have been well thought out, participants are now expected to offer *informed* opinions and to be willing to make tough choices. This understanding has sparked a greater interest in those participation mechanisms that provide opportunities for deliberation that extends over time, as was the case with Burlington's citizens' jury, rather than in mechanisms that merely gather information or involve people in one-shot events such as public meetings. But, this unfolding philosophy also places a greater onus on governments to be accountable to citizens for how public input is used in policy-making.

The new technology of the Internet is creating both new opportunities to reach people and new challenges to ensure equitable access. Is virtual conferencing through the Internet a good substitute for face-to-face participation? Can the Internet provide a useful mix of expert research, background information, and effective participation by citizens? Who gains greater access using this technology: primarily the affluent with their own personal computers and primarily men? Will the new technology revolutionize the process of public participation, or is it merely the latest fad in communication techniques whose utility for the purpose of citizen involvement in decision-making will soon fade quietly away?

These vignettes also underscore the challenge, too often ignored in the past, of determining the basic goal of public participation in the first place and the criteria for evaluating its success or failure. Is its purpose to get concrete and detailed information in order to make "better" decisions? Is it to allow people to feel engaged in the process? Or is the main objective of participation to leave something lasting – enhanced leadership capacity, a sense of political efficacy, or new organizations – in the community? For instance, after consulting with thousands of residents, Vancouver's CityPlan produced a vision based on a "city of neighbourhoods" that would offer affordable housing, good jobs close to home, more parks, clean air and water, and more money for arts and culture. As many critics asked, did it really take a massive public-participation exercise costing $1.9 million to produce this set of platitudes?[5] Are people able to make difficult choices among alternatives, or are these generalities about all that we can expect? Or, are these generalities precisely what we need? Many critics of public consultation see public participation activities as a *chimera* – some might say a cop-out – for a lack of political leadership by elected officials. At minimum, critics are asking what the relationship should be between public participation and the political level. How is public participation actually used in arriving at policy decisions? The fact that these kinds of questions are being posed with considerable regularity points to an emerging backlash in some circles against the value and costs of public participation.

Winnipeg's experiment of reaching out to marginalized populations highlights a final recurring theme for public-participation practitioners. Who is the public? Faced with growing cultural diversity, most local governments have worked hard to broaden participation – to reach out to the non-white, non–middle class, and non-suburban citizens who normally have little contact with city hall. But in many cases, the relationship of local governments with cultural communities or marginalized groups remains tangential and sporadic. The Winnipeg example also shows that *within* city hall, public participation is being rescued from being the almost exclusive domain of planners and public-participation "professionals" to involving a wider array of front-line staff who interact more frequently with marginal and diverse groups. As we will see, working in an environment of diversity requires us to address questions such as where and how citizens, in fact, access or have contact with their local governments. How do different groups use services and how can they be brought into the policy process to express their concerns?

It also forces us to think about how both individuals and interest groups are heard. In many cases, public participation is used as an attempt to hear from individual members of the public as a means of counterbalancing, sometimes even downplaying, participation by groups that are already mobilized and vocal on the issues. Thus, a critical challenge for local governments is to find constructive ways to work with both individuals and interest groups and to situate public participation activities in the broader politics and ongoing political processes.

This collection explores the evolving art of public participation in local governments in Canada. By "public participation" we mean the deliberate and active engagement of citizens by the council and/or administration – outside the electoral process – in making public-policy decisions or in setting strategic directions. Increasingly, public participation cannot be thought of as a single event or series of events, such as public meetings or citizens' panels, through which citizens are involved. Rather, it is an ongoing approach to doing civic business. As the new challenges and persistent problems raised by the opening vignettes indicate, public participation is at a point of critical reassessment by politicians, managers, interest groups, and citizens alike. Due to rapidly changing urban environments and fundamental rethinking of the nature of governance, municipalities need to re-visit and re-evaluate some of the basic issues of why and how they engage citizens in policy-making and service delivery. The attempt to respond to many of the challenges outlined in this volume – to make participation more deliberative, inclusive, innovative, and central to governance – has begun to produce a shift in language. At all levels of government, the language of "public participation" is giving way to that of "citizen engagement" as a signal that these challenges are being taken seriously.

As a first step in rethinking and re-designing public-participation practices for local governments, it is important to understand how we arrived at this critical juncture and what baggage has been acquired along the way. This introductory chapter proceeds by briefly reviewing the basic assumptions on which the public-participation practices of the 1990s have been built and re-visits some of the recurring dilemmas outlined in the literature. It then explores in more depth some of the emerging challenges of a changing environment to which local governments must respond. It concludes with an overview of the case studies that form the backbone of our research and that are presented in their full form in subsequent chapters.

LOOKING BACK

Rethinking future directions for public participation requires an appreciation of its origins so that the essential debates and tensions that have been formative in determining contemporary practice may be better understood. As a starting point, it is essential to remind ourselves that local governments are very different from provincial or federal governments in the conventional ways in which they relate to citizens. Based on underlying principles of open government, municipal council meetings are open to the public, and a citizen can make representation to council or its committees simply by requesting a place on the agenda. Few people hesitate to call up their councillors if they have a concern or a complaint. In addition, most municipalities have provisions for direct democracy that allow citizens to vote on important issues through plebiscites or to petition council to force on the ballot a question on an issue of community importance. In many of the larger Canadian cities, there are highly developed networks of neighbourhood organizations that serve as liaison between citizens and council and that can be vocal advocates for their communities if ignored. Finally, it is relatively easy for citizens to appeal the decisions of municipal councils to an independent quasi-judiciary body or, in some instances, to the provincial legislature.

Given these multiple avenues for political involvement outside of the electoral process, it may seem strange that organized public participation is required or even encouraged by city councils and administrations. But, the politics of local government is also the politics of everyday life. Development projects, zoning amendments, reductions in service delivery, or the pursuit of particular economic-development strategies are highly visible, and their potential effects seem intuitively and immediately tangible to citizens who want to have a say in how quality of life will be affected by municipal decisions. And citizens have also come to expect that they will be heard. Ironically, then, rather than producing public complacency, open government has produced stronger demands by the public for participation.

Canadian municipal governments were encouraged to make public participation a component of their decision-making processes in the late 1960s and early 1970s for two reasons: growing citizen involvement in 1) the municipal land-use planning process; and 2) community development and activism. Public input in land-use planning was seen by municipal governments as an additional source of information, and, by incorporating more information into the planning process, better plans and decisions could result. Furthermore, allowing public input in the early stages of the planning process was a more productive use of time and resources. As cities in the 1970s proceeded with development plans, they often encountered at late stages in the planning process community groups bent on stopping a particular development. Thus, it seemed more efficient to give citizens information about the proposed land-use plan, get their reaction early in the process, and avoid organized protests or appeals later on, after much time and money had already been invested. Provincial governments eventually mandated municipal governments to include public participation as a requisite part of the development of official plans.

Municipal government initiatives to involve citizens were paralleled by community activists' efforts to involve the public in community development. The thinking was that community-development initiatives that involve citizens in decision-making build healthier communities and nourish democracy by enhancing civic education and by producing effective citizens who are less alienated from political institutions.[6] This was understood by Saul Alinsky, a Chicago community activist in the 1930s through 1950s, who stressed and developed techniques for community empowerment.[7] During the late 1960s and early 1970s, the Canadian federal government promoted "social animation" activities by providing grants to local organizations and by supporting activists in the Company of Young Canadians who were helping to expand the organizational capacity of disadvantaged communities.[8] Urban-reform movements of the 1970s were fuelled by the notion of neighbourhood control, as groups of citizens tried – with considerable success – to stop major urban-renewal projects such as Toronto's Spadina Expressway or the razing of Vancouver's Chinatown.[9] More recently, the importance of community organizing has been revitalized under the concept of "social capital," a term first used by Jane Jacobs in 1961 and made popular in the 1990s by the work of Robert Putnam.[10] Social capital refers to horizontal networks of volunteer community-based organizations. In his study of democracy in Italy, Robert Putnam provides both a good theoretical and empirical case that social capital builds social trust and mutual cooperation among citizens, bolsters performance of the polity, and contributes to more efficient government and a stronger economy.[11] Indeed, he argues that "good government in Italy is a by-product of singing groups and soccer clubs."[12]

Over time, much to the delight and largely because of planners, public participation was routinized and became a regular, sometimes mandatory, feature of local planning. As it became routine, participation was also "professionalized" and thereby came to be the almost exclusive purview of planners and a new industry of other professionals who specialized in facilitating and organizing participation exercises for governments. This professionalization is widely regarded as one of the reasons for the failure of public participation in the 1970s: professional planners were unwilling to share their technical expertise (which gave them control over the planning process) with communities, whose expertise was based on popular knowledge. The planners' solution was to control the participation process as well.[13] A more charitable view is that most planners were genuinely interested in making participation work, but professionalization was a natural result of making participation part of their repertoire of planning techniques. Because this "professionalization" of participation has forced a focus on refining appropriate techniques, much of what has been written on public participation has missed many of the big issues of governance and the changing nature of community life. Governments often measure the effectiveness of participation by counting the number of people who participated, no matter how shallow the involvement – attending a meeting or calling a 1-800 number is usually sufficient to be counted. Thus, while there were many innovations in participation and expansion of who participated over the course of the 1970s and 1980s, the standardization of practices meant that participation also became more narrow in its definition and limited in its impact.[14]

At the same time, community activists, for the most part, were preoccupied not with the question of defining the kind of communities they wanted and of developing lasting social capital but with the NIMBY syndrome – "not-in-my-back-yard" – and thus with using community power to stop particular projects and prevent the siting of unwanted facilities, such as group homes, in their neighbourhoods.[15] Because the type of public participation undertaken by local governments seldom involved real power-sharing, many community activists acquired a deep sense of mistrust of planners and of the planning process. To activists, invited participation often seemed little more than "a ritual dance of tell and sell."[16]

The two means through which public participation became an integral part of the decsion-making process in municipal governments – the land-use planning process and the impact of community activism – have left a lasting legacy on practice. This has been evident in the literature since the first contemporary taxonomy of public participation – Sherry Arnstein's classic ladder of participation – was published in 1969.[17] This legacy consists of an ongoing tension between the view that more information from the public should be obtained in order to produce better decisions and the view that real power in decision-making should be shared with citizens. This basic tension is played out in the literature on public participation and in practice, through a series of recurring themes and questions.

When to Undertake Public Participation?

Is public participation appropriate for all policy decisions and for all departments? This central question arises from the dangerous temptation by many local governments to play it safe by featuring a participation component on every issue, even if public involvement is primarily a token gesture. This is a strategy that almost surely backfires. In general, the literature concludes that conducting public participation is legitimate only if it can actually make a difference to the policy decision at hand and only if the sponsoring government is prepared to commit the requisite time and resources to make it effective. If a decision needs to be made very quickly, if the local government has minimal room to manoeuvre or is unwilling to dedicate the resources required to make it meaningful, participation is pointless.

Why Have Public Participation?

Public participation has been designed with a diversity of objectives in mind, including information-sharing, accountability and legitimization, education, community empowerment and actual power-sharing. Perhaps the most common source of conflict and disappointment in public participation is that citizens believe they are engaging in power-sharing and will have a real impact on the agenda and outcomes, while government officials presume that they are merely gathering information on a fixed agenda under restrictive terms of reference. Thus, a vital concern is to have goals and expectations clarified. It may seem naïve to think that goals and expectations will always be declared or will otherwise be transparent. Experience suggests, however, that effective public participation is best approached as a kind of "contract," with the potential and limitations as clearly identified as possible, so that people can properly assess whether it will be worthwhile being involved at all. The delineation of parameters includes spelling out the real limits on public participation by indicating what is really negotiable and what aspects are beyond the authority of local government to decide or deliver. Then, the methods for participation need to be selected to match the goals. While some techniques, such as ongoing relations with neighbourhood associations and citizen advocacy groups, may help to empower communities, others, such as surveys and meetings, can do little more than access information.

Who Should Participate?

The issue of who should participate has been a persistent one in both the literature and in practice. One paradox of participation, as Walter Rosenbaum pointedly observes, is that administrative discretion allows officials to ignore some publics while privileging others: "Often agencies seek to avoid defining the 'publics' to be included in participation activities by retreating into a preoccupation with procedures (public information, notices, hearings, and the like), but the effect, nonetheless, is to create, or perpetuate, an influence structure indulging some interests at the expense of others."[18] Defining and targeting an audience involves deciding whether public participation is to be extensive (i.e., involving large numbers of people but allowing fairly minimal individual contributions) or intensive (i.e., involving few people but allowing a large donation of time by each participant). Sponsors must also decide whether to involve citizens speaking and participating as individuals or as representatives of interest groups or constituencies, speaking on behalf of others. These alternatives encompass important trade-offs. While the advantages of reaching large numbers of people are that awareness of an issue is raised in the population as a whole and people have an opportunity to vent their feelings, the minimal commitment involved in going to a public meeting or responding to a customer survey seldom changes people's views or empowers communities.[19] In contrast, small groups of participants selected by the government may be likely to develop innovative solutions and to reach a consensus, but they also run the risk of being condemned by those on the outside as élitist or as unrepresentative. In the current political climate, the ability to be representative and to reach out to traditionally underrepresented communities is absolutely essential. Yet, government departments often avoid these difficult questions of representation, relying instead on the methods chosen to draw out those who are interested. It is often wrongly assumed that lack of involvement is due to apathy rather than due to techniques that are ill-suited to involving the target populations. In short, getting the right people in the right context, and vice versa, is key to effective engagements.

What Resources are Required?

Public participation does not come naturally to most government departments. Whereas participation requires openness, flexibility and responsiveness, traditional bureaucracies are built on foundations of hierarchy, with authority flowing from the top down, secrecy, professional autonomy, and rational planning that values experts and technical information over popular knowledge. Consequently, most government departments need to prepare themselves for participation by initiating some degree of institutional and attitudinal change. Effective participation can seldom merely be grafted onto traditional bureaucracies.[20]

Many local governments solve this problem by creating teams or units of participation experts or by hiring consultants. The process is handed off to these experts, who are not only the behind-the-scenes organizers of participation activities, but the front-line personnel interacting with citizens. As experience indicates, the danger in this approach is that the actual policy-makers are isolated from the process such that public input is simply another report compiled by – and mediated through – the participation experts. Thus, the likelihood that new ideas will emerge or that attitude change will occur where it is most needed – at the level of senior managers and politicians – is greatly reduced.

The literature also reveals that the capacity of citizen organizations may need to be developed or expanded before they can be effective participants. The comparative analysis of participation in American cities by Jeffrey Berry and his colleagues demonstrates that an increased capacity of neighbourhood associations contributes to a sense of empowerment in relations with government and is thus a critical vehicle in making public participation work effectively.[21] An important resource in building this capacity is information. The open provision of information from the department to the public in an accessible form and the responsiveness to requests by citizens for further information is vital. But government agencies also need to reassess what is regarded as legitimate "data" provided to them by citizens. The role of many potential participants is often restricted, because government will only deal with information that is codified, refutable and validated by experts. Popular knowledge, by contrast, often has been treated as myth, mere opinion or emotion, rather than as one form of useful data.

What Works?

The final dilemma posed in the literature is how we assess whether public participation "worked." In most cases, a very broad definition of success is required. Effective public participation is not simply obtaining good information. It also involves asking how the process affected relations with citizens, contributed to individual and community effectiveness and resources, and whether it made government agencies more responsive to the public. These outcomes need to be evaluated, even if they were not the intended objectives of the exercise. The problem, of course, is that many of these impacts are difficult to measure. Enhanced community empowerment and better government–citizen relations may only become evident over the longer term, long after the evaluation of the process has been completed, and many of the factors that contributed to positive (or negative) results, such as the casual conversations over dozens of cups of coffee between the community planner and community leaders, may be relatively invisible.

Evaluating the effectiveness also requires that administrators look hard at their own organizations. It is too easy to assume that because only five people came to the public meeting held by the department, people do not care about the issues at stake. More critical examination might reveal that people were not provided with adequate, accessible information in order to fully comprehend the potential effects of the issues on their lives. Finally, it should not be presumed that because a consensus was not reached, the process failed. On many issues, consensus can never be obtained, because there are fundamentally different views on the origins and nature of the problem and there is a diversity of community needs and interests. Even in the presence of deep divisions over desired policy outcomes, however, the participation process may still be regarded as successful, if people feel that they had a fair and meaningful opportunity to be involved.

Given these guidelines, which have already been developed by the existing literature, is there anything new to be learned about effective public participation? The need for reassessment and new directions, however, is not merely a result of the failure of practitioners to heed the recommendations offered by the literature and past experience. Rather, it is necessitated by the changing contexts of local governance and cities themselves. Consequently, there is still considerable scope for learning.

LOOKING AROUND

In this section, we explore the four most significant changes in governance, urban life and technology that are re-shaping how local governments interact with citizens.

The Nature of Governance

The first major change is in the very nature of governance, a change that has been taking shape since the late 1980s. This shift has been propelled, in part, by the fiscal crisis that has resulted in cuts to transfers by the federal and provincial governments and the offloading of responsibilities to both local governments and the voluntary sector. It has also been shaped, in part, by the "customer-service revolution" and the experimentation by municipalities with a wide variety of alternative service delivery (ASD) mechanisms. The customer revolution has meant that residents are no longer seen as passive users or even as "shareholders" for whom government, usually as a monopoly provider, determines what kind and level of services they should receive for their share of property taxes. Rather, they are now viewed as "customers." What customers value most is choice and responsiveness. Thus, local governments have embraced the use of citizen surveys, focus groups, and other tools from the marketer's kitbag to get to the specifics of local preferences and have sought a multitude of ways to enhance choice and improve service. For local governments, ASD has also included co-production of services with voluntary organizations, becoming more entrepreneurial and enterprising, contracting-out services, providing one-stop shopping for building and other permits, and the creation of integrated service-delivery teams.[22] As a result of reduced grants and taxpayer revolts against higher taxes, most municipalities have also been forced to make difficult choices about which services to provide and which to cut or make subject to user-fees. Although federal and provincial governments have also joined the movement for better customer service and ASD under the rubric of the "new public management" – a term made enormously popular by David Osborne and Ted Gaebler in their 1992 book – it is important to note that local governments are not newcomers to this change in governing style. In fact, they were pioneers of it. Indeed, Osborne and Gaebler essentially reported the existing practices of city managers rather than presenting entirely new ideas that revolutionized local approaches.[23]

These changes in governance have significant implications for the conduct of public participation. First of all, local governments have had to undertake public participation in entirely new spheres of policy, such as budgeting, economic development, delivery of services, and the reform of municipal and regional institutions, in which they previously had made few serious attempts to involve the public at all. However, the standard procedures for engaging the public had been designed to be applied in land-use planning. As we will see in the case studies, this mismatch has necessitated considerable innovation.

Second, the desire to be responsive to customers and the need to make fundamental choices about which services to continue to provide and which to eliminate requires that local governments know their communities and community preferences well. This has not necessarily been the case in many municipalities. For instance, in his examination of participation in the budgeting process in this volume, Michael Fenn relates the amusing results of a customer-service survey done by the City of Burlington that canvassed councillors, senior management, and a cross-section of city staff, as well as the general public. The results indicated close congruency in views about services between council and senior management and between rank-and-file employees and the public, but there was a big gap between the perspectives of council/senior management, on one hand, and the staff/public, on the other. It appears that local governments cannot always rely on their commissioners or councillors to have an accurate perception of the needs of the customer.

Third, local governments increasingly are entangled with community groups, not just as consumers and customers, but as co-producers of services as well. These new relationships require both a new respect for the voluntary-sector partners and methods for ensuring that they can fulfil their roles as service providers.

Finally, local governments recognize that they need to re-establish their credibility with the public, because credibility has been greatly diminished in the past decade as part of the public's general scepticism towards politicians and political institutions. This should give politicians a renewed, vested interest in making public participation work and a reason to be involved directly rather than leaving it to the professionals. At the same time, however, there is a growing political backlash against public participation as it historically has been practiced. In part, this is due to severe financial constraints, which means that councils are unwilling to commit large sums of money for participation exercises. But, it is also a result of a rising populism among elected officials who feel that they can adequately represent their constituents by building one-to-one relationships with them. The intermediaries of organized interest groups or organized public participation led by the bureaucracy are sometimes seen as unnecessary. A classic pluralism underpins this populism, leading to the supposition that people who have something to say will come forward and be heard by their council so that there is no need to cajole them out to public meetings as part of an institutionalized effort. In many municipalities, such populism is producing a growing tension between the political level and the administration over how their relationships with citizens are managed.

The Emerging Philosophy of Governance

Local governments need to realize that the customer-service revolution has almost run its course and is beginning to give way to another philosophy of governance. Gradually, the *customer* is being supplanted by the *citizen*, but an active citizen, rather than the passive recipient of old. The emerging philosophy of governance emphasizes reciprocal obligation between government and citizen and the assumption of responsibility by citizens and communities.[24] In this perspective, as David Prior, John Stewart and Kieron Walsh note, "the activity which defines the citizen is *participation in collective purposes* rather than choice of individual purposes. The key arena for citizen participation is the political community of which the citizen is a member."[25] This gives renewed meaning to participatory democracy, deliberation and accountability. In one sense, it represents a return to the original value of participation as civic education but with a new emphasis on the responsibility of citizens to become informed before and while they participate and, in the process of deliberation, to take account of the interests and concerns of others.[26]

This emphasis on responsibility is already manifest in the growing interest in deliberative techniques such as deliberative polling and citizen juries or panels. Traditional polling is a one-shot event that simply asks people to state opinions with no consideration of whether these people are giving informed opinions that have weighed trade-offs among choices. In contrast, deliberative polling brings together a group of representative citizens (usually chosen by stratified random sampling); provides them with carefully balanced background materials that discuss the costs and benefits of various choices; allows intensive discussion among participants in small groups with skilled moderators; and gives people the chance to question competing experts and politicians.[27] When participants are then polled at the end of several days of this kind of deliberation, they can provide informed input into policy decisions. Experience with the method reveals that participants often change their views, sometimes dramatically, as they acquire information and gain perspective based on discussions with other people. Often the process is videotaped and shown on television to a wider public that also gains deeper understanding of complex issues.

Citizen juries operate in a similar manner, using the key of deliberation.[28] Although they are quasi-institutions, juries and panels are different from traditional citizen advisory boards in at least two ways: first, citizens are randomly chosen on a representative basis rather than being self-selected; and, second, the membership rotates so that views do not become entrenched and the body a staid institution unto itself.[29] The longer-term goal is to try to inculcate a sense in the public at large that to serve on these panels from time to time is part of their civic duty, just as it is their responsibility to perform jury duty if called. Both of these new mechanisms increase the public's expectation that governments will follow their recommendations and that politicians will be more directly accountable for the public-participation process and its use in decision-making.

Another implication is a revival of attention to the voluntary sector – including neighbourhood associations, issue-oriented groups and identity-based social movements, and local service clubs – as vehicles for citizen engagement. They provide opportunities for deliberation within communities and thus increase the level of preparation for more formal interaction with governments. But there is a paradox in this. In recent years, governments have been undermining the organizational capacity of voluntary associations by cutting their funding, attacking their credibility by branding them in a derogatory way as "special-interest groups" (thus connoting a narrow, vested self-interest), and placing heavy demands on them for service delivery. Ironically then, precisely at the time when local governments need community organizations and interest groups more than ever to play a part in citizen engagement and to assume responsibility, the ability of these groups to do so has been significantly compromised.

Changing Communities

The third major factor to which local governments must respond has to do with the changing nature of community and social life, especially in the large urban centres. The multicultural diversity of Canada's larger cities is expanding remarkably quickly; for example, visible minorities already constitute almost a quarter of the populations of greater Toronto and Vancouver. And the visible-minority population in major cities is expected to double by 2016. In addition, many Canadian cities, notably Winnipeg, Edmonton, Vancouver and Regina, have large populations of off-reserve aboriginal people, most of whom experience shockingly high rates of unemployment and poverty. This diversity requires that public officials approach cultural and racial issues with greater sensitivity to differences than ever before. Diversity also demands that public officials better understand what kinds of services different communities value and how people are most comfortable interacting with state institutions.

Not only has the diversity of communities expanded, but *who* is to represent these communities has also become a critical issue. In recent years, a new aspect of representation has arisen that is sometimes referred to as the "politics of difference."[30] It is no longer considered legitimate by minority communities, now quickly acquiring political acumen, to be represented by élites – whether politicians or distant interest-group leaders – no matter how sensitive they are to cultural differences. Rather, these communities are seeking direct representation by members of their own constituencies, who personally and directly share the experiences of the communities, and they are demanding opportunities to have real input in decision-making processes. The politics of difference places a greater obligation on public officials not only to understand the composition and nature of communities but to help communities develop the leadership and opportunities to speak for themselves.

The social life of urban communities has also been significantly transformed as a reflection of demographic shifts and the changing nature of work. The difference in wealth, job opportunities and perspectives on life between the older population and youth places new demands on policy and participatory mechanisms to bridge intergenerational conflict. The majority of households are now either dual wage-earner or single-parent families. In large cities, people often face very long commuting distances between home and work. Consequently, people have less and less time for participation in civic affairs.[31] Potentially, however, the large cohort of youthful fifty-five-year-old retirees, if often involuntary, may add to the new dynamism of public participation in coming years an injection of people with the time, relevant experience and interest in being involved.

Finally, as a result of the segmentation of the labour market into "good" jobs and low-end service jobs, there is more marked differentiation between the rich and poor in cities. In combination with globalization and the "internationalization" of cities, this segmentation has given rise to a new élite that includes highly mobile knowledge workers who are likely to find themselves living in Toronto one year and in Paris or Tokyo the next. Christopher Lasch argues that this new élite is in revolt against the rest of society.[32] In contrast to the traditional élites who were often philanthropists and leaders in community and political life, the new élites have little attachment to place, preferring to seclude themselves in homogeneous enclaves of walled suburbs and private schools. They are less dependent on public services (being able to purchase many of these, such as security guards, privately) and are less willing to make sacrifices for the community at large: "The new élites are at home only in transit, en route to a high-level conference, to the grand opening of a new franchise, to an international film festival, or to an undiscovered resort. Theirs is essentially a tourist's view of the world – not a perspective likely to encourage a passionate devotion to democracy."[33] If Lasch is correct in his assessment, the challenge for public participation will be to re-engage these placeless élites in deliberative processes that encourage them to be more understanding and tolerant of other segments of society and to reinstate a willingness to make sacrifices for the broader community.

New Technology

Technology is re-shaping the medium for participation. The Internet has substantially broken down barriers of place and time. In addition to being a vehicle for conferencing on-line between local governments and citizens, the Internet also affords a democratization of information. People can cheaply obtain information from disparate sources and enter into discussions with others via newsgroups, thus facilitating greater sharing of experiences across communities and across space. As an information resource, the Internet also allows local governments to circulate their own documents, without reams of paper. Indeed, all major Canadian cities now have a home page on the World Wide Web and, along with much smaller centres, are connected in municipal discussion groups such as British Columbia's CivicNet. As a way of connecting citizens to city hall, e-mail provides an instantaneous way of registering a complaint, offering a viewpoint or asking a question, thus enhancing access for those who might not take the time to mail a letter or make a phone call.

The critical question of the Internet is whether it will be used primarily as an information resource or whether it will empower citizens. As a means of empowerment and participation, most local government policies lag far behind the technology. Many policy questions still need to be addressed. The first relates to access. Although the "Net" is widely assumed to increase access (to information, institutions and other people), this may turn out to be highly differential access. While the homeless may be able to participate in an on-line conference using public terminals in a library, access is obviously much more convenient for people who can afford to have a computer and modem at home. As Monica Gattinger observes in her chapter, there is also a significant gender imbalance among users of the Internet, as revealed by the fact that eighty-two per cent of those surfing the National Capital FreeNet in Ottawa-Carleton on any particular day are men. Local governments have also encountered internal differentiation in access, because they have had considerable difficulty in getting elected officials to go on-line. Use of the Internet for public participation may render the citizen as disconnected from the political level as were traditional means of participation.

A related issue is the impact of the technology on public expectations. The use of e-mail has spawned its own "netiquette" in which senders have come to anticipate great speed of response (a day's response time is usually considered an outside limit). Will these norms heighten public expectations about the speed of responsiveness from city departments and elected officials? The ironic effect may be that the use of the Internet makes local government seem less responsive, because it cannot get back to people as quickly as Net norms dictate. Local governments are just beginning to develop administrative policies about the priority accorded e-mail versus traditional modes of mail and telephone communication. To a large degree, the politics and practices that local government develop in these still-early days of the technology will determine the democratic potential of the Internet as a vehicle for citizen engagement. In the enthusiasm for the new worlds opened by the Web, however, it is critical to keep in mind that the technology is merely a vehicle and, by no means the only one, for public participation.

LOOKING AHEAD

This is a time of both retrenchment and expansion of public-participation practices by local governments. In some municipalities, there is a marked backlash against participation. Under conditions of severely limited funding and resistance by populist politicians, there have been dramatic cuts to many of the "frills" of participation. But, due to the emergence of new deliberative methods, new technologies, a changing philosophy of governance, and a growing cultural diversity of urban environments, this is also an exciting time of considerable innovation. And given financial constraints, practitioners are not only finding more innovative ways but less expensive ways of conducting public participation. Given this nexus of closure and opportunity, this is certainly the time to ask serious questions about current practices and how they can be improved to meet the challenges of changing contexts.

With this in mind, we proceed to the case studies. Each case speaks for itself. In the concluding chapter, we return to some of the basic issues and fundamental questions posed earlier in this introduction. By synthesizing the recurring themes and reviewing the failures and successes discussed in the cases, we offer practically oriented lessons to local governments for the improvement and future directions of public participation.

THE CASE STUDIES

This collection consists of nine case studies, written by both academics and practitioners, that provide concrete examples of contemporary experiences of local governments with public participation across the country, from the Miramichi to Vancouver. The focus is on the involvement of citizens in planning and policy-making outside of the process of municipal elections and the casting of individual ballots. This definition potentially covers a wide array of practices, from traditional public hearings to newer methods of deliberative polling and citizen juries. As is reinforced throughout the chapters, however, public participation is seldom a one-shot event or a single technique but necessitates a series of steps and variety of methods. We have resisted presenting a hardfast definition of public participation due to the degree of experimentation and innovation taking place today. And, as you will see, the contributors have slightly differing perspectives on the boundaries of public participation. But, the contributors consistently note that public participation is, at minimum, interaction and two-way communication that entails some potential for influencing policy decisions and outcomes. Thus, while survey research, on one hand, and the provision of information to the public about a government's policy options, on the other, may be vital components of a public-participation exercise, these initiatives are viewed by the authors in this collection as information-gathering, not as sufficient and stand-alone methods of public participation.

The cases examine four of the major issues facing local governments in Canada today: 1) economic development; 2) land-use planning; 3) the fiscal squeeze and disentanglement of municipal finances and services from other orders of government; and 4) political restructuring. For each subject area, one case is written by an academic and the other by a practitioner who was directly involved in the participation exercise. Collectively, the chapters are intended to offer practical advice to practitioners and students of public participation as to what contributes to effective participation and what kinds of improvements need to be made.

In the first chapter, we begin with a look at public participation in economic development. **Jeff Fielding** and **Gerry Couture** lead us through the public"s involvement in the City of Winnipeg's economic-development strategy, from its inception in 1989 to its implementation over the following six years. Theirs is a success story. Not only did the public shape the initial agenda and forge a community consensus around an economic-development strategy, but council actually acted on the recommendations that flowed from the participation process and continued to involve the public in the implementation stages. Based on a detailed discussion of each of the major phases of the strategy, Fielding and Couture share twenty concrete lessons they learned as planners on the front lines. **Patrick Smith** examines two cases of citizen involvement in economic development in the Greater Vancouver area. His first case study examines the five-and-a-half-year process to develop a new strategic plan for the Greater Vancouver Regional District, marrying concerns with economic development and environmental sustainability. He points to this process as an example of the success of a "consensual model" of regional planning. The great amount of attention paid to public involvement in this process – particularly in setting goals and making major policy choices – offers very useful lessons in metropolitan problem-solving without imposing structural reform on constituent municipalities. The second example of the City of Vancouver's efforts at economic development in the international context provides a sharp contrast. In this case, we see the nuanced role of different segments of the local community in promoting and sustaining the city"s international economic-development initiatives at different times. Smith's analysis highlights the need for economic-development initiatives to be salient to particular communities for its constituents to become involved. Success, in the City of Vancouver case, resulted from interplay between community initiation or support and some city action to cement economic-development links based on cultural affinity, the emergence of particular social movements or business concerns.

We then turn to a more traditional arena for public participation: the land-use planning process. **John Sewell** explores three attempts to involve the public in big official plans in the 1990s: by the City of Toronto, by Metropolitan Toronto, and by the City of Vancouver. In Sewell's assessment, each was a bitter disappointment, and none produced a plan capable of providing strong direction for either councils or citizens. He contrasts these with the relative success of Ontario's Commission on Planning and Development Reform, which he chaired. The critical differences, Sewell suggests, were that the commission involved the right members of the public, got them to resolve their differences, and the commission demonstrated a real willingness to listen and learn from the public. **Jean Dionne, Céline Faucher** and **André Martel** chronicle the emergence and contribution of ward councils in Quebec City. They focus on the experience of two pilot councils, established in quite different neighbourhoods, following city council's adoption of a formal policy of public consultation and the creation of the office of public consultation, in 1991. In contrast with earlier practice, city councillors had no direct role in determining the membership or agenda of these ward councils. The two councils emphasized different issues, ranging from the state of neighbourhood streets and heritage preservation in the Vieux-Limoilou ward, to planning issues related to large-scale development in the Saint-Jean-Baptiste ward, which includes the national assembly and Quebec's conference centre. Two years after their creation, the ward councils were well regarded as constructive influences on city affairs and on community building. Through the hard work and practical projects they had undertaken, they had both influenced city council's priorities and decisions. The principle of allowing ward councils to have politically independent membership and to develop their own agendas was also well established. The city now intends to mandate a similar council in each of its wards.

The next two chapters examine recent innovative experiments in involving the public in the budgeting process and the restructuring of municipal services. **Michael Fenn**, chief administrative officer of the Regional Municipality of Hamilton-Wentworth, explores how local governments have undertaken customer-first approaches to governance. Specifically, he reports on the creation of citizen committees to review the budget and on the use of customer surveys to decide priorities in making decisions about the delivery of services in both the City of Burlington and the Regional Municipality of Hamilton-Wentworth. These examples clearly show how new roles and arenas for public participation need new tools. In a companion chapter, **Edward LeSage** analyses a similar experiment of involving the public in budget preparation in Edmonton – a municipality that has suffered big cutbacks under the Ralph Klein government. LeSage concludes that while the quality of budget-making was not greatly enhanced by Edmonton's public involvement initiative, it did provide new and useful information, increased diversity of views and greater political and administrative accountability. Perhaps the greatest value of public input, the author suggests, has been symbolic. In spite of a certain pessimism about experiences to date, LeSage concludes by suggesting three specific ways in which practices could be improved.

One of the greatest pressures facing city regions in the late 1990s is to restructure their political institutions and boundaries in order to sort out the relationships between municipal and regional governments and to improve the overall governance of the region as a whole. London, Ontario, a single-tier municipality, went through a major annexation in 1993 to become a form of single-tier region. Strangely, the outcome of the annexation process gave the city even more territory than it initially had been seeking. **Andrew Sancton's** analysis of this case finds that although there were "joyfully participatory" public hearings, they had no impact. Citizen participation was countermanded by narrow terms of reference, important decisions made beforehand, and by the sheer technical complexity of the issue. In his compelling assessment, Sancton offers an important cautionary note about the sometimes uneasy relationship between public participation and representative democracy. **John Robison** examines the restructuring of the communities of the Miramichi River in New Brunswick into the City of Miramichi on 1 January 1995. In spite of historic rivalries and failed previous attempts at amalgamation, residents worked together to ensure the process remained community-driven. The community advisory committee to the provincial study team not only was instrumental in determining the approach taken by the provincial study but shaped its recommendations as well, indicating that considerable community goodwill and collective effort can be mobilized in political restructuring.

In the final chapter, **Monica Gattinger** explores the implications of going "on-line" for democracy in local governments. She draws on the experiences of the City of Ottawa and the Regional Municipality of Ottawa-Carleton, two forerunners among municipalities in using the Internet, to consider whether a "wired" local government electronically accessible to citizens represents a change in the democratic nature of governance and whether the technology is being used to empower citizens. Or, are local governments simply using the medium to disseminate information that they would otherwise put on paper? Although its full potential has yet to be realized and some elected officials have so far been quite resistant to going on-line, Gattinger argues that this experiment seems to be headed in the right direction.

We now proceed to the details of these cases. In the concluding chapter, we will consider lessons learned from the cases and the implications for the transition from "participation" to "engagement."

NOTES

1 This example is discussed in detail in the chapter by W. Michael Fenn in this volume.
2 This vignette is drawn from the chapter by Monica Gattinger in this volume.
3 John Sewell mentions the role of children in the planning process in his chapter.
4 On the development of Winnipeg's economic-development strategy, see the chapter by Jeff Fielding and Gerry Couture.
5 For estimates of the costs of the public-participation activities surrounding the development of official plans in Vancouver and Toronto, see the chapter by John Sewell in this volume.
6 This was first trenchantly argued by John Stuart Mill.
7 Saul Alinsky, *Rules for Radicals* (New York: Random House, 1971).
8 Leslie A. Pal, *Interests of State* (Montreal and Kingston: McGill-Queen's University Press, 1993), p. 106.
9 For a discussion of the fight to stop the Spadina Expressway, see John Sewell, *The Shape of the City: Toronto Struggles with Modern Planning* (Toronto: University of Toronto Press, 1993), pp. 177–82; and on the struggle to save Vancouver"s Chinatown from massive urban renewal, see Shlomo Hasson and David Ley, *Neighbourhood Organizations and the Welfare State* (Toronto: University of Toronto Press, 1994), pp. 112–36.
10 Jane Jacobs, *The Death and Life of Great American Cities* (New York: Vintage Books, 1961).
11 Robert Putnam, *Making Democracy Work: Civic Traditions in Modern Italy* (Princeton: Princeton University Press, 1993) , p. 173; see also Francis Fukuyama, *Trust: The Social Virtues and the Creation of Prosperity* (New York: The Free Press, 1995), p. 356; and Jeffrey M. Berry, Kent E. Portney and Ken Thomson, *The Rebirth of Urban Democracy* (Washington, D.C.: The Brookings Institution, 1993), pp. 264–70.
12 Putnam, *Making Democracy Work*, p. 176.
13 David Prior, John Stewart and Kieron Walsh, *Citizenship: Rights, Community and Participation* (London: Pitman Publishing, 1995), p. 142.
14 Christopher Howard, Michael Lipsky and Dale Rogers Marshall, "Citizen Participation in Urban Politics: Rise and Routinization," in George E. Peterson, ed., *Big-City Politics, Governance, and Fiscal Constraints* (Washington, D.C.: The Urban Institute Press, 1994), p. 154.
15 On the emergence of the NIMBY syndrome in participation, see Pierre Filion, "Government Levels, Neighbourhood Influence and Urban Policy," in Henri Lustiger-Thaler, ed., *Political Arrangements: Power and the City* (Montreal: Black Rose Books, 1992), pp. 169–83; and Glenda Laws, "Community Activism Around the Built Form of Toronto's Welfare State," *Canadian Journal of Urban Research* 3, no. 1 (June 1994), pp. 1–28.

16 Henry McCandless, president of the Centretown Citizens' Community Association in a presentation to the Ottawa branch of the International Association for Public Participation, Ottawa, 3 April 1996.
17 Sherry Arnstein, "A Ladder of Citizen Participation," *Journal of the American Institute of Planners* 35, no. 4 (July 1969), pp. 216–24.
18 Walter A. Rosenbaum, "The Paradoxes of Public Participation," *Administration and Society* 8, no. 3 (November 1976), p. 370.
19 Mary Grisez Kweit and Rovert W. Kweit, *Implementing Citizen Participation in a Bureaucratic Society* (New York: Praeger, 1981), p. 60.
20 Barry Checkoway and colleagues argue that while there is a significant relationship between effective participation and agency resources, it is not simply the level of resources but the *commitment* by senior management and staff training and experience that are the critical factors. See Barry Checkoway, Thomas W. O"Rourke and David Bull, "Correlates of Consumer Participation in Health Planning Agencies: Findings and Implications from a National Survey," *Policy Studies Review* 3, no. 2 (February 1984), pp. 306–307. Similarly, a comparative analysis by Sharon Varette of consultative practices in two federal departments, Agriculture Canada, and the Treasury Board Secretariat points to the importance of a supportive corporate culture. In addition to lack of time, financial resources and skills-training, between one-quarter and one-third of the respondents in Varette's study cite lack of cooperation from management as an important barrier to participation. See Sharon Varette, "Consultation in the public service: a question of skills," *Optimum* 23, no. 4 (Spring 1993), pp. 28–39.
21 Berry, Portney, and Thomson, *The Rebirth of Urban Democracy*.
22 For examples of some of these innovations, see City of Calgary, *Responding to the Challenge: City Business and Operational Initiatives 1992–1994* (Calgary, Commissioners' Office, 1995). Vancouver has been one of the leaders in creating integrated service-delivery teams, groups of front-line staff, including police, fire, building inspectors and public health officials, who work together in teams to solve problems on the ground. See City of Vancouver, *Integrated Service Teams, Orientation Session* (Vancouver: City, 1995).
23 David Osborne and Ted Gaebler, *Reinventing Government: How the Entrepreneurial Spirit is Transforming the Public Sector from Schoolhouse to State House, City Hall to Pentagon* (Reading, Mass.: Addison-Wesley, 1992).
24 This philosophy is taking hold at the federal and provincial levels as well. See Susan D. Phillips, "Making Change: The Potential for Innovation under the Liberals," in Susan D. Phillips, ed., *How Ottawa Spends 1994–95: Making Change* (Ottawa: Carleton University Press, 1994), p. 13.
25 Prior, Stewart and Walsh, *Citizenship: Rights, Community and Participation*, p. 17 (emphasis in the original).
26 Ibid., p. 80; see also Anne Phillips, *The Politics of Presence* (London: Oxford University Press, 1995).

27 The deliberative polling technique was developed by James S. Fishkin in *Democracy and Deliberation* (New Haven; Conn.: Yale University Press, 1991). See also Daniel Yankelovich, *Coming to Public Judgement* (Syracuse, N.Y.: Syracuse University Press, 1991). For a discussion of its use in Canada, see Canadian Policy Research Networks, *The Society We Want* (Ottawa: CPRN, 1996); and Maureen O'Neill, "Democracy Needs More Deliberation," *The Ottawa Citizen* 14 February 1996.

28 On citizens' juries, see J. Stewart, L. Kendall and A. Coote, *Citizens' Juries* (London: Institute for Research on Public Policy (IPPR), 1994); on panels, see Ned Crosby, Janet M. Kelly and Paul Schaefer, "Citizens Panels: A New Approach to Citizen Participation," *Public Administration Review* 46, no. 2 (March/April 1986), pp. 170–78; and Lyn Kathlene and John A. Martin, "Enhancing Citizen Participation: Panel Designs, Perspectives, and Policy Formation," *Journal of Policy Analysis and Management* 10, no. 1 (Winter 1991), pp. 46–93.

29 Crosby, Kelly and Shaeffer, "Citizens Panels," *Public Administration Review*, pp. 171–2.

30 Iris Young, *Justice and the Politics of Difference* (Princeton, N.J.: Princeton University Press, 1990). For an application to Canada, see Anne Phillips, *The Politics of Presence*, pp. 115–43.

31 Robert Putnam explores the reasons for what he argues is a significant decline in social capital (participation in associational activities) in the United States in recent years. After examining the impact of a number of factors including the pressures of time and money, residential mobility, more women in the labour force, and the rise of the welfare state, Putnam concludes that the culprit is television. Not only does television have a major effect on time displacement, but it has changed the outlook of a generation. See Robert D. Putnam, "Tuning In, Turning Out: The Strange Disappearance of Social Capital in America," *PS: Political Science and Politics* 28, no. 4 (December 1995), pp. 664–83.

32 Christopher Lasch, *The Revolt of the Elites* (New York: W.W. Norton, 1995).

33 Ibid., p. 6.

2

Economic Development: The Public's Role in Shaping Winnipeg's Economic Future

Jeff Fielding and Gerry Couture

BACKGROUND

Winnipeg was once a dominant force in the growth and economic development of this country. Known as Canada's "Gateway to the West," Winnipeg prospered in the early part of this century, as the Canadian frontier moved first farther west and later into Canada's North. By the early 1900s, Winnipeg had become one of the world's fastest-growing grain centres and one of the largest rail centres in North America. In 1904, Winnipeg was the fastest-growing city in Canada; in 1905, it was the fastest-growing city of its size in North America. Having become the third-largest city in Canada, it was fully expected that Winnipeg would become one of North America's most important economic centres. The First World War slowed its growth, however, and, with the opening of the Panama Canal in 1913, there was a new route for shipping goods from eastern Canada to the west coast, which diminished Winnipeg's role as a transportation hub. Winnipeg's relative importance in the Canadian economy has been declining steadily ever since.

Over the past few decades, Winnipeg has developed a very diversified economy that has protected it from boom-and-bust cycles experienced by other cities but that has generated very modest growth. Nevertheless, Winnipeggers came to pride themselves on this stability, recognizing it as the basis for a comfortable quality of life, free of the anxieties associated with fast-growing urban centres. In recent years, however, it became clear that the city's quality of life was being jeopardized by slow economic growth. Winnipeg's tax base could no longer support the services deemed vital in maintaining the standard of living that the city's residents had come to expect. Within the community, there was a growing consensus that economic development had to become Winnipeg's highest priority. Community leaders believed that attention to a number of critical economic issues was needed if Winnipeg, once again, was to compete successfully with other cities in North America. It was recognized, as well, that the public had an important role to play in shaping Winnipeg's economic future.

In Winnipeg, perhaps more than in any other Canadian city, it is expected that decisions of importance will be shaped through public processes. The community has a history of activism and strong social consciousness, beginning with the General Strike of 1919 that shook the nation. More recently, the city's regional form of government was replaced in 1970 with a single-tier system that entrenched participation in political decision-making processes. In the new structure, all councillors are elected by ward, creating a strong link between council and local neighbourhoods. The wards are amalgamated into larger communities reflective of the former municipalities. Those elected must not only sit on the city council but must also sit on community committees that allow councillors to deal with local issues at the neighbourhood level, thereby facilitating close contact with the community. Furthermore, the community committees are guided in their decisions by formalized resident advisory groups elected within the communities. This system has led to high expectations of participation. As a result, public consultation must be part of any planning process if it is to be seen as credible.

SETTING THE STAGE

In February of 1989, city council commissioned a new economic-development strategy for Winnipeg. Previously, in 1978, the Winnipeg chamber of commerce recommended an economic-development strategy to city council that resulted in the creation of the Winnipeg Business Development Corporation, an organization aimed at bringing together resources from both the business community and the municipal government. In the intervening period, changes in the business and economic climate, coupled with the city's weakened economic position, led council to question the merit of continuing its funding of the Winnipeg Business Development Corporation. In keeping with the tradition of public participation, a task force was established, with members drawn from business, labour, education and government, to undertake the assignment under the chairmanship of the then-deputy mayor. The task force completed its work in 1990 and submitted a series of recommendations to council. The proposed strategy had five basic components:

- *building leadership* through the creation of the Leaders Committee, consisting of business, government, labour, education and other sectors;

- *targeting specific key sectors* by focusing efforts in eight areas considered to be Winnipeg's competitive strengths;
- *improving communities* by creating a positive business climate through taxation and labour legislation, education, a long-range airport strategy, and a strong, vibrant downtown;
- *improving communications and marketing* by reinforcing the "open-for-business" mandate through communications and a focused marketing strategy; and
- *taking advantage of emerging opportunities* through sustainable development and aging rehabilitation servicing, which, in particular, were seen as having strong foundations in Winnipeg.

The task force confirmed that, as a result of Winnipeg's diverse economy, there was a strong base on which to build. Diversity meant that there would always be opportunities for seeking out new enterprise in support of existing economic activity within the city. In the end, the task force was convinced that Winnipeg's valued quality of life could only be sustained and improved in the long term by a strengthened pursuit of new jobs, especially quality, higher-paying jobs.

BUILDING CONSENSUS IN THE COMMUNITY

City council adopted the Economic Development Strategy in February 1990. The primary objective was to strengthen the leadership for economic development within the community, based on the understanding that the public and private sectors had different roles to play. While the public sector had to provide support for economic-development activity, the primary thrust had to come from the private sector through the pursuit of economic opportunities. Therefore the Leaders Committee was established, with strong private-sector representation. Funding for an arm's-length organization, called Winnipeg 2000 (which replaced the Winnipeg Business Development Corporation), was provided by the municipal and provincial governments to support the work of the Leaders Committee.

Winnipeg 2000 quickly undertook its responsibilities as mandated through the Economic Development Strategy. A number of programs were soon formulated, and initiatives were implemented for business retention and recruitment. Research programs were developed to identify and pursue emerging opportunities, and a strong marketing and communications program was introduced.

Meanwhile, momentum began to build in the community. The membership of the Leaders Committee included key players in the community who were instrumental in getting the ball rolling. The airport, for example, became a focus for immediate action by the private sector. Leaders within the business community began discussions with the federal government to assign control of the airport to a local airport authority. An effort, led by the owner of a large trucking firm in the city, was undertaken to exploit the potential of the airport as an air-cargo hub for international cargo distribution. As well, the concept of business-improvement zones was rapidly catching on. The Downtown Winnipeg Business Improvement Zone, which represented over seventeen hundred businesses and was entirely self-funded, initiated a number of programs to strengthen the competitiveness of the downtown core.

ESTABLISHING A POLICY CONTEXT

Work began concurrently on the issues assigned to the City of Winnipeg. While the city's primary responsibilities lay in community-development initiatives, it was necessary to begin by establishing a policy context for economic development. The city had provided financial support for an economic-development organization in the past and now was contributing similarly to the new Winnipeg 2000 group. However, aside from its contribution as a funding source, the city's role in economic development had never been fully defined. What initiatives could the city undertake on its own to complement those of Winnipeg 2000? This was a question that needed to be asked of the public. As part of a comprehensive review of its development plan, known as Plan Winnipeg, the city set out, first, to confirm that the community considered economic development a priority and, second, to determine what the city could do to improve its economic future.

In the past, Plan Winnipeg had focused primarily on land-use issues. Through quiet, informal discussions with key organizations such as the chamber of commerce, Tourism Winnipeg and the social planning council (eighteen different groups in all), it was recognized that a broader perspective was needed. Five study-areas were identified early on: environmental stewardship; social equity; urban-development management; urban image; and economic development. Because it was council's responsibility to establish policy relative to Winnipeg's long-term future, a coordinating committee was struck comprising eleven councillors (two councillors assigned to each study-area, together with a committee chair). It is worth noting that the chair was a particularly strong councillor who could command the attention and respect of the other members. Furthermore, he helped select each pair of councillors, which consisted of two individuals with generally opposing ideologies. The intent was to ensure that all views were fairly represented and that, in the end, this group of eleven councillors could sway the entire twenty-nine-member council to adopt the plan. Each pair of councillors cochaired a committee to deal with its area of study. These committees included representation from a variety of interests; for instance, the Economic Development Strategy committee included twelve members.

The consultation process involved numerous committee meetings (called "brown bag" sessions, because they were usually held over lunch), where guests, knowledgeable in particular topic-areas, were invited to share their ideas with the committee. The focus of discussions was on specific strategies that could be employed to make improvements in areas such as employment retention and growth, job training and re-training, research and development, and city finances and regulations. Focus groups were also held. At these sessions, invited guests from a variety of backgrounds were encouraged to discuss the general issue of economic development, while staff sat by as observers and recorders of the proceedings. This was intended to validate the overall direction that was to be established. Another avenue of consultation involved more structured workshops, where invited guests were guided by a facilitator to determine the group's consensus on topical issues such as the airport or the downtown. The intent here was to seek agreement on strategic direction.

Two public-attitude surveys were carried out: one locally, and the other nationally, to provide comparative analysis with other cities. Several open-forums were held to inform the general public and to solicit input. As well, a call for written briefs resulted in a number of high-quality submissions that complemented, and helped validate, what was being heard through the workshops and focus groups. As this process was being carried out, a parallel process was followed. For the plan to be successful it would have to accommodate input from those individuals and groups who would assist in its implementation. Consequently, discussions were carried out with the senior levels of government and with a number of city departments to seek their concurrence with the direction and strategies being proposed.

Through all of this, a clear consensus emerged that economic development was a top priority. Winnipeggers said that in order to achieve progress, a strong commitment would be required on the part of government, business and labour. Each had a role to play, and their efforts had to complement one another. The public wanted the city to demonstrate leadership, to communicate direction effectively, and to maintain consistent policy on which business could rely. Winnipeg's residents and businesses also expected the city to demonstrate sound financial management, with predictable results in its day-to-day operations. The community expected cooperative working relationships between government and the private sector. Winnipeggers knew that no matter how well-intentioned public-sector initiatives might be, they stood little chance of success unless they were supported and endorsed by the private sector. And finally, the public expected that weaknesses in education, training and employment would be addressed, that the quality of the downtown would be improved and that the city's advantages in transportation (rail and truck), including the further development of Winnipeg International Airport, would be pursued. Policy was established to support this direction, and a new Plan Winnipeg was adopted unanimously in June 1993. The plan, for the first time, had a strong economic-development component. Most importantly, in the minds of councillors, the consultation process had confirmed and built public consensus around the direction established in the economic-development strategy.

As a measure of the success of the process, the council chamber was filled to capacity with supporters of the plan, most of whom had participated in the process in one form or another. As well, the media, normally quick to pick up on criticism, was noticeably subdued in their reporting of the event. It was an indication that there were few vocal critics in the audience.

The work of the city on its development plan served not only to validate the public's interest in economic development but to strengthen the resolve of community leaders to follow through on their commitments. The community understood the issue of economic development and was supportive of the need to address it. The public debate generated through the Plan Winnipeg review consolidated many of the ideas that had been put forward. Winnipeggers, business and government now agreed on direction. This understanding within the community was significant, because it set the agenda for future economic-development initiatives in Winnipeg.

ACTING ON COMMUNITY CONSENSUS

The city was prepared to continue to fulfil its responsibilities in setting the stage for economic development through community-improvement initiatives, as recommended in the Economic Development Strategy and entrenched in its development plan. An effort was made to generate improvements in four areas:

1. *Taxation*. Prevailing labour legislation and municipal taxes were considered to be impediments to business retention and recruitment efforts. Winnipeg was seen as having high taxes and, therefore, uncompetitive.

2. *Education.* The out-migration of young, well-educated people had left behind an older population below-average in education and training levels.

3. *Winnipeg International Airport.* The airport's potential to become a major cargo hub needed to be pursued aggressively, and, to accomplish this, its twenty-four-hour operating status needed to be protected.

4. *Downtown.* The coordination of downtown interests was considered essential if the city was to become more economically competitive.

The last two were addressed through planning programs that provided further opportunity for public involvement.

The chronology of events in Winnipeg's economic-development strategy is outlined below:

Chronology of Events

February 1989	City of Winnipeg establishes an economic-development task force.
February 1990	City council adopts the task force's recommendations and appoints a steering committee to implement the strategy.
February 1990	Winnipeg 2000 is created with funding from the city and province to provide the administrative support for economic development.
April 1991	The City of Winnipeg undertakes a major review of its development plan.
December 1992	The Winnipeg Airport Authority Inc. is created to manage the Winnipeg International Airport.
June 1993	"Plan Winnipeg ... toward 2010" is adopted by city council.
June 1993	The City of Winnipeg undertakes a process to explore opportunities associated with the airport.
June 1993	The City of Winnipeg undertakes a process to build consensus around a direction for the downtown.

May 1994   The Airport Vicinity Development Plan is adopted by city council.

December 1994   "CentrePlan" and its first-year action plan is adopted by city council.

December 1994   A private-sector group called WinnPort is formed to develop Winnipeg as an international air-cargo distribution centre.

March 1995   The Winnipeg Development Agreement is signed by the three levels of government, committing $75 million to thirteen separate programs, including $4 million for downtown revitalization and $5 million for airport development.

The Airport Vicinity Development Plan

The private sector took the lead in advancing the opportunities that could be realized if the Winnipeg International Airport was developed as an air-cargo hub. Winnipeg was recognized as having the distinct advantage of a central geographic location that places it at the crossroads between Asia, the Pacific Rim, and the European Union and the quick, low-cost truck and rail connection into the Mid-Continent Trade Corridor that leads as far south as Mexico. The airport also operates on an unrestricted twenty-four-hour basis, which was recognized as a tremendous advantage if the air-cargo opportunity was to be fully explored.

Recognizing the inherent opportunity, a powerful local businessman emerged with a strong vision of Winnipeg recapturing, and even surpassing, its historical importance as a transportation centre. The stage was no longer North American, it was global. He was able to instil confidence in others that the airport's potential could be realized if action were taken quickly to capitalize on the opportunity. Other local businessmen gave their support and lobbied hard for federal and provincial government assistance. The success of those efforts yielded funding for the creation of a private-sector organization, known as WinnPort, that was mandated to develop plans for air-cargo and intermodal facilities. WinnPort is now leading the way on airport development, but the influence of the business leader and the quality of his vision were largely responsible for overcoming the initial hurdles.

The civic government was given the task of ensuring that land-use in proximity to the airport was compatible with airport operations and that a development plan for the vicinity was established. Extensive public consultation was carried out in support of this work. The vision, "Winnipeg International Airport: Canada's New Major Transborder Air Hub," was clear from the outset and agreed to by all. The process was designed to identify issues that needed to be addressed and to develop strategies in response to those issues. In other words, an abbreviated strategic-planning process was followed.

The process was driven by a steering committee comprising stakeholders, including industry leaders, private-sector interests, residents, and senior political representatives from the City of Winnipeg and the neighbouring rural municipality (since development of the airport would likely extend beyond the city's boundaries). The deputy mayor of the city, a particularly strong advocate for airport-related development, chaired the committee and proved instrumental in building support among other participants. The committee reported to council's standing committee on planning and community services. The support group responsible for delivering the process included fourteen administrators from the three levels of government.

The steering committee met on numerous occasions with their support team, and these forums became the primary source of stakeholder input. As well, over fifty participants from industry, business and local residents contributed to a specialized workshop to identify actions that were required to realize the vision. Special effort was made here to include representatives from all important stakeholder groups. The existing industrial area surrounding the airport was recognized as the healthiest and most successful in the city. It was particularly critical that industry leaders were able to share their concerns and their expertise regarding the potential expansion of that zone. The results were refined by the steering committee and formed the basis of the final plan.

The sensitivity of airport-related operations to the surrounding residential communities was stressed by many participants. As a result, five public open-houses were held in the neighbouring communities to share information and to garner local resident support. The adjacent rural municipality also held a series of open-houses for their residents. Members of the steering committee, including the elected officials, were on hand at these sessions to field questions and address concerns.

Through these discussions, we heard that the land-use concerns on the west side of the airport were different from those on the east side and warranted separate strategies. As well, if the air-cargo hub concept was to become a reality, primary attention needed to be paid to the provision of infrastructure, particularly to the upgrading of the street system. From the local community, residents expressed the need for some assurance that noise mitigation measures would be put into place.

Four specific products emerged from the process: an Airport Vicinity Development Plan, including a series of specific actions and commitments from various jurisdictions for their implementation; an amendment to Plan Winnipeg to recognize noise contours and to accommodate the boundaries of the plan; an amended buildings by-law that required acoustic insulation for new construction in proximity to the airport; and a zoning by-law amendment to ensure no increase in residential densities around the airport.

Participants in the process were able to identify the critical factors that needed to be addressed if that vision were to become a reality. From these discussions, the original focus on compatible land-use in the vicinity of the airport was broadened to ensure that steps were taken to capitalize more aggressively on the economic opportunity that presented itself. In response to concerns by nearby residents, noise management was also addressed. Furthermore, participants stated that the city's commitment had to be made explicit through policy and by-law amendments. Less than a year after the process was launched, the Airport Vicinity Development Plan and associated by-laws were adopted by city council in May 1994.

The plan faced its first major test in early 1996. An application came forward to re-zone a parcel of land containing three single-family properties located within close proximity to a flight path. The developer proposed a medium-density condominium project. The plan, however, was intended to restrict multiple-family development in this area while not necessarily eliminating it altogether. At the hearing on the proposal, many of the participants in the planning process, including airport officials, transport industry representatives, and the chamber of commerce, appeared in opposition and expressed their ongoing commitment to airport protection as stressed in the plan. Councillors, as well, remained firm in their commitment by rejecting the application.

CentrePlan

Concurrent with the preparation of the development plan for the airport, council initiated a planning process, known as CentrePlan, for the city's downtown. Winnipeg's Economic Development Strategy stated that the downtown established the city's image and identity and that it determined Winnipeg's competitive position within the rest of the country. Civic leaders agreed that a vibrant and healthy downtown required a long-term commitment to a vision and a plan, and they were aware that a plan could only be successful if it reflected the consensus of all downtown and community interests. Again, the public was invited to share its hopes and aspirations, this time directed towards a revitalized downtown.

CentrePlan was always intended to be a downtown-community plan and not a City of Winnipeg plan. Many groups were active in the downtown and allocated resources towards projects that affected the downtown. The plan had to coordinate agendas among these groups. It would not be sufficient to articulate the city's role and to commit the city's resources towards various initiatives, because the city was only one of many stakeholders in the downtown. Rather, the plan had to define roles and responsibilities among a number of groups and had to coordinate the allocation of their resources. Even if no new resources were provided, it was expected that a downtown plan could make better use of existing resources. To strengthen this concept of community ownership, participating groups were asked to contribute to the funding of the planning program (although it was not mandatory for their participation). In the end, six different groups helped to fund CentrePlan.

CentrePlan was led by a steering committee of thirty-five downtown stakeholders who were selected by the mayor and included political representation from all three levels of government, together with prominent downtown leaders and members of various downtown boards. The committee was equivalent to a board of directors and was cochaired by the mayor and a private-sector leader. This committee was guided in its decision-making by a forty-seven-member advisory committee with large representation from the civic administration, together with administrators from a number of downtown organizations and representatives of various interests groups. For the sake of continuity and communication, the chair and co-chair of the advisory committee also sat on the steering committee. The city provided the staff resources to support the process.

A strategic-planning formula was followed whereby considerable effort was placed at the outset to articulate a long-term vision for the downtown. Issues then needed to be identified that, when addressed, would allow progress to be made towards that vision. Finally, specific strategies and actions to deal with the issues needed to be established. This was taken to the point of assigning responsibilities and allocating resources. Public consultation was used in all three phases: to establish the vision, the issues, and the strategies. It is important to recognize, however, that the process was not strictly linear with consecutive steps. The vision was still being refined even as issues were being identified and strategies were being considered.

Workshops were held with forty different stakeholder groups (nearly five hundred individuals) over a four-month period. Participants were asked three questions: what did they like about the downtown; what did they not like; and what did they think the downtown needed in order to be improved. Their responses were recorded on flip charts, and the group was then asked to establish priorities in each of the three areas. Each participant was also asked to describe the ideal downtown, using three separate adjectives (e.g., vibrant, safe, prosperous). These words were similarly recorded and prioritized. Together these two exercises yielded tremendous insights and exposed consistent thinking among many participants, which allowed the vision, issues and strategies to be drafted.

Following the format established in these workshops, a workbook was developed that listed the three questions used in the first exercise described above. This workbook was distributed generally to any individual expressing an interest, or stake, in the CentrePlan process. In doing so, it was important not to ignore those more marginalized residents – particularly the transient, aboriginal and poor residents of downtown – who had little contact, and perhaps little trust, in civic institutions. In order to make contact with these individuals, their primary point of contact with the city administration – public-health nurses – was used. An orientation session was held with the nurses, and they were given copies of the workbook. At downtown clinics and as part of their house-to-house visits, nurses were able to ask their clients these fundamental questions about the downtown and to record the results in the workbooks. Although the overall response was quite limited, this tactic yielded some valuable insights and provided an opportunity for future contact. It also helped establish a cooperative working relationship between two disparate groups within the civic administration.

A large public forum with over three hundred participants from the city at large was held to further explore the values held by the community and to help refine the vision statement. This refined vision, which was adopted by the two leadership committees, had five components. What became clear was that the downtown ought to have a sense of community and belonging; exhibit prosperity and innovation; be a model of effectiveness and efficiency; display a soul and personality all its own; and be led with strong direction and commitment.

For each of the five components of the vision, strategy teams were formed to continue to identify strategic direction and to outline a series of possible actions. Over one hundred and fifty people participated on the strategy teams, including members of the steering and advisory committees. A sample survey of five hundred people was used to validate, in the community at large, all that had been heard. The results were incorporated into the main CentrePlan document: *Vision and Strategies*. A smaller public forum with fifty participants was held to further refine the strategies and to establish a sense of priority among them. The advisory and steering committees then developed the results into a two-year action plan that committed time and financial resources from a number of downtown stakeholders. The advisory committee was particularly useful in this exercise, since it comprised managers and executive directors familiar with the mechanisms required to get things done. Those actions for which each group was responsible were extracted and taken to their respective boards for ratification. (Having a member of these various boards on the steering committee facilitated this process.) Similarly, those items for which the City of Winnipeg was responsible were put before council for adoption. Council committed its support for CentrePlan at the end of 1994, and the implementation of some of those actions began immediately afterward.

The main issues identified through the consultation process and validated through the public-attitude survey included safety, parking, cleanliness and maintenance, accessibility and leadership. The process also identified the retail and office sectors as strengths of the downtown but not necessarily as areas of growth. Meanwhile, areas of potential growth were identified as urban tourism; arts, entertainment, and culture; education and training; and information technology.

Three documents were packaged together as CentrePlan: the main one articulated the vision and strategies, broken down according to the five components of the vision; the second was a two-year action plan that laid out thirty-five discrete actions, together with the responsible jurisdiction(s), the necessary resources, the expected benefits, and the required first steps; the third listed all the possible actions that had been identified in the process. (A fourth complementary report provided documentation of the process, including all the details of the public consultation.)

INFLUENCING FURTHER ACTION

In March 1995, independent of the planning initiatives that had taken place, the three levels of government came together and signed a new tripartite agreement – the Winnipeg Development Agreement – that would contribute $75 million over a five-year period to community priorities. Not coincidentally, the Winnipeg Development Agreement focused on all the same priorities that the community had identified through their involvement in the various public processes conducted during the past few years. (See Table 1.) As the agreement was being developed, a short public-consultation exercise was carried out that served to verify that economic development was a priority. The community also wanted financial resources to be committed to education and training, public safety in the downtown and adjacent neighbourhoods, and downtown revitalization. The process of gaining consensus in the community on how public money should be spent was made easier because of the past involvement of the residents in a variety of participatory activities.

Table 1. *Expenditures on Community Priorities by the Tripartite Winnipeg Development Agreement*

Program	Expenditure in $ millions
North Main street development	10.0
Urban safety	3.5
Neighbourhood improvement	7.0
Housing	1.5
Job access	9.0
Career access	1.0
Innovative demonstration projects	6.8
Innovative child and family services	4.5
Transportation (primarily airport)	5.0
Information technology applications	4.8
Downtown revitalization	4.0
Tourism	4.2
Heritage resources incentives	6.2
Strategic initiatives	6.0
Total	75.0

In the span of six years, the community-improvement initiatives identified by the task force on the city's Economic Development Strategy have been addressed substantially. Winnipeg will have a new training and continuous learning centre in its downtown that will improve the educational services in the city. The airport will be transferred to community ownership, and efforts are under way that may result in the city becoming an international air-cargo hub. Revitalization activities for the city's downtown have been funded and commenced in 1995.

LESSONS LEARNED

Public participation has been encouraged in Winnipeg, and it has produced successful results. The expectation of participation and consultation is such that the city essentially provides that opportunity as a service to the public, much like any of its other services – police protection, public transit, and garbage collection. As such, there must be a measure of customer satisfaction to the provision of that service; that is, the public must value the service and feel that it is getting good value for tax dollars.

But who is the public? There is a strange misconception here. It sometimes appears that anyone who actively participates in a process somehow abandons his or her status as a member of the public. In reality, the public comprises anyone outside the jurisdiction of the agency that is running the planning process. A process led by a steering committee that includes a cross-section of residents, business leaders and academics, among others, is one that has incorporated public participation into its organizational structure. The ideas generated by that group represent a legitimate form of public input. So too does the result of a public forum, a workshop with an interest group, or a public-attitude survey. In providing the service of participation and consultation, planners must recognize that the public has the potential to occupy many roles in the process.

In working with the public, the planner plays a vital role as well. It is the planner's responsibility to recognize and seek out the visionaries who are capable of articulating the grand ideas that have merit; to bring these ideas forward for scrutiny and refinement by decision-makers; and to pull together strategists capable of bringing the ideas to fruition. In doing this, the range and form of consultation can vary greatly depending on the circumstance. Through the experiences described above, insights have been gained and much has been learned. On the basis of this experience, we propose twenty lessons for municipal policy-makers and practitioners of public participation.

Lesson 1: Trust the process

A credible process will produce reliable results each and every time. Credibility stems from the open exchange of ideas and opinions and the honest conveyance of those ideas into a final product. Public consultation cannot be used to justify preconceived ideas and established positions. As representatives of city government we learned not to interject our own views and consciously avoided shaping the outcome of the consultation process in favour of our own convictions. The participants in the process would feel manipulated and would withdraw their support and involvement. We have learned to trust the process; it will deliver the "right" results.

Lesson 2: Know your stakeholders

The involvement of the stakeholders is essential to the success of the consultation process. Every effort must be made to engage those individuals or groups in the dialogue about the process, their participation in the process, and its outcome. It is easy to identify and involve organized groups; it is a much more difficult task to engage those that are unorganized. However, failing to reach all stakeholders in a meaningful way will deny the process the credibility it requires to be effective. In the CentrePlan process, it became apparent that the downtown residential community was not represented adequately on the steering committee. They immediately criticized the process and distanced themselves from it. The residents then had to be approached repeatedly to participate. Considerable effort was made to gain their confidence and to assure them that their participation would be legitimate. Overlooking these stakeholders at the beginning of the process was a mistake, however; not pursuing their involvement would have resulted in the failure of the process.

Lesson 3: Keep it simple; make it clear

The public is not an amorphous mass; it is a collection of individuals. As an individual, the person participating in a workshop, forum, or other venue wants to know very clearly and simply what is going on. What is this project all about? What do you expect from me? What will you do with the results? How does it fit into the overall process? These are some of the questions that need to be answered at the outset, in a personal manner. In the CentrePlan process, over three hundred people attended a public forum. Thirty-three tables were set up, with a facilitator at each. Upon entering the hall, each participant was given a workbook that clearly explained how the evening would unfold, and they were directed to sit anywhere. The facilitator at the table provided personal contact by greeting each participant individually and answering any questions that were raised. As well, the overall project was explained to the entire assembly at the beginning and, at the end of the evening, the results were summarized for the entire group. The next step of the process was explained and participants could submit their names if they wanted to continue their involvement.

Lesson 4: Build on challenges not promises

The public has been asked to participate in many different initiatives over the years. All too often, these processes did not seem to go anywhere. As a result, members of the public have become jaded. They question whether their input will be meaningful. They want to see results and will only be willing to participate if they have some assurance that their recommendations will be acted on. It is important not to make promises that cannot be kept. If the resulting plan must be approved by city council, for example, let them know that this is the challenge. And, ask them how best to meet it. As well, let them know that it is their collective responsibility to ensure that action results from the process they are embarking on. Their continued support and commitment can make it happen.

Lesson 5: Expect resistance

If a planning process runs its course smoothly, there may be something wrong with the process. We have learned to expect resistance along the way, and we have come to recognize the pattern. A newly formed group, whether it is a steering committee or participants in a workshop, needs to coalesce. Before that happens, one or more hurdles often need to be overcome. Members will question the process and question the composition of the group. And, of greater concern, they will be reluctant to accept their assignment. When charged with a difficult responsibility, participants often respond by saying that they do not have enough information or that they do not have enough time. This resistance needs to be overcome before the process can continue. It requires persistence and patience.

Lesson 6: Spend time preparing, and keep looking ahead

Preparation is the key to any successful consultation process. In the review of Plan Winnipeg, a tight, six-week program was devised and delivered with considerable success. While participants were appreciative of quick results, the intensity of this compressed program was difficult on staff. At the end of the six-week segment, the energy level was low and much time was wasted. The momentum that was generated was lost. We learned that while intensive consultation can only be sustained for short periods of time, it is critical to continue to plan ahead in order to ensure the next segment is well thought out and can follow suit with minimum time lost. As a consultation process unfolds, the tendency is to be overwhelmed with day-to-day administrative details. We learned that one group of staff members must be entrusted to manage that operation, and another group must continue to plan the process months ahead of process delivery. It is critical to establish targets and to hit them.

Lesson 7: Manage the process

Staff involved in public consultation must be experts in process development and management. In the CentrePlan process, members of an advisory committee continually questioned the expertise of the staff in designing and delivering the process. To address their concerns we formed a subcommittee called the Process Team to advise staff on how to proceed. This was a mistake. It led to ongoing conflict between staff and the Process Team. We learned that, as managers of the process, we have a responsibility to do just that: manage. The process cannot be given to others to manage. Participants are responsible for content, and the staff is responsible for allowing that content to emerge. In doing so, staff members must be experts in managing complex processes, in understanding of theory, and in their ability to apply it. And participants must be confident that the staff knows what it is doing.

Lesson 8: Work hard to get people out

Providing the opportunity for participation is not enough. Hard work is required to ensure that meaningful participation takes place. During the CentrePlan process, we conducted a very successful interactive public forum, with thirty-three facilitators and over three hundred participants. With media present, we wanted to build excitement and importance around the event. We had to make sure that the hall was full. We could not afford to only advertise the event in the newspapers and take our chances. To ensure attendance, personalized invitations were sent from the mayor's office to everyone on our mailing list, and this was followed up with phone calls to each. We used the grapevine to spread the word to colleagues and asked them to do the same. We provided (and advertised) day-care service. Since the forum ran from 5:00 pm to 9:00 pm, we provided (and advertised) a modest buffet. We monitored interest and were well prepared for the number that showed up. Good attendance does not just happen, it requires hard work.

Lesson 9: Match technique to desired output

There are many reasons to invite the public into a consultative process, so begin by asking, "What are we trying to accomplish?" Consultation can be used to identify public expectations, community needs, expert advice, issues and strategies. Consultation can also be used to validate what you have already heard. Once the purpose is clear, techniques can be selected or devised to achieve the desired result. We learned, for example, that the general public can provide insights into community values – values that distinguish that community from others. During the CentrePlan process, we devised a technique to identify these values. In small-group workshops, we asked participants to write down three separate adjectives that would describe the downtown the way they would like it to be. We asked for these words, one by one, and wrote them on a flip-chart. After grouping words of similar meaning, a simple priority-setting exercise was conducted whereby each participant placed dots beside their three favourite words from the complete list. The top-rated words were a reflection of that group's values. Know what you want to get, and pick a technique that will get it for you.

Lesson 10: Match style to group

Each group you work with in a public-consultation process will warrant a different style of facilitation. Coming from the public sector, our style was professional yet somewhat informal. During the Plan Winnipeg review, we learned quickly that a meeting with the chamber of commerce, for example, warranted a less casual, more business-like style. It was necessary to ensure that meetings started promptly, that an agenda was presented (and adhered to), that presentation material was professional looking, and that the meeting unfolded expeditiously (usually no more than an hour). Meeting with a resident group in the evening at a community centre was a different story. Here, a white shirt and tie could become a barrier, and efforts to stick to a specific time-frame could inhibit the willingness to share points of view. During the CentrePlan process, we established five strategy-teams to come up with ideas related to the components of the vision. The team responsible for the form and function of the downtown chose to limit its membership to a manageable number of fourteen, met twice, and submitted its report. The team responsible for social well-being chose to have an open membership that grew to nearly fifty, met nine times, and had considerable difficulty bringing its discussions to closure. Different groups; different styles.

Lesson 11: Convince the sceptics; ignore the cynics

Many members of the public are naturally sceptical of consultation processes and may be hesitant to participate. They often have legitimate doubts that, if addressed, can cause them to become your greatest allies. Other individuals are consistently cynical, will never participate, and will, passively or actively, seek to promote your failure. During the review of Plan Winnipeg, many organized groups and associations were approached and asked to participate in the review process. Many of these groups were sceptical about their involvement and were concerned that their efforts would be unproductive and a waste of time. The business community, in particular, was critical of the city's planning initiatives. Establishing a working relationship with Winnipeg's chamber of commerce was an immediate priority. Continued effort to build a credible relationship resulted in the chamber of commerce being a supporter of the review process and a "driver" of the two planning initiatives that followed. In the CentrePlan process, it soon became apparent that certain individuals would forever remain outside. They expressed cynicism and refused to 'legitimize a flawed process,' regardless of concessions that were offered. Be prepared to walk away from these people, but before you do, assure yourself that they are not merely sceptics.

Lesson 12: Keep your steering committee busy

When leaders are assigned responsibility for the outcome of the planning exercise, efforts must be taken to ensure that a sense of ownership is developed. It is difficult for this to occur if they are passive observers of the process. We found that it is critical to set an ambitious agenda for the steering committee to follow. They must have important decisions to make on a regular basis, or they will lose interest. Direct involvement in the consultation process helps as well. In the CentrePlan process, we encouraged each of our thirty-five steering-committee members to participate (with additional members from various interest groups and the public at large) on their choice of five strategy-teams that had been established. In fact, each strategy-team was chaired and cochaired by steering-committee members. In this way, they were able to experience first-hand the breadth of ideas that was put forward and to participate in the negotiation required to achieve consensus on priorities. In the end, having the leaders involved greatly facilitated the adoption of the plan and gave them a greater sense of satisfaction.

Lesson 13: Strive to learn

The reason for engaging in consultation is to tap into the collective wisdom of the community. It is a means of gaining insight into their aspirations, their concerns, and their solutions. Staff members involved in delivering the process benefit the most as they acquire knowledge that could not be gained any other way. In developing the plan for the airport, we would have erred had we followed our initial instincts and imposed a plan of strict land-use controls to regulate development in proximity to the airport. Instead, we were encouraged to consult with a variety of industries, businesses and residents. As a result of their input, a better understanding emerged of what needed to be done. In the end, land-use regulations were only one component of a more comprehensive approach to securing the long-term potential of the airport.

Lesson 14: Build consensus around good ideas

Not every idea agreed to by consensus is necessarily good or right. The objective must be to recognize the good ideas (which may be few in number) and to build consensus around them. Experts will need to be consulted. The Economic Development Strategy identified the airport as our window to the world. But it took five more years of exploration by the business community to uncover the particular niche of opportunity. Research by experts, together with continued validation through community consultation, resulted in the identification of specific air-cargo and intermodal potential. This, in turn, provided the necessary conditions that allowed government to financially support and invest in the venture. Consensus around a good idea, in this case, was built over a period of years.

Lesson 15: Use experts to build knowledge

The effectiveness of a consultation process is dependent on the knowledge of experts to point out the relative merit of the ideas that are generated. If these experts are part of the process they can provide a valuable resource. During the airport process, over fifty representatives from airport-related business and industry were pulled together to share their unique perspectives on the future of the airport. Many of the insights they offered were a reflection of their in-depth knowledge about their business or industry and the markets within which they operate. Each of the participants benefited from shared knowledge, which they would not have been privy to in any other way. We also benefited from the experts' opinions, because they eliminated the need for expensive and time-consuming research. In the end, the group formed an association that is now the driving force behind the airport initiative, and it has been granted financial support from government. Through this experience, we were somewhat surprised to learn that experts are often eager to share their knowledge. Take advantage of them.

Lesson 16: Numbers count, to a degree

Consultative processes always boast their numbers. There is merit in doing so. A high number of participants lends credibility to a process and helps garner political support. However, quality is more important than quantity, and one-on-one dialogue works best. To achieve good results, a consultative process must include opportunities for small-group, face-to-face discussions. Certainly, numbers are important, but there is a limit to the number of participants that is needed to ensure reliable results. We learned that public participation is a lot like survey work: there is a point beyond which the reliability of the results improves very little. However, continued participation is still important to build your store of good ideas. During the CentrePlan process, we conducted workshops with forty different organizations and interest groups. With only small variations, each workshop followed the same format, focusing on what participants liked and disliked about the downtown, and what they felt it needed in order to improve. The priorities identified in each of these areas changed little after fifteen or twenty workshops. But the repetitiveness strengthened our convictions that what we were hearing was legitimate, and we continued to pick up good ideas along the way.

Lesson 17: Build the product as you go

It is generally necessary at the end of a planning process to produce a final report. To maintain the support of those who participated, it is critical that the report accurately reflect their input. We learned that the best way to ensure this is to build the report as you go. If a vision statement has been articulated, place it in a draft report and feed it back to participants for verification. If that is followed by the identification of issues, list them in the next draft and send it back. Whatever feedback is received must be incorporated into the next draft. Keeping track of drafts can be very confusing, but participants will recognize that it is their words that are being recorded and that their ideas are shaping the direction of the document. As well, it is important to get design advice early so that the appearance of the document, in terms of style and graphics, does not change substantially from beginning to end. The only thing that should change at the end is the quality of the printing – there should be no surprises.

Lesson 18: Record everything

In a successful process, participants are confident that their ideas have been properly recorded and have influenced the result. Several months after the completion of CentrePlan, a student from the University of Winnipeg approached us to talk about the process. His was one of over sixty written submissions mailed into the CentrePlan office. He wanted to know what became of his ideas. We were able to present a document, entitled *Participation Results*, that included in detail all that we had heard throughout the process. He could see that his name and his suggestions had been accurately recorded and that the summary of the written submissions included his thoughts. He was convinced, rightly so, that his input had made a difference. Careful documentation can silence potential critics.

Lesson 19: Don't quit till you're satisfied, but ensure closure

The quality of any process is a direct reflection of the integrity and dedication of those who participate in it and those who manage it. We learned to set high standards and to continually push the participants until those expectations were met. In the review of Plan Winnipeg, one component of the plan dealt with corporate-management philosophy. There was resistance to include this in what amounted to a development plan, and, once that hurdle was overcome, there was difficulty articulating the philosophy in a way that fit well into the plan. Much hard work (and about a dozen drafts) resulted in a stronger document that now encompasses not only the policies that outline what the city intends to do over the long term, but the operating principles under which those policies will be implemented. Perseverance pays off. One caution, however, is to avoid unnecessary extensions in the duration of the process. Closure is critically important to participants. They need to know that action is forthcoming from the recommendations they provided. As one of our colleagues stated, "There are too many round tables, and not enough end tables!"

Lesson 20: Build on the relationship

The most important outcome of a consultative, participatory process is the relationship that is fostered with the community. That relationship should be one of trust, respect and commitment. While the process you run must be brought to closure, contact with the participants need not. Through newsletters that provide updates on progress, or through follow-up workshops that refine and validate the direction, or through personal contact with the participants, the dialogue initiated by the process can continue. Consultative planning processes grant you access to community leaders, which can be a tremendous resource in the future. Make the effort to keep up the relationship.

CONCLUSION

People want to have a say in decisions that affect their lives, and there may be nothing that affects their lives more over the long term than their city's ability to promote economic development. We learned over the last six years that Winnipeggers are impassioned about their city. They do not want Winnipeg to be anything other than it is (or perhaps was) – they are not asking for drastic change. They recognize that their city affords them a high quality of life and provides many of the benefits of other large urban centres without the accompanying problems. They have affordable housing, world-class arts and cultural facilities, great restaurants, numerous parks and open spaces, vibrant neighbourhoods, high-quality educational institutions, clean air and uncongested streets. They want these benefits to continue to be provided, but they recognize that the current economic situation in the city does not allow that to happen. The city is losing ground, and aggressive economic-development efforts are needed simply to maintain the present level of services. In short, Winnipeggers support economic growth as a means of maintaining their quality of life. And, they have some very strong thoughts about where and how that growth should occur. It is important for us in government to understand what they are saying. We must make the effort to listen.

3

More Than One Way Towards Economic Development: Public Participation and Policy-making in the Vancouver Region

Patrick J. Smith

INTRODUCTION

The changing realities of economic development in contemporary societies have posed a variety of dilemmas for urban policy-makers. These new realities confronting our city regions have also produced a variety of processes and policy choices. Added to this mix is the issue of local public involvement in determining such choices.

In this chapter, the contention is that different types of economic-development emphases may involve differing degrees and forms of public involvement; as such, policy responses on economic development – and public involvement in their determination – may vary according to focus and type. This assessment is based on local and regional policy choices and reactions in the metropolitan Vancouver region (Greater Vancouver). Two types of cases form the basis for this analysis: 1) *local* economic-development efforts – primarily at the regional but also at the local and provincial levels within Greater Vancouver; and 2) the *global* activities at the municipal level of the City of Vancouver, as these relate to the economic-development strategy of the city. Both are examined through the prism of public participation. The argument here is that public participation does matter – where it is allowed to occur or where there is some local insistence on it – but that examination of such activity in our city regions needs to recognize that different economic-development policy foci may be supported by differing degrees and forms of public involvement. This examination of economic development within Greater Vancouver suggests that local variations in public participation do exist, depending on the type of involvement and the setting, and that the regional experience itself may differ from that of individual municipalities in the region. Evidence with regard to Vancouver's global activities supports a conclusion that different segments of the community may be particularly active in sustaining different policies for distinct municipal–international activities on economic development across alternative global-policy phases. Evidence concerning more local economic-development efforts adds to this notion, suggesting that the more "niche-based" community support/participation evident in the various international policy phases is also different from the broader community base essential in developing and implementing a successful regional strategic-planning exercise. These variations say a good deal about the impact of public involvement in agenda setting – on economic development and, more generally, for urban governance. The case evidence reported here supports the notion that different forms of community involvement play important roles in sustaining policy outcomes – an important aspect of measuring the success of public participation in local governance.

THE SETTING

Greater Vancouver is Canada's third-largest metropolis. It is one of the four fastest-growing urban areas in North America and Canada's fastest.[1] It is projected that this region will grow to 2 million by the end of the century, and to 2.5 million by 2025. This region is the core of British Columbia's "Lower Mainland." Over half of the citizens of the province (2.1 million people – 54.4 per cent) reside in the Lower Mainland, which comprises two regional districts (reconfigured from four) along the Fraser River Valley adjacent to Vancouver.[2] The Lower Mainland represents the economic engine of the province.[3] Politically, the region elects just over half (50.7 per cent) of the members of the legislative assembly of the province. In Jane Jacobs' terms, this Vancouver-centred Lower Mainland forms one coherent "city region."

The Vancouver census metropolitan area now essentially corresponds to the recently re-defined Greater Vancouver Regional District (GVRD).[4] Established in 1967, the GVRD is an amalgam of twenty municipalities and two unincorporated electoral areas, covering 3250 square kilometres. The GVRD contains a little under half (1.867 million people – 48.2 per cent) of the provincial population and a majority (eight of twelve) of the largest (over 50,000 population) local authorities in the province. As of the May 1996 B.C. general election, the Vancouver metropolitan region had thirty-six of the seventy-five legislative seats, forty-eight per cent of the provincial total.

Whatever its substantial growth potential, the fastest-growing areas in the Vancouver metropolis are in the Fraser Valley suburbs within and beyond the eastern boundaries of the GVRD. By 2010, for example,

GVRD projections have the Greater Vancouver suburb of Surrey surpassing the central-city Vancouver in population. Adjacent non-GVRD outer suburbs, such as Mission, Abbotsford/Matsqui and Chilliwack are the fastest-growing areas in the province. One by-product of this rapid growth is that the ethnic makeup of the Vancouver-centred region's population has become increasingly multicultural; almost half of the public-school population of Vancouver has English as a second language, for example, and other municipalities are not far behind. This translates, increasingly, into politics around who will represent these communities. In metropolitan Vancouver, this has produced new representatives for the Indo-Canadian communities and the first provincial representative from the Chinese community (in the May 1996 B.C. general election).

In terms of the development of metropolitan Vancouver's economy, there has also been a growing dichotomy between the Lower Mainland and the rest of the province: much of B.C.'s economy is resource extractive, with heavy reliance on logging, mining and fishing. The economic base of the Lower Mainland, on the other hand, is increasingly service-oriented, with a strong reliance on personal and corporate services, including tourism, and province-wide distribution of goods and service.[5] Combined with its significant internationalist population, a more interdependent – and internationally oriented – regional economy, and its Pacific port location (the Port of Vancouver is the second-busiest in North America, and the busiest on the west coast of the Americas),[6] metropolitan Vancouver has become an "international city."[7] The internationalist orientation of the city has had an impact on its economic-development orientation, as I will discuss below.

One additional factor that affects local economic-development decision-making in the Vancouver-centred region is the fact that most of the best arable land in the province is found in the Lower Mainland. Only one-quarter of the land in the province is suitable for *any* form of farming, and most of this prime agricultural land is in the Vancouver region. Thus, the potential for policy conflicts and the necessity of devising regional solutions to resolve urban-development problems as part of any economic-development strategy become immediately apparent.

"REGIONAL" ECONOMIC DEVELOPMENT IN GREATER VANCOUVER: PUBLIC PARTICIPATION AND A HOLISTIC POLICY APPROACH PRODUCE RESULTS

Background

Regional economic development has always been linked with strategic land-use planning. Increasingly, as both the private sector and urban governments recognize that quality of life is the key factor in promoting economic development and that development must be based on a sustainable model, these links are becoming even stronger. Local public involvement in defining and defending urban quality of life is thus increasingly important as well.

A community base and public involvement have been essential in sustaining municipal "global" economic-development policy activity over time in the City of Vancouver. Efforts at the regional level in metropolitan Vancouver to develop a new "strategic plan," including an economic-development component, were premised on extensive public participation and "local buy-in," and they produced positive results. The regional planning exercise had provincial support but was locally inspired. It produced local support and a sense of ownership largely because of the public consultation on which it was based, a process that took almost five and a half years. It achieved this degree of success because there was recognition that a more holistic approach to ensuring regional "livability" was required, one that combined thinking about land-use and transportation planning together with economic development and green-space preservation, air, water quality and waste.

Two significant events occurred in 1995 to produce this positive result. A new provincial planning legislation, the Growth Strategies Statutes Amendment Act, was passed in British Columbia. It required municipalities to plan regionally and allowed the province to establish mediative forms when local–regional agreement was not forthcoming. This new provincial legislation was the result of an extensive consultative process that included consideration of other planning and governance models. The results of this research agenda and consultation was agreement on nine basic principles, which underpin this important provincial legislative reform:

1. *no new institutions*: partly a by-product of recent political and fiscal realities and partly a recognition that B.C. already had a strong local planning system;[8]

2. *voluntary participation, most of the time*: premised on the notion of voluntary planning and the idea that "planning works best when there is buy-in" but allowing for provincial requirements for regional growth strategies in instances of "extreme" growth or where local governments are slow to react cooperatively;

3. *compatibility, a bias towards agreement*: to ensure compatibility and consistency among local and regional growth strategies. Subsidiarity prin-

ciples are included here, with an "interactive" system giving "equal weight" to official community plans and regional strategies;

4. *dispute resolution, as a last resort*: recognition of the need for a "closure" requirement, while preferring locally negotiated "collaborative solutions," a provincial capacity – and mechanism – to ensure "differences" are, in the end, "resolved";

5. *broad-based consultation, early and often*: a commitment that "everyone – municipalities, community groups, and other interested publics – who has to live with the outcomes should have a say in the development of plans";

6. *regional diversity/regional flexibility*: a planning system flexible enough to accommodate regional diversity in economy, geography, objectives and issues;

7. *provincial direction and support*: a provincial commitment to stating all its expectations clearly;

8. *early provincial involvement*: recognition that a wide range of provincial decisions – for example, on capital expenditures for highways/transit, health/education facilities or energy projects – can significantly affect settlement patterns; and a provincial commitment to come to the table early and stay involved continuously throughout the regionally led planning processes; and

9. *provincial commitment*: an acceptance that the province should itself be guided by regional growth strategies and ensure its actions/investments are consistent with local governments' initiatives.

Also in 1995, the GVRD arrived at the end of a more than five-year-long local–regional process of consultation and discussion to establish the Livable Region Strategic Plan. This "Creating Our Future" process produced broad policy agreement. Greater Vancouver's Livable Region Strategic Plan was approved by the provincial government in the spring of 1996. A second-phase regional context round followed.

Both the new B.C. provincial planning legislation and the GVRD's agreement on a new strategic plan speak directly to arguments about metropolitan governance, growth management reform, sustainable economic development, and the role of public participation in ensuring successful policy outcomes. In addition, the Greater Vancouver regional experience offers a rebuttal to suggestions by Anne Golden and her fellow commissioners on the Task Force on the Future of the Greater Toronto Area (GTA) that the consensual model, as exemplified by Greater Vancouver, was "inherently weak" and suffered from a "lack of mandate," lack of representation and "an inability to achieve consensus on matters of specific policy."[9] The Greater Vancouver and British Columbia experience of the 1990s suggests alternatives to metropolitan restructuring, to economic development, and to major policy initiatives premised on truncated public participation.

This case study explores the recent experience of Greater Vancouver in regional economic development and planning and comments on the relationship between these efforts and the public participation on which they are based.

Beginning with the intermunicipal agreement among the City of Vancouver and three neighbouring municipalities to form the Burrard Peninsula Joint Sewerage Committee in 1911, the early history of cooperation in the Vancouver region was largely locally inspired. It also had at least one significant by-product – the development of a regional political culture and identity.[10] Subsequent local action resulted in a regional water district being created in 1926; this was followed by the establishment of four area health/hospital boards, between 1936 and 1948. And following significant flooding in 1948, the Lower Mainland Regional Planning Board was formed the following year.[11]

The regional identity was important in Greater Vancouver, where the planning role of the regional district, established by the provincial government in 1967, was substantial and involved working with provincial agencies, such as the new Agricultural Land Commission set up in 1973 by the David Barrett NDP government to administer and help preserve all arable lands in the province. The first GVRD plan was the Livable Region Plan (LRP), completed in 1975. The existence of this regional identity was even more important after regional planning was abolished by the province in the early 1980s. Regardless, the GVRD sustained its political commitment to regional planning.

From the late 1960s to the mid-1970s, the GVRD concentrated on a new form of planning to arrive at its LRP. This plan was based on five strategies, with economic development and land-use links at its centre:

– establishing various core areas and job targets for these;

– creating regional town centres;

– allocating residential growth so it was consistent with jobs and services;

- preserving farmland, parkland, significant view sites; and

- establishing a light-rail system as the key to achieving the other four strategies.

Based on an extensive public-consultation process, this first LRP had widespread public support. Its effects were lasting, the most obvious of which were the implementation of an economic-development strategy based on a regional town-centre concept and GVRD support for farmland preservation in the metropolitan region and beyond, into the rest of the Lower Mainland.

Ironically, it was largely around policy disagreements with the rightist Social Credit provincial government over agricultural farmland preservation in the region that the GVRD, and, as a result, all other regional districts, lost regional planning responsibilities. The province made this decision in 1983, as part of a broader package of "Restrained Government." The broadly based process and agreement on regional planning goals achieved in the late 1970s/early 1980s within the Greater Vancouver Region played a crucial role in preserving regional planning in the absence of regional planning authority. This included further expansion of the regional town centres; agreement on the alignment of rapid transit to complement these growth centres; an extensive acquisition program for regional parks – even extending beyond the boundaries of the Vancouver region; and, as by-products, initial steps towards improvements in air quality/air monitoring, and waste disposal and treatment. Within the GVRD, this regional focus was encouraged primarily by the development services department, the successor to its disbanded planning component, and by its parks department.

Creating Our Future

Despite the success of ongoing regional planning in Greater Vancouver, even with the loss of regional district planning *authority* in 1983, the GVRD concluded that a major update of the 1975 LRP was needed by the end of the 1980s. Changes in the region and a significant increase in development pressures led to a GVRD decision in spring 1989 to begin an extensive process of public consultation for a revised regional plan. Proceeding without formal authority helped determine the GVRD's consensual approach and its public participation component. In March, the region published *The Livable Region: A Strategy For the 1990s* as an initial discussion paper.[12] In July, the same year, the GVRD board approved seven broad "Livability Goals" as part of this citizen-participation exercise:

1. *a region in nature*: blending urban development and preservation of the natural environment;

2. *an economy of growth and change*: blending livability, economic growth and diversity amidst interdependence;

3. *accessibility for people and goods*: ease of communication, job-housing links, etc.;

4. *a healthy and safe region*: air and water quality, good social services, functional space patterns, etc.;

5. *a region of diversity and vitality*: support for social and physical diversity;

6. *an equitable region*: sharing the region's livability across all communities; and

7. *an efficient region*: ensuring effective spending and intergovernmental cooperation among the region's municipalities and with senior jurisdictions.[13]

The early public meetings and other measures of community priorities identified considerable support for an economic-development strategy that was environmentally sustainable. Numerous groups – including The Bike People, a regional bikeway lobby, SPEC (Society Promoting Environmental Conservation), the Sierra Club of Canada, Greenpeace, other air- and water-quality advocates and various mass-transit proponents – pushed this sustainability agenda. These first documents led the Choosing Our Future consultation process, which continued for the next fourteen months. The process had the following elements:

- a series of seven "regional challenge" seminars, involving over four hundred participants from a broad range of community interests, on various policy dilemmas (e.g., urban mobility, the environment, culture, health and aging, urban design and suburban development, changing values, and community life);

- the Urban Futures Public Attitude Survey of thirteen hundred regional residents on regional development issues and whether citizens were willing to pay for improvements;

- the Children's Vision Poster Program, with input from over eight hundred young people in the region;

PUBLIC PARTICIPATION AND POLICY-MAKING IN THE VANCOUVER REGION

- a subsequent regional forum, held over a day and a half, involving more than four hundred people who were given responsibility to refine the actions needed on issues from the regional economy to the environment. The forum had local cable coverage and phone-in capacity for others to participate and comment from their homes;

- six community meetings, involving seven hundred more participants;

- subsequent presentations to the GVRD planning committee;

- various research reports;[14] and

- a subsequent (June 1990) region-wide television program with public phone-in on the preliminary recommendations for regional development.[15]

The use of the local community cable networks on two occasions during this period to create an *additional* window for public involvement – beyond informational mailings to keep citizens updated and various, more traditional opportunities such as the community meetings – was one of the more innovative elements in the GVRD Choosing Our Future planning process.

Following this huge effort, the GVRD announced a consensus on "54 Steps to a More Livable Region." These included limitations to private automobile-use in the region, the creation of more "complete communities," conserving land resources, including farmland and accessible green areas, helping to ensure clean air and water, sustainable waste-disposal and treatment, and maintaining the region's economic health. The latter linked environment and economic development as regional priorities. Perhaps most importantly, the involvement of such a broad cross-section of the region's interested publics was an excellent example of public participation at the normative planning level: what Graham Smith has defined as "a reconsideration of the value premises underlying decisions; the definition of desired ends and ideals; and decisions that determine what ought to be done."[16] In such a lengthy and complex enterprise, this normative agreement, and the broad base on which it was established, were essential ingredients in the degree of subsequent success.

Between autumn 1990 and spring 1991, each of the then-eighteen municipalities in the GVRD also conducted their own local reviews of what had been agreed. The earlier "Livability Goals" and "action steps" had, by early 1993, been condensed into five major themes and thirty-six strategic/operational policies option.[17] The five themes included the following:

- *maintaining a healthy environment*: thirteen policy directives for better water quality, solid-waste management and cleaner air;

- *conserving the region's land resource*: five policy statements for green-space preservation, agricultural land maintenance and containment of urban sprawl, and five steps towards transportation investments, which would reinforce regional goals and values;

- *serving a changing population*: six policy choices to more effective social policy – research, health planning, equitable service provision, improved policing, and housing, particularly regarding affordability, an important issue in a region where average single-family home prices had increased $56,000 over the previous twenty-nine months of the Livable Region Plan (LRP) review process;

- *maintaining the region's economic health*: three policy directives to help ensure global competitiveness, ensuring an economic-growth distribution that supports LRP objectives and develops dialogue with the province to share growth with other parts of the province; and

- *managing the region*: a new approach based on six principles: a strengthened intermunicipal federation; clear, effective and fair working relationships with the province; mandate changes to the GVRD; regional land-use/transportation-planning mandates that do *not* impinge on municipal authority; fiscal integrity; and ensuring an informed public. Four policy options were set out to achieve these principles: on consultation regarding land-use, transportation and social-development mandates; maintenance of cooperative planning and decision-making in the region; implementing broad public communication on regional choices; and ensuring that regional expenditures and debt management relate to the region's capacity to fund its "livable" future.

These themes and potential actions were posed in another regional consultation in May 1993. Six "Critical Choices" forums were held simultaneously in different parts of the Greater Vancouver region. To ensure the widest public input, this process also encouraged citizens to complete a newspaper insert questionnaire that was distributed to every home in the region through community newspapers. As with the first round, local input was sought by allowing all citizens in the region to view the public consultation on region-wide cable television. The major outcome of this participatory exercise was a focus on growth management and on ensuring that any development in the region preserved its livability.

Over the next two years, the GVRD members worked on achieving consensus on five major choices to ensure regional livability:

1. an air-quality strategy;

2. a Transport 2021 plan to ensure that public-transportation investments coincided with the agreed regional livability values;

3. establishing financial priorities – on water, sewers and solid waste, hospitals, transit and other regional investments – to reinforce the region's future;

4. adopting a Livable Region Strategic Plan; and

5. re-defining/restructuring the role/mandates of the regional government.

Public participation during this phase included a policy conference, in January 1992, on regional governance, with more than two hundred participating, and a May 1992 conference on regional growth and transportation, involving three hundred participants from across the region and from adjacent regions. Here, as with other conferences, invitations went out to all who had expressed any interest in any of the previous participation exercises. The conference was also open to newly interested people. The event also included regional cable coverage. In July 1992, over three hundred and thirty people were involved in a further public conference, on regional governance. This concluded that the "active involvement of citizens" at all levels is essential to the process.

On transportation, regional consensus was achieved during 1993 (on a medium-range plan) and 1994 (on a long-range plan, increasing public transit's share, modestly, from thirteen per cent to eighteen per cent by 2021). This was the first instance in Greater Vancouver "of regional land use and transportation ... being planned interactively by local government and provincial authorities together."[18] Various staff reports and public meetings formed the basis for these changes. For example, in October 1992, over three hundred people participated in a public forum on regional bicycle issues. Thirty-three presentations were made by representatives from bicycle clubs and advisory committees, environmental groups like the Sierra Club and Greenpeace, bicycle commuters, couriers, and recreational and mountain bikers. All this was supplemented by an ongoing Regional Bicycle Task Force and by information from a survey of twenty-three hundred cyclists in the region.[19]

Other public meetings and conferences were held at each subsequent phase on each key issue. For example, the "Critical Choices" conference in November 1992 involved GVRD politicians and staff, municipal representatives, a wide range of interest and community groups, Fraser Valley representatives, and provincial government representatives, four hundred and fifty people in all. In December 1992, all of the previous several years' work was reviewed by the Greater Vancouver Council of Councils – a first-ever meeting of all elected representatives within the GVRD. Ninety-one of one hundred and fifty-four were able to participate.[20] On the basis of all of this ongoing public input, the GVRD was presented with continually revised technical reports reflecting changes accepted from the consultations. A second Council of Council meeting was held in March 1993. It occurred prior to six public forums held in May 1993. These six forums, involving over 630 participants, were held simultaneously on 15 May. They were connected via satellite. Every household in the region could also participate via return of a questionnaire distributed prior to these public meetings, or through their cable involvement. A third Council of Councils, with seventy-one councillors from across the region, was held in June 1993, to review the May public responses. Draft proposals came out of these meetings throughout late 1993 and 1994, with further public input at events such as the Pacific National Exhibition in August-September. All citizens continued to be informed about planning progress. In October 1993, another insert was included in all community newspapers throughout the region.[21]

The year 1994 saw resolutions on the planning and transportation initiatives before the GVRD board. The provincial government also made important policy statements concerning transportation in 1995. Despite the lack of full agreement on these matters, many of the transportation goals identified through the consultative process have begun to be implemented. Many of the decisions, particularly on transportation-demand management and public transit, were taken with air-quality improvements in mind,[22] and with clear awareness that they were premised on the normative planning agreement achieved earlier. Other major regional investment decisions on infrastructure and environment, on sewage treatment, for example, were taken by the GVRD in 1995, pushed by federal and provincial environmental requirements. On land-use and growth management, both the province, with its Growth Strategies Statutes Amendment Act of June 1995, and the GVRD, with the approval of its Livable Region Strategic Plan in October 1995, put in place legislative and policy decisions to ensure implementation of the four fundamental strategies contained in Greater Vancouver's strategic plan:

1. *protect the green zone* through major parks, farmland and watershed preservation and thus establish a long-term boundary for urban growth, an important consideration in a region expected to more than double in population (from 1,317,000 to 2,676,000) over the plan's twenty-five years;

2. *build complete communities* to ensure better job-housing balance through extension of such initiatives as town centres, better public transportation and public services, and more affordable housing;

3. *achieve a compact metropolitan region* to concentrate growth in just under half the region's municipalities, a growth concentration area. Here, work remains to be done: over one-quarter of the 650,000 additional population anticipated in this growth concentration area remains "unaccommodated"; and

4. *increase transportation choice* in all forms of transportation – walking, cycling, public transit, and goods movement – to take precedence over private automobile-use. Transportation-demand management is intended to "help change travel habits."[23]

Implementing the 1995 Plan

To implement its strategic plan, the GVRD anticipates continuation of its consensus/partnership-based planning process (self-described as "preparing plans by consensus and implementing them through partnerships"); delivery of GVRD services and through local/provincial/federal government and other forms of partnerships; monitoring change and progress towards Livable Region Strategic Plan goals and targets; and public reporting. It is also committed to a five-year review of progress towards achieving the regional goals and targets.[24]

Challenges within Greater Vancouver remain, not only on "sharing" population growth, but in achieving transportation goals. Financing these also remains a significant question. Increasingly, as they move on self-governance, First Nations' initiatives for their own economic development in metropolitan centres do not always coincide with their municipal–regional neighbours. In Delta, for example, a significant debate has emerged between the municipality and the Tsawwassen First Nation Band. From the perspective of the band, efforts of the municipality to ensure zoning compliance with its by-laws contradicts moves towards band self-government. The view of the city is that major development on band lands, which do not take into account local transportation, education and other service needs, should not proceed. The debate has left the band to develop its own services for sewage, fire and other needs, and the city refusing to supply the band with water. Because much of the development is occurring on the Pacific flyway for migratory birds and near the Fraser River, with its major salmon runs, calls for senior environmental reviews are added to the discord. This also occurs while Delta is negotiating its Regional Context Statements to ensure that local planning and development coincides with the recently agreed regional strategic plan. The GVRD has become involved through a request from the Tsawwassen Band for water and other services. The GVRD has declined to intervene. Possible First Nation involvement in casino construction, an apparent provincial but not municipal priority, further complicates matters.

Despite ongoing political debates, the Livable Region Strategic Plan and related transportation, environmental and economic-development decisions in the mid-1990s represent "a fundamental shift in direction from the accommodation of current trends to an approach that will conserve the region's strategic resources in land, air, water, energy and financial capital."[25] Agreement on and implementation of the Livable Region Strategic Plan has been based on consensual decision-making, local buy-in, strategic planning, and economic-development goals, all through extensive public participation. Tests, such as in the regional context statements and on transportation, financing and governance, remain. However, the Vancouver region experience supports the conclusion that achieving agreement on sustainable economic development requires public definition of the goals on which it is based, at both the normative ("what ought to be done") and strategic ("what can be done") levels. It also must involve ongoing public consultation and input at the operational/implementation level – what Graham Smith calls "decisions that ... will be done."[26] The results of the November 1996 municipal election suggest that some local differences continue but that prior agreement on the goals for the region certainly contributes to resolution of such real and potential policy differences. Because of its commitment to public involvement, the Greater Vancouver Regional District is assured at least of the capacity to achieve the goals of its strategic plan through transitional and other legislative changes brought forward by the province under its Growth Strategies Statutes Amendment Act. An early history of planning success, based on several decades of public participatory dialogue and normative-level agreement on regional development goals, has produced broad consensus on the development of the metropolitan region over the next quarter-century.

Part of that consensus has included an understanding that economic development in the Vancouver region must also recognize and respond to increasing globalized interdependence. Beginning with an ad hoc, largely non-economic response to locally sponsored municipal international activity in the 1940s, a considerable component of Vancouver's economic-development strategy has come to contain a "global" element. This international economic-development focus has also come to include broader sustainability features.

PUBLIC PARTICIPATION IN "GLOBAL" ASPECTS OF ECONOMIC DEVELOPMENT IN THE CITY OF VANCOUVER

A growing literature emphasizes the international activity of local governments. Much of the literature accentuates the argument that such activity is simply a required municipal response to the external forces of interdependence and globalization and the internal fragmentation of political power. To a considerable degree, local business has been characterized as the engine that has come to drive "global" ideas and policy directions. Critics have suggested that contemporary local decisions about economic development are primarily a variation of local business boosterism from an earlier age. They have also suggested that its emphasis is not one that is particularly inclusive or based on popular definitions of community needs. Yet, both old, and now new, emerging policy phases, where policy has had success, have always had a community base. As the following discussion shows, difficulties in sustaining some of this global activity at the municipal level attest to the importance of community involvement.

It is generally thought that a focus on global policy and capacity at a global level are relatively new among municipal governments. In reality, a global focus by Canadian municipal governments (sometimes called "constituent diplomacy")[27] is more than a half-century old. Vancouver's 1944 twinning with Odessa is the oldest such international link among Western democracies.[28] That cities have become significant global actors contradicts many of the traditional views about the natural order of governance where, constitutionally, foreign policy-making has been the primary responsibility of national governments. It also runs counter to the fact that in Canada, local authority derives from provincial governments, which have had international agendas for a long time.[29] In Canada, senior constitutional authorities, particularly the provinces, have been prone to see any significant policy divergence by municipalities as conflictual.[30]

What has been most intriguing about the global economic-development activities of most Canadian municipal governments, however, is how little conflict local international policy innovations have so far generated with the provincial or federal governments.[31] In the Vancouver case, as well as in others, this relative intergovernmental calm has accompanied expansion in the extent and type of international economic-development activity by local government:

- *in extent*: from the time of Vancouver's twinning in 1944 to 1967, only nine Canadian municipalities had twinned themselves with non-Canadian communities. Over the past thirty years, this pattern has accelerated considerably to include several hundred such formal subnational international exchanges and many other less formal ones.[32] Throughout Greater Vancouver, there has been considerable variety in the degree of municipal international activity. In Vancouver itself, five formal international twinnings and a number of other less formal "strategic" economic-development links have been developed;

- *in type*: more importantly, as the number of municipal governments involved internationally has grown, so too have the types of global activity and exchange. Initially often cultural and educational, these have shifted to more strategic, business-oriented and economic-development forms and have begun to show distinct signs of an emerging and broader "globalist" policy phase. The differing "types" have each included varying degrees of public involvement. As this case study of Vancouver's international-policy phases suggests, the degree and form of community support in each instance helps explain the capacity of particular "types" to sustain themselves over the longer term. In the Vancouver region, both the extent and type of municipal international policy activity fit various forms and reflect differing degrees of community involvement over time. In Vancouver, four policy phases can be identified: the ad hoc policy phase (1940s–1970s); the national policy phase (1980–1986); the strategic policy phase (1987–1990); and the globalist policy phase (1990s).

The Ad Hoc Policy Phase: 1940s–1970s

The first phase was ad hoc in nature and extended from the 1940s to the early 1970s. The ad hoc phase was indicative of relatively immature policy intent and capacity and was oriented primarily towards cultural and educational exchanges. It worked best where it had a clear community base and ongoing community support. The rationale for Vancouver's 1944 twinning with the city of Odessa was rooted in humanitarian assistance to a war-devastated sister port. Several community interests approached council to act to establish a link. Business and labour interests around the port supported the initiative. There was also an important cultural link between the Jewish communities in both cities. Vancouver's Jewish community promoted to council the idea of city-based assistance to Odessa. Cold War relations after 1945 limited further contact, but this sister-city link was never broken.[33] It was re-established with Soviet perestroika and glasnost in the 1980s.

During this early phase, Vancouver added two other sister-cities: Yokohama, in 1965, and Edinburgh, in 1978. In each instance, the incremental pattern was the same: intense initial involvement by parts of the community, creating pressure for formal municipal linkages to be established. These were sometimes followed by periods of relative neglect. The Yokohama link was promoted by local business interests wishing to establish stronger economic links with the emerging Japanese economy. The relatively small Japanese cultural community in Vancouver has not been particularly active in sustaining the Yokohama link. The business interests, which convinced city council to initiate it, have shown levels of attention varying between intensity and neglect over the intervening years. In the case of the Edinburgh connection, the local Scottish community was the catalyst for pressuring council to adopt a sister city link. Its motivation was essentially cultural, including involvement in the Edinburgh Festival and related Scottish events. The local ethnic base was enough to sustain the connection, but efforts to expand the range of mutual activities much beyond the educational and cultural have not materialized.

The basis of these early international exchanges for Vancouver was substantially cultural and educational. The incremental phase was, as Vancouver alderman Libby Davies stated, "never a set program; it was just a matter of evolution."[34] Particular councils were approached (at a rate of fewer than once a decade), and little thought was given to downstream benefits and costs. As such, this policy phase was consistent with Federation of Canadian Municipalities (FCM) objectives for twinnings at the time: to provide direct contact between diverse peoples to foster international understanding; to expand contact between homelands of new Canadians and Canadian communities; to develop an appreciation of foreign culture, history and traditions; and to develop better perspectives on problems/opportunities at home.[35] Increasingly for some, particularly city officials, by the end of the 1970s, this was increasingly "not enough."[36]

The Rational Policy Phase: 1980–1986

The second phase, marked by efforts to develop a more *rational* approach to international activities, extended from the latter part of the 1970s to the mid-1980s. The rational phase emphasized the development of an institutional capacity and a greater focus on economic linkages. In 1980, Mike Harcourt was elected as Vancouver's mayor, with substantial leftist support. During his three terms (1980–1986), Harcourt sought to put the city's internationalist links on a less ad hoc basis. Apart from active participation in the FCM, and in the discussions of "Big City" mayors, Harcourt promoted Vancouver as Canada's "Pacific Gateway." As a result, the city's international focus began to shift to a more economic rationale. This involved work with the then-new Conservative federal government to establish Vancouver as one of two Canadian international banking centres and to strengthen Vancouver's Pacific Rim links.[37] The link with Yokohama was revitalized under Harcourt, and, in 1985, Guangzhou, China, was added as a sister-city. Guangzhou's central place in the emerging Guandong provincial economy and its increasing ties to the dynamic Hong Kong region were important considerations. This twinning had widespread support within the local Chinese community, which is eighty per cent Cantonese. The Guangzhou case demonstrates the importance of a local champion, as well as the significance of niche community support. In 1982, elected alderman Bill Yee became the first Chinese-Canadian elected to Vancouver city council. A political ally of Mayor Mike Harcourt, Yee contested a council policy that there be no new twinnings until after Vancouver's 1986 World Exposition. He felt that there was considerable value – economic as well as cultural – in promoting exchanges between the local Chinese community and China. As a high-profile representative from the local Chinese community, Yee was able to convince a significant portion of the community that a formal twinning with either Shanghai or Guangzhou would be a good idea. Not surprisingly, that consultation indicated strong support for the latter. To push this initiative before council, Yee was instrumental in creating a committee made up of Chinese community leaders, together with local academics and individuals with possible business interest in southern China. To ensure that Guangzhou would be receptive to such an approach, Yee and others made a number of preliminary trips to the Chinese city. With this work done, community support in place, and a committee to promote the twinning before city council, Yee was able to convince his ally Mayor Harcourt and others on council to initiate the formal sister-city relationship.[38]

The same rational approach to twinning, focusing on economics and the Pacific Rim, was evident in the choice of Los Angeles as Vancouver's American twin in 1986. Despite a number of local proposals for other U.S. relationships, Harcourt pushed for Los Angeles because of business opportunities, particularly in the film industry. In this, the mayor had initial local board of trade support. He also had a strong push from the emerging B.C. film industry, much of it centred in metropolitan Vancouver. Here, the mayor himself was an important local champion, seeing the Los Angeles link as consistent with his Asia/Pacific orientation and with important local economic-development opportunities.

Three features of the Los Angeles link stand out:

1. Vancouver participation was essentially from within parts of the business community;

2. The City of Vancouver pursued its Los Angeles and Southern Californian interests with some vigour. The much larger city of Los Angeles – which now has over twenty-five formal sister-city links, all maintained by some form of local niche-community interest and little city involvement – took only limited notice of its northern twin;

3. The Los Angeles link was, and remains, largely business based. It has provided a significant payback for limited local investment. For example, the Vancouver's economic-development officer, working with B.C. Film, created a "pot" of $300,000 by levying everyone in the local film industry. They invested this money in bringing twelve Los Angeles–based independent film producers, each year for six years, to Vancouver. That particular investment is calculated to have produced $150 million in local film-related business to date.[39]

The Los Angeles case suggests that a shift to a more economic interest did mean that broader community involvement in helping to define the international policy orientation of Vancouver declined in importance. Although some form of community base within Vancouver – whether primarily business as with Los Angeles or combined cultural–business as with Guangzhou – was essential to initiate international city-based economic-development activity, it was more important for *maintaining* the link. These bases became even more important as financial constraint hit cities like Vancouver in the 1990s. In the case of Guangzhou, though its local champion Bill Yee left council just after the mid-1980s, he continued to chair the local sister-city committee. And while there were periods subsequently when Vancouver–Guangzhou activity was more muted, Yee was always able to call on its community support if something was needed: if a Chinese vice-mayor visited, for example, Yee could draw on the close-knit local Chinese community.[40] The value of this city link from a local perspective was that the various delegations taken to Guangzhou by both Mike Harcourt and his successor, Gordon Campbell, were not only able to open economic-development doors for Vancouver business in China but also in the vibrant Hong Kong market, a collateral stop on each Guangzhou trip.

The more rational character of this policy phase was also reflected in the organization and funding of city–international initiatives, between 1980–1986. Prior to 1980, there had been no obvious organizational centre for this activity; prior to 1982, budgetary allocations had also been ad hoc. In 1982, Harcourt had city council establish an annual budget for Vancouver's international program. Initially set at $30,000, this grew to $100,000 (out of a total city budget of $300 million) by 1985. Despite the apparently limited nature of city funding, when private-sector multipliers (such as hosting dinners, arranging air travel, etc.) and senior governmental grants (such as travel funding for cultural/artistic groups to participate abroad) were added, the impact of this city seed-funding was considerably greater. Organizationally, day-to-day staff responsibility for Vancouver's global activities was shifted to the city's economic-development office, with protocol placed in the city clerk's office; there was involvement by the mayor's office, as program needs dictated. The very success of this more rational city diplomacy under Harcourt highlighted the limitations of the first incremental phase, with its emphasis on formal sister-city links. The confluence of increased interdependence, a proactive, internationalist mayor (and a committed fellow councillor), senior governments with increasingly coincident Pacific-policy goals, and, in important respects, community involvement created a base for these global economic-development policy initiatives for Vancouver. From an economic-development perspective, the most successful of Vancouver's sister-city links under Harcourt were Los Angeles, with a reasonably active business-community base and the mayor as a champion, and Guangzhou, with clear support in the local Cantonese community and councillor Bill Yee as champion. The Yokohama connection was recognized by the local business community as having considerable potential. There was, however, no champion in this case. The relatively small and diffuse character of the Vancouver Japanese community contributed to the absence of a strong community-based nexus between ethnocultural and business interests. Cultural exchanges continued to dominate the Edinburgh association. Lacking both a local champion and a strong cultural or business base, the Odessa link languished again.

Harcourt's departure to lead the provincial New Democratic Party, the October 1986 re-election of the rightist Social Credit Party to lead the provincial government, and the November 1986 election of business-backed Vancouver mayor Gordon Campbell all paved the way for a new phase of economic development.

The Strategic Policy Phase: 1987–1990

The third phase focused on the development of a more *strategic* internationalist policy position in the late 1980s. Municipal constituent diplomacy in this strategic phase began to place much greater emphasis on a business-oriented economic-development approach. Thus, Vancouver shifted from adding more formal sister-city twinnings (still limited to the five established in the mid-1980s) to establishing less formal linkages with cities that were identified as "gateways" to significant regional and national economies. The strategic policy phase undertaken by Campbell involved a "quiet moratorium" on additional sister-city links and a new emphasis: "a sister-city rationale for the 1980s must recognize that, in addition to friendship, economic and cultural opportunities must be reenforced. It is vital that governmental and non-governmental institutions coordinate their efforts to optimize their economic benefits."[41]

To ensure this policy goal, Campbell had council create a Sister City Commission and five sister-city citizen committees, one for each twinning agreement. This was followed by a top–down major policy review, which produced the Strategic City Program in August 1987. Among its key policy goals were flexibility (as opposed to the formal requirements of more twinnings); stronger business links (as opposed to a mixed range of relationships, with business often a limited priority); and access to foreign cities that act as gateways to significant national and regional economies and that could provide a discernible niche for Vancouver business.[42]

Broad public involvement in this policy shift was limited but not insignificant. Each sister-city committee included a strong ethnocultural community and business component. Local business interests now combined with many other community elements. This resulted in institutions such as the Asia Pacific Foundation that bridged business, cultural, academic and governmental areas and provided community input in developing long-term relations to contribute to economic development in the Vancouver region.

The Globalist Policy Phase: 1990s

The fourth phase, beginning in the early 1990s is more comprehensive than the earlier phases. This phase is still in the process of developing, and it confronts an alternative local state that is often retreating from responsibilities. Yet, the globalist phase represents a significant expansion in policy content, from a cultural/educational and business/economic focus, to include additional emphases on world peace and disarmament, international aid, and environmental-sustainability components. More than the second and third phases, which increasingly emphasized and were supported by business components in the local community, the globalist orientation has been premised on a broader community involvement. This broader community base also has linked a range of city–international actions with more local planning and economic-development initiatives.

Promoters of this globalist phase have increasingly suggested that local communities – and their municipal governments – are no longer prepared to passively wait for senior governments to take action on pressing global matters.[43] Equally, they have identified that preserving local livability through more sustainable economic development contributes significantly to urban solutions to global problems.[44] Pushed by their citizen movements, municipalities like Vancouver are becoming directly involved in a variety of issues to counter threats to humanity (e.g., environmental degradation) and to improve the quality of life for individuals locally and beyond. Linking local economic development and sustainability, more generally, a variety of interests have pushed issues like ecology back onto municipal and metropolitan agendas. As discussed above, local opponents of reliance on extensive private automobile-use have succeeded in having alternative forms of transportation, both public and non–internal combustion, as a part of discussions on planning and city–regional economic development. Their actions are tied to local solutions to global environmental problems. Emerging "globalist" city stances challenge more traditional "international" definitions. The policy reality of the 1990s and beyond suggests the need for an expanded city–international role. The experience of Canadian cities like Vancouver suggests the likely characteristics of this emerging globalist policy phase. Not all have explicit economic-development aspects; yet each suggests a more complete municipal global citizen.[45]

Four components of the globalist perspective are showing varying prominence:

1. *a world peace/disarmament component*: Vancouver is home to a strong local peace community that has significant public support. Council agreement to designate Vancouver a Nuclear Weapons Free Zone, despite its desirability as a port-of-call for United States navy ships, is a manifestation of this. This designation occurred in 1983 but has been maintained and augmented by successive municipal councils of different political stripes.

2. *a foreign-aid component*: the local economic benefits of activities such as municipal professional staff exchanges with Third World cities or pro-

viding aid to re-build war-torn villages are clearly limited. Vancouver and surrounding municipalities have nonetheless been involved in such initiatives. For Vancouver, the roots of such efforts are in its community-based 1944 humanitarian aid to war-ravaged Odessa.

3. *a global ecological component*: in Vancouver, the 1960's debate/defeat of freeways, led by community activists and the region's long-standing commitment to preservation of regional farmland were forerunners for broader local environmental concerns. Greater Vancouver's 1989–96 review and implementation of its Livable Region Strategic Plan, discussed above, placed emphasis on such policy concerns as air and water quality, waste treatment/disposal and preservation of green space and arable land. These concerns were premised on a broad local participation, and regional recognition of its potential to ensure local economic development contributed to such global issues as planetary warming. Similarly, the international city-based Urban Carbon Dioxide Project, with Vancouver and Toronto as members, "hopes to develop a blueprint for the rest of the world to follow" in dealing with carbon dioxide gases. "[W]ith their power over zoning and land use, transportation and building approvals, cities have their hands on the levers which can turn down the global warming tap."[46] More importantly, citizens in places like Vancouver and Toronto are no longer prepared to wait for senior governments to act. The international city-links developed over fifty years are being used to encourage local policy initiatives on recycling, automobile-alternative transportation, newer waste disposal forms and other sustainability measures. The policy push, reinforced at the 1996 UN Conference on Human Settlements (Habitat II) in Istanbul, is for economic development while preserving livability in cities locally and globally.[47] In Vancouver, aspects of each of these global components currently exist. In October 1990, for example, the city council released *Clouds of Change*, a report containing thirty-five recommendations on atmospheric change; many were outside the formal jurisdiction of the city, but their inclusion indicated Vancouver's determination to deal with air quality and other environmental problems in the region, irrespective of where authority resided.[48] The push of various local environmental groups, for example, the cyclist lobby has helped create a policy climate requiring such city initiatives.

4. *a global economic component*: a significant component of any city-based international activity remains explicitly economic development. That has been the case in Vancouver since the Harcourt "rational phase"

changes of the early 1980s. Although such international policy-making has been discussed in this chapter in terms of four *distinct* phases, the phases in reality are overlapping. For example, while the strategic phase emphasized business and economic benefits, cultural exchange (from the ad hoc phase) was also seen as contributing significantly to economic-development opportunities. In the globalist phase, economic exchange continues to be a central aspect of municipal international activity, despite its broader environmental and peace/aid dimensions. Each policy phase has reflected a different set of choices by Vancouver, in keeping with shifting policy climates. While some condensing or broadening of public involvement occurred, the experience of Vancouver's international efforts suggests that those linkages that have the strongest community bases are the ones with the most capacity to have an impact on economic development for the city.

CONCLUSION: ECONOMIC DEVELOPMENT AND PUBLIC PARTICIPATION

The two cases discussed in this chapter demonstrate the extent to which globalism and localism in world cities are linked. It is increasingly true that national economies have become substantially premised on the economies of a nation's major city regions.[49] For some, the conflicting trends this has created has meant that the "traditional boundaries between countries ... [have] become increasingly meaningless, ... cities [have] become independent of their countries and deal directly with other parts of the world, [and] city and regional interests ... will be far more important that national and provincial economic policies."[50]

Municipal responses to perceived global dimensions of economic development in Vancouver demonstrate this. In Vancouver, global experience began largely because of perceived community interest and involvement. That interest, initially among particular cultural elements in the city, and later with business support, produced five formal city–international linkages and a considerable range of other less formal exchanges. The downturn in city support for such ventures, caused by budgetary squeezing in the mid-1990s, supports a conclusion that those links with the strongest and widest community bases – both cultural and business – have the best chance of success. The economic restructuring current in the former Soviet Union has meant that the Odessa link has been weakest, although City Peace Movement interest brought about a 1980s revival, and, in 1996, local business interests in post-Soviet investment have initiated another re-examination. The local Scottish community has helped sustain the Edinburgh link, but its relative lack of a strong economic-development "add-on" has also meant that the impact of this exchange has been limited. In contrast, two of the three formal Asia Pacific twinnings – Guangzhou and Yokohama – have both community cultural support and important economic-development business components, coinciding with provincial and federal government economic/trade orientations.

In each instance, success has been premised on an interplay between some degree of community initiation or support and some city action to cement such cultural, educational and economic-development links. A local champion – either as community leader or financial supporter – is also important. All participants emphasize the interrelationships between each of these aspects, although developing relationships over time through cultural and educational exchange and enhanced cultural understanding are important preludes to any subsequent mutual economic-development exchanges. The latter cannot long be sustained, particularly with Asia Pacific jurisdictions, without this local community participation.

It is also increasingly true that urban quality of life is the critical factor in promoting economic-development, particularly in international cities. Thus, strategic planning that promotes quality of life and sustainable development at the regional and local levels is an integral part of global economic-development strategies. Successful development implementation of regional strategic plans, in contrast to the case of twinning, requires more inclusive and widespread local public participation, rather than leadership by a specific community with a self-identified interest. The GVRD's Livable Region Strategy Plan experience provides a constructive model for achieving strategic planning that integrates economic development and sustainability, municipal buy-in to a regional process and plan, and broadly based citizen engagement.

NOTES

1 The Canadian Dicennial Census of 1991 confirmed the Vancouver census metropolitan area as the third-largest metropolitan region in Canada, and the twenty-ninth largest in North America. (In comparison, the Toronto metropolitan region, Canada's largest, is eighth in North America; Vancouver's neighbour, Seattle, is nineteenth.)
2 The Lower Mainland is bounded on the south by the U.S. border, on the north by mountains that extend virtually without interruption to Alaska, on the east at Hope by similar mountain ranges, and on the west (including the City of Vancouver) by the gulf waters of the Pacific Ocean.
3 See David Bond, "Sustaining the Metropolitan Economy," in P.J. Smith, H.P. Oberlander and T. Hutton, eds., *Urban Solutions To Global Problems: Vancouver –*

Canada – Habitat II (Vancouver: Centre for Human Settlements, University of British Columbia, 1996), Chapter 12, pp. 68–71.

4 In July 1995, Maple Ridge and Pitt Meadows (1996 population: 75,000) were formally added to the GVRD. They had previously been members for water/sewers (both) and parks (Maple Ridge only). Langley Township and Langley City (1996 population: 106,395) had also joined the GVRD in 1989. All current population figures are from BC Stats, a division of the Ministry of Finance and Corporate Relations, Province of British Columbia. Only Matsqui, outside the GVRD, continues to participate in GVRD functions, for parks.

5 On the changes in the Lower Mainland and B.C. economies, see M. Howlett and K. Brownsey, "British Columbia: Public Sector Politics in a Rentier Resource Economy," in Keith Brownsey and Michael Howlett, eds., *The Provincial State: Politics in Canada's Provinces and Territories* (Toronto: Copp Clark Pitman, 1992), pp. 265–95; and P.J. Smith, "British Columbia: Public Policy and Perceptions of Governance," in James Bickerton and Alain-G. Gagnon, eds., *Canadian Politics* (Peterborough, Ont.: Broadview Press, 1994), pp. 506–26.

6 For a more extensive discussion of this, on Vancouver, see P.J. Smith, "The Making of a Global City: Fifty Years of Constituent Diplomacy: The Case of Vancouver," *Canadian Journal of Urban Research* 1, no. 1 (June 1992), pp. 90–112.

7 See P.J. Smith and T.H. Cohn, "International Cities and Municipal Paradiplomacy: A Typology For Assessing the Changing Vancouver Metropolis," in Frances Frisken, ed., *The Changing Canadian Metropolis: A Public Policy Perspective* (Berkeley: Institute of Governmental Studies Press, University of California, 1994), volume 2, Chapter 19, pp. 725–50.

8 British Columbia, Ministry of Municipal Affairs, "Context For the Growth Strategies Act: Principles underlying the Legislation," in *An Explanatory Guide to BC's Growth Strategies Act* (Victoria: Queen's Printer, 1995), p. 4.

9 Task Force on the Future of the Greater Toronto Area (GTA), *Greater Toronto: Report* [Golden Report] (Toronto: Queen's Printer, 1996). Anne Golden and her GTA commissioners did note that differences in regional political culture helped explain the relative success of "consensual decision-making" in the Greater Vancouver case. The GTA task force's general conclusion, however, was that such an approach was "weak."

10 For an historical overview, see H. Peter Oberlander and P.J. Smith, "Governing Metropolitan Vancouver: Regional Intergovernmental Relations in British Columbia," in Donald Rothblatt and Andrew Sancton, eds., *Metropolitan Governance: American/Canadian Intergovernmental Perspectives* (Berkeley: Institute of Governmental Studies Press, University of California, 1993), pp. 329–73.

11 See Robert North and Walter Hardwick, "Vancouver Since the Second World War: An Economic Geography," in Graeme Wynn and Tim Oke, eds., *Vancouver and its Region* (Vancouver: University of British Columbia Press, 1992),

pp. 200–233; and Oberlander and Smith, "Governing Metropolitan Vancouver," in Rothblatt and Sancton, *Metropolitan Governance*.
12 Greater Vancouver Regional District, "Who Are We? What Do We Do?" *The Livable Region: A Strategy For the 1990s* (Burnaby: GVRD, 1989).
13 Greater Vancouver Regional District, *Livability Goals*, (Burnaby: GVRD, 1989).
14 See, for example, Greater Vancouver Regional District, *Choosing Our Future* (Burnaby: GVRD, 1990), a series of reports; and *Creating Our Future: Steps to a More Livable Region – Technical Report*, "Choices Make a Difference" (Burnaby: GVRD, 1990).
15 There are various GVRD documents detailing this process, among these, *Creating Our Future: The History, Status, and Prospects of Regional Planning in Greater Vancouver* (Burnaby: GVRD, 1994) and *Establishing a Regional Strategic Plan: A Review of the Process* (Burnaby: GVRD, 1994) are particularly useful.
16 See Graham Smith, "Mechanisms For Public Participation at a Normative Planning Level in Canada," *Canadian Public Policy* 8, no. 4 (Autumn 1982), pp. 561–72, definition at p. 562.
17 Greater Vancouver Regional District, *Creating Our Future: Steps to a More Livable Region* (Burnaby: GVRD, 1993).
18 Greater Vancouver Regional District, *Creating Our Future: The History, Status, and Prospects of Regional Planning in Greater Vancouver*, p. 15.
19 Greater Vancouver Regional District, *Establishing A Regional Strategic Plan*, pp. 51–2.
20 Ibid., pp. 65–6.
21 Ibid., p. 81.
22 See Ken Cameron, *The Future Evolution of the Strategic Planning Function* (Burnaby: GVRD, Strategic Planning, 1996).
23 See Greater Vancouver Regional District, *Livable Region Strategic Plan* (Burnaby: GVRD, 1995). An August 1996 decision by new NDP highways minister Lois Boone (Prince George) to allow a major high occupancy vehicle (HOV) lane investment between Port Moody and Burnaby to be used by vehicles with only two passengers, "because it will be underutilized much of the time," provoked GVRD, VanPool and other transportation-change advocates to protest, suggesting that not everyone at the provincial level has bought in to the regional vision. See, for example, David Marsh, "Van Poolers Cooled By Barnett Express-Lane Decision," *Burnaby News Leader* 21 August 1996, p. 2; and Scott Simpson, "Barnet Link: A Fast People Mover or a Trojan Horse?" *Vancouver Sun* 23 August 1996, pp. B1–2.
24 Ibid., p. 8. The five-year review – and update – provision is for consideration at each fifth year in the twenty-five-year Livable Region Strategic Plan.
25 Cameron, *Future Evolution of the Strategic Planning Function*, p. 5.
26 Smith, "Mechanisms for Public Participation at a Normative Planning Level in Canada," *Canadian Public Policy*, p. 562.

27 John Kincaid argues for this less pejorative term in describing subnational international activity: "[T]here is no settled terminology describing the international activities of 'constituent' or 'subnational' governments. ... Constituent diplomacy is 'preferred' as such terms as micro-diplomacy and 'paradiplomacy' imply that constituent diplomacy is inferior to nation-state diplomacy and exhibits a nation-state bias. ... Constituent diplomacy is intended as a neutral descriptor, one that avoids the implication that the activities of constituent governments are necessarily inferior, ancillary or supplemental to the 'high politics' of nation-state diplomacy." See John Kincaid, "Constituent Diplomacy in Federal Politics and the Nation-State: Conflict and Co-operation," in Hans Michelmann and Panayotis Soldatos, eds., *Federalism and International Relations: The Role of Subnational Units* (Oxford: Clarendon Press, 1990), pp. 54–75.
28 P.J. Smith, "The Making of a Global City: Fifty Years of Constituent Diplomacy: The Case of Vancouver," *Canadian Journal of Urban Research* 1, no. 1 (June 1992), pp. 90–112.
29 T.H. Cohn and P.J. Smith, "Subnational Governments as International Actors: Constituent Diplomacy in British Columbia and the Pacific Northwest," *BC Studies* 110 (Summer 1996), pp. 25–59; Victor Jones, "Beavers and Cats: Federal-Local Government Relations in the U.S. and Canada," in H.P. Oberlander and H. Symonds, eds., *Meech Lake: From Centre to Periphery – The Impact of the 1987 Constitutional Accord on Canadian Settlements* (Vancouver: Centre for Human Settlements, University of British Columbia, 1988), pp. 80–126.
30 P.J. Smith, "A View Through a Kaleidoscope: Local–Federal Government Relations – Canadian Perspectives, American Comparisons," in Oberlander and Symonds, *Meech Lake: From Centre to Periphery*, pp. 127–40.
31 P.J. Smith, "Policy Phases, Subnational Foreign Relations and Constituent Diplomacy in the United States and Canada: City, Provincial and State Global Activity in British Columbia and Washington," in Brian Hocking, ed., *Foreign Relations and Federal States* (London: Leicester University Press, 1993), pp. 211–35.
32 T. Cohn and P. Smith, "Developing Global Cities in the Pacific Northwest: The Cases of Vancouver and Seattle," in Peter Kresl and Gary Gappert, eds., *North American Cities and the Global Economy: Challenges and Opportunities* (Thousand Oaks, Calif.: Sage Publications, 1995), pp. 251–85.
33 Smith, "The Making of a Global City, *Canadian Journal of Urban Research.*
34 Libby Davies, Vancouver alderman. Interview, 6 October 1988.
35 Federation of Canadian Municipalities, *A Practical Guide to Twinning* (Ottawa: Federation, 1988).
36 Sid Fancy, manager, economic development, City of Vancouver. Interview, 27 October 1989.
37 For a detailed discussion on this, see Michael Goldrick, "The Impact of Global Finance in Urban Structural Change: The International Banking Centre

Controversy," in Jon Caulfield and Linda Peake, eds., *City Lives and City Forms: Critical Research and Canadian Urbanism* (Toronto: University of Toronto Press, 1996), pp. 195–214.
38 Bill Yee, former city councillor. Interview, August 1996.
39 Colleen McGuinness, former Vancouver economic development officer, currently with contract responsibility, via the City Clerk's Office, for the city's sister-city activities. Interview, August 1996.
40 Bill Yee and Colleen McGuinness, interviews. In mid-1996, Yee passed the chair of the Vancouver–Guangzhou Committee to another long-time member. He has taken up chairing the BC–Guandong Province Committee. Guangzhou is the capital of Guandong province.
41 Janet Fraser, executive assistant to Gordon Campbell, mayor of Vancouver. Interview, 30 September 1988; and Gordon Campbell, mayor of Vancouver. Interview, 17 October 1988.
42 Patrick Smith, "The Making of a Global City," *Canadian Journal of Urban Research*.
43 See, for example, Heidi Hobbs, *City Hall Goes Abroad: The Foreign Policy of Local Politics* (Thousand Oaks, Calif.: Sage Publications, 1994) on this for U.S. municipal settings.
44 This theme – Urban Solutions to Global Problems – formed the basis of the 1996 United Nations Conference on Human Settlements (Habitat II) in Istanbul. It also is the title of a review of the twenty-year environmental, social, economic and governmance legacy of the Habitat I Conference in the Vancouver regions. See Smith, Oberlander and Hutton, *Urban Solutions to Global Problems*.
45 On the concept of a municipal global citizen, see Chadwick F. Alger, "Linking Town, Countryside and Legislature to the World," *International Studies Notes* 13 no. 0 (Fall 1987), pp. 57–63.
46 See, for example, n.a., "Cities join to fight global warming," *The Toronto Star*, 13 June 1991, p. A10.
47 For an extensive discussion of this in metropolitan Vancouver, see Smith, Oberlander and Hutton, *Urban Solutions to Global Problems*.
48 City of Vancouver, *Clouds of Change* (Vancouver: City, 1990).
49 Jane Jacobs, *Cities and the Wealth of Nations: Principles of Economic Life* (New York: Random House, 1983).
50 M. Seeling and Alan Artibise, *From Desolation to Hope: Pacific Fraser Region in 2010* (Vancouver: Board of Trade, 1991).

4

Helping the Public to Participate in Planning

John Sewell

INTRODUCTION

One widely agreed-upon principle of contemporary city planning is that citizens must be consulted as the plan is prepared. There are fairly simple models readily at hand for consultation about neighbourhood issues, but plans with a larger intention – plans for a city, say, or for a region – pose larger problems. Municipal governments have spent considerable sums trying to get public participation in the preparation of these plans "right," usually unsuccessfully.

This chapter will consider three attempts to involve the public in the creation of "big" plans in the early 1990s: Toronto's Cityplan '91 exercise; Metro Toronto's work leading to the adoption of The Liveable Metropolis plan; and Vancouver's CityPlan process. It then reviews the work of the Commission on Planning and Development Reform in Ontario (of which I was chair) and the methods the commission used to involve the public in shaping its recommendations. The three municipal processes share several common characteristics. They all concluded with the adoption of a general plan. They all made deliberate efforts to engage a wide cross-section of people, spending considerable sums of money in the process. However, the promise of each planning-exercise disintegrated – some quickly, some less so – as the process unfolded. None concluded with a plan that seemed capable of providing strong direction for citizens, whether elected or unelected. Instead, public disappointment and lethargy has been the more likely result. By contrast, the New Planning in Ontario exercise (as it was referred to) seemed much more successful. This chapter will conclude with some suggestions as to what led to such unfortunate results at the municipal level and, after reviewing the work in the early 1990s of the Ontario commission, proposes how things might be done better in the future.

THE IRONIES OF ENCOURAGING PUBLIC PARTICIPATION

There are two considerable ironies in the notion that governments should reach out and include citizens in planning-exercises. On the one hand, there has been an underlying belief for most of this century that governments are incapable of planning for the longer term, because political leaders are only worried about the short term leading to the next election. This assumption, which found strongest expression in the first half of the century, led to the creation of "independent" planning-boards, consisting of citizens appointed by politicians, to have carriage of long-term planning-matters. In the late 1960s and early 1970s, the burgeoning citizen movement claimed that these boards acted mainly as a buffer to protect elected politicians from decisions they did not want to be seen to be making themselves, and the boards began to lose respectability and influence. Soon after, the idea of citizen participation was born, and citizen advice was again sought, although more directly than through the device of the planning-board. As often occurs, things came full circle, and the citizen again re-entered the picture as part of planning decision-making.[1]

On the other hand, citizen involvement in planning-decisions in the late 1960s came as a challenge to municipal politicians and their staff. It first burst onto the Canadian municipal scene as a strong reaction by local residents to urban-renewal plans that were thrust on unsuspecting neighbourhoods. The challenge quickly spread to other fronts: fighting expressways; preserving heritage structures and views; preventing highrise intrusions in settled neighbourhoods; stopping downtown megastructures; and, finally, formulating neighbourhood and city plans.[2] It might be said that the rise of the urban-reform movement in Canadian cities in the second half of the twentieth century is integral to the question of decisions about planning-matters. Citizens did not like the impact of the modern or international style on their cities, and they fought back.

As they were elected, reform politicians re-shaped the way planning was done and incorporated consultation and citizen participation into the municipal planning process, thereby changing its tenor. No longer was citizen participation a sign of resistance and change: ironically, it was digested into the way city business was done. The most reactionary politicians spoke well of it, and participation became a potent tool to enforce the status quo – as evidenced in the not-in-my-back-yard (NIMBY) syndrome, which has weighed down municipal decision-making for the past decade. Perhaps one result of NIMBY-ism has been that planners have retreated into the safe haven of platitudes.

These contradictions swirl around the participation of citizens in large plans: advice – but not too much advice – is sought. Participation in decision-making is encouraged until the point of decision. Planning-jargon is dispensed with, until the final report must be prepared. Processes are inclusionary and open, until the real options are finally put to the politicians.

One of the larger questions that is difficult to pin down is the meaning of "public" in public participation. Who is the public? Is it the well-organized interest groups, such as realtors, the chambers of commerce, social-service agencies, and professional planning associations? Is it ad hoc interest groups, such as environmental coalitions, tenant organizations, and property-tax or business coalitions? Is it neighbourhood resident groups or recreation clubs? Is it the "silent majority"? Is it people directly affected, or is it those who have no self-interest?

One might say that the "public" includes all of the above, but the methods used to reach some of these interests are very different from those required to reach others. Well-organized groups rarely have trouble finding someone to attend a meeting, while some neighbourhood groups are not visible enough to outsiders even to be identified for purposes of asking. Further, the value of input is often measured – for obvious reasons – by the previous involvement of the participant, so definitions of the "public" often are based on past response. Added to this is commitment. Petitions signed by thousands carry little weight among those seriously worried about "public" input because of the low degree of commitment required to sign a piece of paper: ten warm bodies are worth a lot more than many pages of names in the political forum simply because of the energy needed to get those ten people in one place at one time. At the end of the day, there is no easy method of determining whether the "public" has been well consulted. Instead, a subjective judgement must be made depending on the complexity and history of the issue, the intentions of the parties, and the local political culture.

The way that participation was encouraged in different contexts in the four cases is described in considerable detail in reports prepared by the planning-staff of the respective cities and of the commission. What follows here is a summary of those events, interspersed with interpretive comment. As a broad generalization, one might conclude that citizen participation in the large municipal plans discussed here is a story of shattered dreams. The provincial attempt seems to have been more successful.

PARTICIPATION IN "BIG" CITY PLANS

City of Toronto

The Central Area Plan, adopted by the city in 1976, was a milestone for

Toronto. It was the product of three years of intense work following the December 1972 election of a council that was very interested in changing direction for the city's downtown. The new direction included a number of different desires: to limit the construction of large office buildings downtown; to build more housing downtown; to preserve older buildings; and to make downtown streets comfortable and friendly for pedestrians.[3]

These directions were foisted on council by active community groups, which were tired of fighting city hall on these issues. In some cases, those elected in 1972 were representatives of these groups; in other cases, they were amenable to the things the groups wanted to see happen and became their spokespersons. Planners had no question about what they were expected to do: they had to find ways of legitimizing these new values in planning-terms and then of ensuring the new plan reflected them.

One of the first initiatives taken was simplicity itself: a by-law was passed in 1973 prohibiting the construction downtown of any building higher than forty-five feet or with a floor area of more than forty thousand square feet. This move was supported by virtually every community organization in the city, although the development industry was apoplectic.

In a few years, the planners had constructed plans that were so complicated that the outside world had difficulty understanding what they were about. When the Central Area Plan was finally presented to council, community groups had trouble knowing how they should respond. On the one hand, the planners said that the values the groups espoused were reflected in the plan; on the other hand, things seemed so confused and contorted that community leaders were not quite sure. The hard-core reformers on council refused to endorse the plan, claiming it did not go far enough, but, in the end, the plan was approved. As has been noted, the plan did mark a significant and positive change of direction for Toronto. Many of the things community groups wanted to see occur have happened: a large increase in housing downtown; a much more friendly pedestrian environment; the retention of many older buildings (or at least their façades).

This process and this plan have been seen as the paragon of large plans for Toronto. It was in this context that the recent Cityplan '91 exercise was undertaken and completed.[4] The 1976 plan was subject to five-year reviews, and the thought was that for 1991 the plan should not simply be tuned-up but re-thought and perhaps re-tooled.

The planners began their work in 1988, when a group in the planning and development department was assigned to the exercise. There was concern about strong inflationary and speculative pressures in the city and about the burgeoning new office buildings, which made those pressures real. But, it was not a stellar time for an active citizenry nor for councillors itching to initiate change. Citizen groups most often arise in boom times, when prosperity abounds and growth can be seen on every corner. Boom times also give rise to reform-minded politicians promising ways to control and channel that growth. In the late 1980s, there was plenty of concern about hyperinflation and over-development, but when the recession came in 1990, that concern quickly disappeared.

In the absence of others, the planners found themselves in the unfortunate position of leading the endeavour. With the support of their advisers, they tagged the planning-process with the logo "Your City. Your Future. Make it *Your* Plan." Many flowery words accompanied that logo, of which the following, released in April 1989, are but a few:

> The preparation of the 1991 Central Area Plan represents a major opportunity for the people of Toronto to fulfil the promise that is their city's future. Those citizens who contribute ideas and opinions can help establish the municipal planning and social policy agenda for years to come. In doing so, they will be influencing the quality of life for this, and possibly future generations of Torontonians.[5]

It seemed to be asking for a re-staging of the events in Toronto during the early 1970s. A task force was created to ensure widespread public involvement and to develop consensus around major issues. Half of city council was on the task force, along with an array of representatives from significant interest groups in the city – developers, environmentalists, non-profit housing proponents, education advocates, and so forth. In fact, the task force was so diverse that the planners were able to garner little direction from it. The task force set up three subcommittees dealing in turn with social equity, quality of life, and growth management. By mid-1989, the task force had produced a print-heavy twenty-four-page statement of goals and principles for public discussion.

This document was used for discussion at a series of community meetings held throughout the city. The platitudinous nature of the document, and the fact that it tried to make a statement on just about every issue of city life one could imagine, did not engender debate or comment. There was no great community excitement exhibited at these meetings nor any general consensus about key issues.

A questionnaire in English and in four other languages was distributed widely. It was mailed with water bills and with a newsletter of the Metro Tenants Federation, and it was put in public libraries. But the response was poor: although 190,000 copies of the questionnaire were distributed (Toronto's population was slightly over 600,000 people), less than 3,000 replies were received – a response of less than two per cent. The replies were of the "conditioned response" variety that can be expected from those who have not thought much about city life: the primary concern was traffic congestion, followed by a wish for more green space.

A forum was held where prominent experts from Toronto and elsewhere in North America spoke on set topics in a generally academic tone. An extensive process called "Kidsview" was undertaken to involve students in elementary and secondary schools. Kids got to see a ten-minute video about Cityplan '91 and received a button stating "I helped plan Toronto's future." Some eight thousand students from one hundred schools participated, and a handsome report, rife with graphics, summarized students views: "We had fun talking, writing and thinking about the city plan," and "We learned how hard it is for the city to think of new ideas and to improve systems," which are two statements quoted in the first three pages of the report.

Special initiatives were made to get the views of Toronto's homeless (including nine meetings in various hostels and drop-in centres), church groups, and multicultural communities. Various reports summarized opinions expressed, and, perhaps to give them some extra legitimacy, they were published in the same grey format as the research documents that had been commissioned on the usual planning-issues for which the planners wanted to have data and information. In all, these background reports occupied some thirty volumes.

By June 1991, the planners completed the proposals report for the politicians' review. The real-estate industry expressed concerns about suggestions in the proposals report to link the approval of new office space with the construction of affordable housing, and it went on to complain about urban-design ideas the planners had included. As it turned out, the recession meant that the linkage idea was not feasible, and it did not survive into the next iteration of the plan. The design ideas were also modified.

A final plan was presented to the council in 1992. It caused hardly a ripple of concern and was approved, followed by the implementing by-laws in 1993. The plan encouraged the redevelopment of main streets, set several broad policies around environmental issues, and proposed a framework for negotiations about larger developments. These were the three aspects of the plan that could be considered "new." It would be stretching things to argue that these ideas arose because of public consultation – in all likelihood the planners would have proposed these on their own, without outside encouragement.

It is not easy to isolate the actual cost of programs to encourage public participation and input, but a figure of $500,000 is generally acknowledged to be a fair estimate of what could have been saved if the planners and council had decided to simply prepare the plan they thought appropriate without attempting to encourage public input.

Did public input have *any* effect on the plan, apart from increasing costs and lengthening the processing time? This question cannot be answered in a scientific manner or with any certainty, but there are several markers that help point to an answer. First, the new plan caused very little political debate. Unlike the 1976 plan, it was not contentious and rarely rose to enough prominence to be reported on by the local media. Second, when the plan was presented by city planners in 1992, community groups did not line up either to denounce it or support it. They gave no indication that they thought this was *their* plan, as the planners had initially urged, because it wasn't. It was something the planners had devised. Third, the plan resulted in little significant change in direction for the city. Things carried on, save that the recession generally brought redevelopment to a halt, leaving little activity around which any planning could occur.

Ironically, the plan has not proven itself to be a particularly useful document to decision-makers in the mid-1990s, because it does not address the issues now confronting the city. It provides little direction for economic development – perhaps the most crucial problem now facing the city. It made assumptions about the continued growth of downtown office space, but office vacancy rates are so high that construction of new office towers is extremely unlikely. It said little about the property-tax problems, which has resulted in many buildings being demolished.

The plan also has some apparent shortcomings. A group of residents is challenging it at the Ontario Municipal Board (OMB), arguing that the plan's continued designation of certain areas as "low-density areas" makes no sense, since these areas have population densities of 8,000 or more residents per square kilometre – a density comparable to that found in London and one that is higher than in many European cities. The plan does little to make the planning-process or planning-decisions clearer to ordinary people, and it makes no steps towards simplifying planning-controls by relaxing convoluted concepts of density and use.

One can argue that the attempts to involve a wider public in plan-preparation ensured that those interested had the opportunity to learn what was going on, giving them less reason for objecting when the final draft emerged. This might be called the "negative" reason for encouraging citizen participation: it saves one from being ambushed later on. That may be useful, but it does not legitimize the citizen participation that was attempted in the formulation of this plan for Toronto.

Metro Toronto

Legislation establishing Metropolitan Toronto in 1953 required the region to have an official plan, but the local politicians from Metro's member municipalities feared that this plan would interfere with local decisions. Accordingly, the council did not press staff to comply with the legislation. For their own guidance, Metro's staff prepared an "unofficial" plan, which had the merit of providing a context for staff decisions without putting any limits on what the politicians could actually decide. The practicality of this arrangement failed to impress those who thought some formality (let alone legality) was needed, but it was not until 1980 that Metro council finally adopted an official plan.

Metro planning-staff had commissioned many reports over the years on key issues confronting Metro. These provided the basis for the 1980 plan, which was created by the planners and leading members of Metro council, without any undue attention to a public process. The public was not excluded, but, apart from making studies widely available and providing notification of formal meetings, nothing special was done to encourage public debate. Apart from the section describing the road network plan for Metro (which was done in very great detail), this plan was general and brief. It did not foreclose many options.

Thus, when it was decided in the early 1990s that a new and more comprehensive plan should be prepared, Metro planners and politicians proposed to undertake a much more public process and to engage as many of Metro's two million residents as possible in debate about key issues.[6]

After appropriate background studies, planners prepared a draft plan entitled "The Liveable Metropolis." In the early fall of 1992, thirty-five hundred copies of this eighty-page document were sent to agencies, boards, groups, libraries and other forums, accompanied by a letter asking for comments. Several thousand copies of a brochure describing the plan were also sent to individuals, and advertisements were placed in many publications in nine languages other than English. One public meeting was held in each of the six area municipalities, and, although each was well advertised, attendance was sparse. Several workshops were organized to create more interest, sessions were held with secondary-school students, and a forum on economic vitality in Metro was organized. A three-day *charrette* on reusing industrial land was held, and a number of meetings were arranged with stakeholders.

The draft plan contained several elements that could have been quite controversial. It proposed a population target of 2.5 million – an increase of half a million people – to be achieved mostly through intensification or "re-urbanization," as it was called. It also proposed Metro's intervention in some development matters, which heretofore had been completely in the purview of the area municipalities. However, the attempts to engage the public in the draft plan and in these issues was not successful: only sixty-eight submissions (from individuals and groups) were received in response, some arguing against re-urbanization, others wanting more focus on economic development.

A revised draft plan was prepared in 1993, and a second attempt was made to engage the public. Press releases, flyers, and summaries (in twelve languages and in Braille) were sent out in the thousands. Four community forums were held, attracting a total of one hundred and fifty people. Special meetings were held with half a dozen interest groups. Metro's economic development and planning committee scheduled a special meeting in March 1994 to receive written and oral comments on the planners' final proposals, but only a few dozen responses from the public were made. In June 1994, council adopted the final plan.

A fair estimate of the costs involved for the participation program is about $750,000. For the response generated, it clearly was an expensive operation.

Of course, it was not an entirely level playing field. Metro faced the historical reluctance of the area municipalities to legitimize what they saw as intrusion by the Metro jurisdiction into "their" planning decisions. Area municipalities might not have actively discouraged citizen involvement in the process, but they certainly did not do anything to encourage it. This has been a continuing problem for Metro: since 1991, when councillors were first chosen by direct election (after almost forty years of being chosen from area councils), they have claimed that no one understands what they do. The failed participation exercise seems to bear out that observation.

Vancouver

The City of Vancouver has used a number of documents to guide planning-decisions over the years – *Goals for Vancouver*, first published in 1980, for example, and the "central area plan," or the "Livable Region Program" prepared by the Greater Vancouver Regional District – but until 1995 it did not have a formal general plan. The creation of this new plan was the product of three years' work and an intensive process of citizen involvement costing $1.9 million. Planners claim that more than twenty thousand people made submissions or attended events, and, according to public-opinion surveys, the choices they made reflect the opinions of the broader society.

A four-step process of participation was designed and carried out. People put their ideas together; they discussed those ideas; they considered main issues and choices; and then their conclusions were reported to council on proposed directions. It was on that basis that CityPlan: Directions for Vancouver was prepared for council's consideration in early 1995 and, after some amendments, adopted that summer.[7]

Step one began with the preparation and wide distribution of the "Tool Kit" in late 1992. This was a package of about fifty background papers, divided into fourteen topic areas, setting out useful facts and outlining various trends. These papers are short and concise, graphically attractive, and readily accessible. More than $250,000 was spent on the publication of the Tool Kit. The concept of "City Circles" was brought forward, and "circles" were formed in early 1993 in an attempt to get people to share ideas in the Tool Kit and to think of proposals. Some circles came together under the initiatives of city planners, others formed from existing organizations. Some 250 circles were created, about seventy of which were from multicultural groups. Students from 150 schools participated in the Youthview Program. This first phase was accompanied by a media campaign to get the word out and by a monthly newsletter. *Ideas Book*, 475 pages long, was published in April. People were asked to summarize their ideas on two pages for inclusion in the book, which also included ideas from the City Circles and Youthview. A second book, entitled *Ideas Illustrated*, contained graphic presentations. Both books were widely distributed.

Step two involved talking about and sorting ideas. During April 1993, "Themes Day" was held, where about one hundred representatives of the City Circles reviewed ideas and pulled them into different themes. Over the first weekend in May, "Ideas Fair" was held in the downtown, and people and organizations were given a chance to exhibit their ideas. About ten thousand people attended, of which two thousand wrote out their priorities in a prepared "Check Book." That was followed a month later by "Ideas Forum," a day-long series of discussions, where issues and choices were further reviewed.

Step three involved making choices. Planning-staff took all of the ideas and grouped them into twelve themes. In each theme, choices were provided, along with the likely effects of that choice. The first choice was always the current trend, which was noted as such. A thirty-eight-page tabloid format workbook, *Making Choices*, was published in January 1994 and distributed to five thousand people who had indicated an interest in continuing to be a part of the planning-process. This step was accompanied by four well-attended workshops, and the workbook was given to five hundred Grade 11 students. There was a reasonable array of media coverage.

By April 1994, almost two thousand responses to the workbook had been received, and choices started to become quite clear, favouring an enhanced public realm and a less auto-dominated city. Planners prepared an eight-page brochure on four different futures for the city. This document was delivered to all city households, and it was translated into five languages for distribution through agencies and non-English newspapers. (Throughout the planning-process, many documents were provided in five languages other than English.) Comments were invited through a questionnaire. "Future Labs" was established, with the hope of running a Future Fair, which, because of labour problems, never occurred. Displays were set up for a number of locations during the summer months, and attendance at "Future Labs" was high. Almost nineteen hundred questionnaires were returned, and respondents were clear about the option they supported for Vancouver – an option known as City of Neighbourhood Centres – which attracted sixty-three-per-cent support. This result was confirmed by a public-opinion survey in September 1994.

Step four was the completion of the draft CityPlan document, which was submitted to city council. This draft, which flowed directly from the work to date, was available for comment in February 1995. With small changes, it was approved by council in mid-1995.

As an exercise that engaged many members of the public, this process was clearly a success. But did it amount to a plan that means much in the city's life? Vancouver's mayor Philip Owen has characterized the plan as a "general, flexible, blueprint," which does not seem an unwarranted statement. Indeed, the plan does consist of a number of general statements, and there seems little in it to restrict the tenor of political decisions that council might wish to make. There is nothing in the plan that states that certain actions cannot be taken or that, if taken, would permit citizens to retaliate with court action. The plan is, as it states, more of a "vision" that requires further action to be implemented and made effective.

Michael Seelig, professor of planning at the University of British Columbia, says "CityPlan is an elaborate polling exercise undertaken for Vancouver's politicians by the planning department." He notes that the plan consists of a long wish-list (perhaps of urban clichés):

CityPlan shows that Vancouverites want a "city of neighbourhoods" with distinctive and affordable housing; good jobs close to home; better health and social services; more parks; clean air and water; more arts and culture money; and all this delivered by a financially sound government. Nowhere is there a reference to sacrificing anything in return for all these goodies.[8]

Seelig states that "[p]lanners should not confuse public consultation with plan making. They have a professional responsibility to suggest what needs to be done and at what costs." While the process of CityPlan may have been superb at involving the citizenry of the city, it resulted in a few general statements, about where the city might head, rather than in a plan.

Shortcomings

In each case, the link between the process and the plan seems to have broken at a point when the matter was passed over to the elected politicians for decisions. In every case, the process of consultation was led by planners, and there was no sense that elected politicians were in control and would pay the price for a process that failed or that arrived at unsatisfactory conclusions. (The contrast with the Central Area Plan in Toronto in the 1970s is remarkable: there, politicians were elected or rejected on the basis of their views about planning.) Thus, when the time came for decision-making, the politicians felt they had a relatively free hand and could decide according to their own predilections.

The process of decision-making is a two-way street. Citizens often do not bother to spend time and energy dealing with official or general plans for their neighbourhoods since they realize politicians will make whatever decisions they want on re-zoning applications, whatever the official plan says. Why waste your time on something the politicians don't care about?

The problem with citizen participation, then, is trying to ensure its energy is directed at the elected politicians, not at the planners. For that to happen, the political decision-makers must be front and centre in the whole process. If that does not occur, then citizen involvement will amount to very little.

It was this kind of force that drove Toronto's 45-foot Holding Bylaw and the ensuing Central Area Plan. It was also the force that drove the Commission on Planning and Development Reform in Ontario and the report it issued in mid-1993. This process will be briefly described in the next section.

THE COMMISSION ON PLANNING AND DEVELOPMENT REFORM IN ONTARIO

The commission was appointed in mid-1991 to make recommendations to the Ontario government on how the planning-system in Ontario, which was badly broken, might be repaired. Lack of trust among the players was endemic, time-frames for decisions were impossibly long, and the system gave no certainty to anyone.

At the outset, the commission decided that problems would be resolved only if there was general agreement about common ground regarding goals, policies, and direction for planning in Ontario and that this agreement would be needed from those most directly involved in planning – developers and environmentalists, for instance – and from the general public, as represented by municipal politicians, community groups, and social agencies.[9]

The process used is described at length elsewhere, and its details are not relevant to this discussion.[10] In short, a number of different working groups were established to set goals and priorities. The conclusions of these groups were published and distributed widely for more public feedback. The conclusions were amended accordingly, re-published and again distributed widely. A draft report was published and was subject to further public input. Within two years of the start of the process, a final report was submitted to the Government of Ontario and was quickly implemented both in policy and in legislation.

Two factors were important to this success. First, those who headed the planning commission and who wrote its final report were intimately involved in the process. They served on all the working committees, attended all meetings and participated in all public sessions of the commission's work. The distance between those many members of the public who agreed to be involved in the process of consultation and those making the commission's recommendations was very small. The decision-makers felt their constituency was the very people they were meeting with on a regular basis.

But, of course, those heading the commission were only making recommendations to the government. Elected members of the government and their aids had not been much involved in the process. Why did they act so quickly to implement the report? This can be explained by the second factor at play: the force of the recommendations came from the fact that they emerged from working committees consisting of leading members of different interest groups in the province. What those committees proposed was a consensus of the interests most directly involved. The commission's recommendations were not just a bunch of good ideas: they were good ideas to which leading lights from all sides had given their consent.

From the government's perspective, the commission had managed to propose recommendations that generally seemed satisfactory to those most interested in planning-matters. None of the significant players stood outside the process or complained. Politically, it made no sense not to proceed to implement the recommendations. The commission had been able to find common ground on the difficult issues relating to planning-policy for the province. Why wouldn't a government jump at implementing these results?

Yet, it should be noted that, perhaps in contrast to the Vancouver process, the commission dealt with matters considered highly controversial, namely, the destruction of good agricultural land by sprawling urban development and the loss of natural features and habitats in and around urban areas.

New provincial planning-policy required municipalities to protect significant natural features from development. It also stated that "prime agricultural areas will be protected for agricultural use" and permits only very limited exceptions. Policy also stated that urban additions on the edge of cities "will have a compact form, a mix of uses, and densities that efficiently use land, infrastructure, and public service facilities" such as public transit.

To many involved in planning-struggles, it might seem somewhat miraculous that agreement could be forged on such divisive issues, which have been at the heart of so many planning-battles. The commission believed it was simply the result of a process that tried to find common ground and discovered that different interests shared a lot more of this common ground than anyone was aware. Better still, members of the general public showed they were willing to respond to this attempt to debate planning-policy options. The commission had many open, public meetings on planning-policy, where lots of people attended for serious discussion. Indeed, on many occasions, more people than the rooms would comfortably accommodate attended. More than twenty-two hundred submissions were filed in response to draft reports.

Why such a good response? Probably because people thought they had been given important and useful information, including intelligent, realistic and practical proposals made by committees of various interests. The policy proposals made strong cases against which to argue, and they also went much beyond the bland generalities that reveal nothing of real intentions. The commission made it clear it wanted feedback and was willing to change its mind (as it did on several notable occasions).

The resulting public discussion led to a refinement of the conclusions and to a presentation to decision-makers at the province of a set of policy recommendations that had most of the key interests onside and in support. The wisdom of agreeing to such policy was clear to politicians, since it was built on the common ground developed by those most interested in the issues and the solutions had a broad enough base of support to be implemented by the government. It is the kind of process and results that seem magic in the abstract; yet, it is neither costly nor time-consuming. It is based on new ways of developing public policy rather than on assuming that a government bureaucracy – with its planners – is capable of doing so.

The cost of the commission was just under $3 million for all of its activities. It is difficult to separate out the actual costs of public consultation, since the process was infused by it, but one could probably say that close to half the budget was spent on encouraging public input through meetings and newsletters.

CONCLUSIONS

Many cities have spent considerable sums encouraging public participation in "big" planning-issues. The results rarely live up to the expenditure. There seem to be two important factors in ensuring that public energy is put to good use. First, a process must be found that minimizes the distance between the interested members of the public (and the input they are generating) and the decision-makers. Handing participation aspects of the process over to the planners is exactly the wrong way to ensure that this happens, and planners should strongly resist attempts of elected leaders to forego the time and political commitment that citizen participation entails.

Several steps can be taken to help this occur. One or two politicians – rather than a clutch – can be put in charge of the process, so they will have a stake in making the process a success (since failure will be noticed, and blame will be attached). Obviously, the more these politicians are in leadership positions, the more successful will be the attempt to bring the process to the fore. As well, it is advisable to put less emphasis on creating a general plan that addresses all problems besetting the city and more emphasis and focus on resolving one or two substantial problems. Working from the specific to the general is advisable in the political realm.

A second suggestion for ensuring that public energy is put to good use is that attempts should be made to get the leaders of various interests to resolve their differences on the major planning-issues in contention. This will ensure that the process deals with the central – rather than the peripheral – questions, which is surely the hallmark of any successful planning-exercise. It will also ensure that the product of the process is something that elected leaders need and will want to implement.

NOTES

1 Graham Fraser, *Fighting Back* (Toronto: Hakkert, 1972).
2 See John Caulfield, *Tiny Perfect Mayor* (Toronto: James Lorimer & Company, Publishers, 1974); Donald Gutstein, *Vancouver, Ltd.* (Toronto: James Lorimer & Company, Publishers, 1975); Elizabeth Perry, *The Battle for Citadel Hill* (Hantsport, N.S.: Lancelot Press, 1979); and John Sewell, *The Shape of the City: Toronto Struggles with Urban Planning* (Toronto: University of Toronto Press, 1993).
3 Sewell, *Toronto Struggles with Urban Planning*, pp. 174–85.
4 Information and reports on the Toronto Cityplan '91 process are available from the city's planning and development department. Unfortunately, there is no single report or newsletter that summarizes what can be found in the almost thirty background volumes of reports or the newsletters or in reports to city council.

5 City of Toronto, *Cityplan '91* [newsletter] (Toronto: Planning, and Development Department, 1989).
6 For information on the Metro Toronto process, see particularly *Report 10* of the economic development and planning committee, considered by Metro Council on 12 May 1993, and *Report 14* of the same committee, considered by Metro council on 23 June 1993.
7 For information on Vancouver CityPlan, see particularly City of Vancouver, *Report 1: Description of the CityPlan Process* (Vancouver Planning Department, 1995). The other materials referred to in the article are excellent examples of their kind and, if possible, should be studied carefully.
8 Michael Seelig, "Citizen Participation as a Political Cop-out," *The Globe and Mail* (Toronto) 27 February 1995, p. A15.
9 For information on the process followed by the Commission on Planning and Development Reform in Ontario, see *New Planning for Ontario, Final Report* (Toronto: Queen's Printer, 1993), particularly pp. 5–7.
10 John Sewell, "Finding a Common Ground for Housing Policy," in John Richards and William G. Watson, eds., *Home Remedies: Rethinking Canadian Housing Policy* (Toronto: C.D. Howe Institute, 1995), pp. 224–31.

5

Les conseils de quartier à Québec

Jean Dionne, Céline Faucher et André Martel

La Ville de Québec regroupe quelque 170 000 habitants. Capitale du Québec, elle est la ville centre d'une région métropolitaine de 650 000 habitants. En 1993, elle initie des expériences pilotes de conseils de quartier dans deux de ses quatorze quartiers (Saint-Jean-Baptiste et Vieux-Limoilou), pour une durée de deux ans.

Leur mandat est de mener les consultations publiques sur les questions d'aménagement du territoire qui touchent le quartier (règlement de zonage, plan d'urbanisme, règlement de circulation et de stationnement ...) et d'entreprendre des initiatives susceptibles d'améliorer la qualité de vie. Finalement, le conseil de quartier est le lieu principal où se font les échanges entre les citoyens et citoyennes et les services municipaux.

Composés chacun de sept membres élus par la population dans le cadre d'une assemblée de quartier et des conseillères ou conseillers municipaux dont le district appartient en tout ou en partie au quartier, ces conseils formulent des recommandations au Comité exécutif de la Ville. Précisons que ces recommandations sont toutes adoptées en assemblée publique. L'amélioration de la qualité de vie dans le quartier constitue la principale motivation des personnes qui postulent un siège au conseil de quartier. Comme l'écrivait dans son bulletin de présentation une candidate au conseil de quartier, propriétaire résidente et mère de jeunes enfants : «Je souhaite m'impliquer à titre de citoyenne pour contribuer au développement de ce quartier, mais surtout, pour en préserver les qualités qui m'ont poussée à m'y installer : un environnement sain et animé, des voisins chaleureux et des services reliés aux besoins d'une jeune famille.» Les conseillères et conseillers municipaux du quartier, eux, sont membres d'office, sans droit de vote, du conseil de quartier. Par ailleurs, les résidents et résidentes sont invités à participer activement aux activités du conseil en s'intégrant à ses comités de travail.

Au plan des ressources, la Ville met à la disposition de chaque conseil une aide professionnelle afin de soutenir ses activités et la préparation de ses documents, de même qu'un local et un budget de fonctionnement. Par ailleurs, dans le cadre des consultations publiques, les fonctionnaires municipaux responsables des dossiers participent aux réunions.

À maints égards, les conseils de quartier mis sur pied à Québec se distinguent des structures de consultation et de participation de la population que l'on retrouve ailleurs au Québec et au Canada, au sein des gouvernements locaux ou municipaux. En effet, en général, les expériences recensées montrent que ce sont les Conseils municipaux ou des commissions de ces derniers qui sont chargés de tenir les consultations publiques sur les questions d'aménagement du territoire. À Québec, ce mandat a été confié aux conseils de quartier. Toutefois, le Conseil municipal se réserve la possibilité de nommer une commission de consultation *ad hoc* pour traiter d'un sujet qui concerne plus d'un quartier ou encore l'ensemble du territoire municipal. Par ailleurs, à l'instar de certains conseils de quartiers américains, ceux de Québec se voient confier un mandat d'initiative à l'égard du développement social et économique du quartier. Ainsi, le pouvoir d'initiative et la place faite aux citoyennes et citoyens comme membres du conseil de quartier singularisent l'expérience vécue à Québec.

Afin de rendre compte de cette expérience, nous présenterons en premier lieu le contexte sous-jacent à la création de conseils de quartier. Cette présentation sera suivie d'une description des expériences vécues dans les deux quartiers mentionnés plus haut. Finalement, la conclusion fera état, à grands traits, des principaux résultats de l'évaluation de cette expérience et des perspectives d'avenir.

LE CONTEXTE RÉGLEMENTAIRE MUNICIPAL AU QUÉBEC

En vertu de l'article 92 de l'Acte de l'Amérique du Nord Britannique, les affaires municipales constituent un champ de compétence exclusif aux provinces. Les municipalités sont des créations des gouvernements provinciaux. Leur existence dépend exclusivement du gouvernement provincial qui peut les créer, les abroger, les contrôler, leur déléguer des pouvoirs ou, au contraire, les leur retirer.

Au Québec, en matière de consultation publique, la *Loi sur l'aménagement et l'urbanisme* prévoit des procédures précises de consultation de la population qui doivent être appliquées par le Conseil municipal au moment de modifier ou d'adopter un règlement d'urbanisme. Le recours au référendum est également possible sur les amendements au zonage et les règlements d'emprunt. Il suffit qu'un nombre suffisant de citoyennes et citoyens signent le registre prévu à cet effet pour que le Conseil municipal retire son projet de règlement ou le soumette à l'approbation d'un vote référendaire. Toutefois, les villes de Québec et Montréal ne sont pas assujetties à cette loi. Elles sont régies par des chartes qui ne peuvent être modifiées que par l'Assemblée nationale. Notons que, dans la pratique, le législateur tient largement compte des avis du Conseil municipal avant de modifier la charte de l'une ou l'autre de ces municipalités. C'est dans ce contexte de relative autonomie municipale que se crée une marge de manoeuvre politique et administrative suffisante pour soulever, à l'échelle de la Ville de Québec, la question suivante : Quel est le niveau souhaitable de participation de la population?

LE CONTEXTE POLITIQUE

À la fin des années 1970, M. Guy Tardif, ministre des Affaires municipales de l'époque, introduit dans sa *Loi sur l'aménagement et l'urbanisme* des mécanismes obligatoires de participation de la population. Par ailleurs, il propose, sans succès, l'introduction de conseils de quartier à Montréal et à Québec. Le Conseil municipal de Québec, sous la direction du maire Jean Pelletier, se prévaut de l'autonomie que lui confère la charte de sa municipalité pour bloquer toute mesure législative qui imposerait à la Ville de Québec des processus ou des structures de participation. Toutefois, le Conseil municipal crée alors des comités consultatifs de quartier formés de citoyennes et citoyens désignés par le Conseil municipal. Ces comités siègent à huis clos et sont chargés d'aviser le comité exécutif de la Ville en ce qui concerne les différents amendements au zonage qui touchent les quartiers.

L'arrivée au pouvoir, en 1989, de l'équipe du Rassemblement populaire et du maire Jean-Paul L'Allier marque un tournant au chapitre de la participation du public. Créé au cours des années 1970, ce parti regroupait alors une nouvelle génération de jeunes professionnels urbains et de gens des milieux communautaires. Cette opposition se cristallise en réaction aux excès modernistes qu'a subis Québec, comme plusieurs villes d'Amérique du Nord, dans les années 1960 et 1970. Son programme politique s'articule autour d'un transfert du pouvoir vers les citoyennes et citoyens et les quartiers afin de leur donner plus de contrôle sur l'aménagement urbain.

Une des premières mesures du nouveau Conseil municipal est l'adoption d'une politique de consultation publique. Ainsi, on retrouve dans le document intitulé «Politique et lignes directrices de la consultation publique,» adopté par le Conseil municipal en octobre 1991, l'énoncé de principes suivant : «La Ville de Québec recherchera de façon systématique les avis de sa population par rapport à des décisions importantes qui doivent être prises par le Conseil municipal.» Également, on y lit que : «La Ville de Québec souhaite donc donner à sa population la possibilité de se prononcer, en dehors du cadre électoral, sur des projets et des interventions qui modèlent son milieu de vie.» En outre, cette politique stipule que les comités consultatifs de quartier siégeront en public et que les règles de nomination des membres seront transparentes. Elles feront entre autres l'objet d'un appel de candidatures auprès du public.

Finalement, la Ville de Québec crée un Bureau des consultations publiques pour assurer la mise en oeuvre de sa politique de consultation publique. Ce bureau est formé d'un superviseur, de quatre professionnelles et professionnels (un agent, deux animatrices et un animateur sociocommunautaires) et de trois personnes affectées au soutien administratif. Le Bureau des consultations publiques coordonne l'organisation des consultations publiques. Il assure aussi la liaison entre les services municipaux, les membres des instances consultatives, les membres du Conseil municipal et la population dans son ensemble.

En 1993, deux expériences pilotes de conseil de quartier sont initiées dans Saint-Jean-Baptiste et le Vieux-Limoilou. Une campagne d'information a été menée auprès de la population des deux quartiers par une animatrice et un animateur du Bureau des consultations publiques. Une première étape a consisté à tenir des rencontres regroupant des membres des divers organismes implantés dans les quartiers. Un second objectif était d'informer la population de la venue de cette expérience dans leur quartier. À cet effet, un dépliant a été distribué dans toutes les boîtes aux lettres des deux quartiers. Plusieurs personnes ont manifesté leur intérêt suite à cette distribution. Finalement, la dernière étape consistait à la tenue de deux réunions publiques : la première réunion portait sur la présentation des conseils de quartier expérimentaux, (il s'agissait d'une rencontre d'information) et la deuxième réunion était consacrée à la consultation publique.

Dans le Vieux-Limoilou, les gens se sont mobilisés dès le départ. Suite aux rencontres tenues auprès des organismes du milieu et à la rencontre d'information publique, plusieurs se sont montrés intéressés à participer activement à la mise en place du conseil de quartier. Un comité d'implantation formé de douze personnes fut actif pendant plus d'un mois. Les objectifs de ce comité étaient de sensibiliser la population du quartier à cette nouvelle expérience, de rechercher l'appui écrit des citoyennes et citoyens et des organismes du quartier et de les inciter à participer à la soirée de consultation publique.

Le champ d'action des conseils de quartier (urbanisme, loisirs, sécurité publique, services aux citoyens) est beaucoup plus vaste que celui des comités consultatifs qui se préoccupaient principalement d'urbanisme. Ils sont aussi invités à prendre des initiatives susceptibles de stimuler le développement du quartier. Dans Saint-Jean-Baptiste et le Vieux-Limoilou donc, les comités consultatifs sont remplacés, à titre expérimental pour deux ans, par des conseils de quartier.

LE VIEUX-LIMOILOU

Quelques caractéristiques du quartier
Le quartier est localisé au nord du centre-ville et de l'arrondissement historique de Québec. Il appartient au bassin hydrographique de la rivière Saint-Charles, un des affluents du Saint-Laurent. Cette rivière borde la partie ouest du quartier avant de terminer sa course quelque cinq kilomètres plus loin, au pied du Cap-Diamant que surplombe le Château Frontenac. Quelques kilomètres de distance et quelque cinquante mètres de dénivellation, mais néanmoins un monde de différence, séparent le Vieux-Limoilou de l'arrondissement historique qui assure l'image de marque de la Ville de Québec.

Bien qu'en 1535, l'explorateur français Jacques Cartier ait passé l'hiver dans le Vieux-Limoilou, à l'embouchure des rivières Saint-Charles et Lairet (ce fut d'ailleurs la première fois qu'un européen hiverne au Canada), le développement urbain ne s'y amorce véritablement que vers 1915. C'est le développement des transports en commun, notamment du tramway, qui permet cette expansion urbaine vers Limoilou.

Le quartier présente une trame urbaine quadrillée et la majorité des rues sont caractérisées par des sens uniques et de nombreuses ruelles. On y retrouve principalement des triplex mitoyens avec des escaliers extérieurs en fer forgé. Les rez-de-chaussée sont souvent occupés par des propriétaires et les autres étages par des locataires.

Le Vieux-Limoilou est un quartier populaire. Sa population s'élève à 16 375 personnes, soit 15 % de la population de la ville. Sa densité résidentielle est la plus élevée des quartiers de Québec. Plus de 40 % de la population y vit sous le seuil de la pauvreté. Les familles monoparentales représentent près de 15 % des familles. Les personnes âgées représentent aussi près de 15 % de la population.

Le Vieux-Limoilou possède deux artères commerciales. Quelques commerces sont aussi localisés dans les secteurs résidentiels. Les industries, dont la papetière Daishowa et l'incinérateur de la Communauté urbaine de Québec, sont situées dans sa périphérie Est. Les rues sont bordées d'arbres. Toutefois, la majorité des espaces verts sont localisés en périphérie du quartier, le long de la rivière Saint-Charles.

Pouvoir d'initiative
Dès le début de son mandat, le conseil de quartier a tenu deux rencontres publiques afin de consulter la population sur ses besoins et ses préoccupations. Les ateliers de discussion portaient sur différents sujets tels l'aménagement urbain, l'environnement, la sécurité dans le quartier, la vie communautaire et culturelle, les artères commerciales. Suite à ces rencontres, le conseil de quartier a soumis son plan d'action en consultation publique. Les priorités retenues ont été la bonification des activités de loisirs offertes aux jeunes, le recyclage en centre culturel d'une caserne de pompiers abandonnée, l'aménagement des ruelles et le patrimoine urbain. Des comités de travail formés chacun de deux membres du conseil de quartier et de citoyens et citoyennes volontaires ont été constitués à cet effet. Nous reprenons ici plus en détail deux des thèmes principaux : l'aménagement des ruelles et le patrimoine urbain.

Parmi les dossiers retenus, le projet d'aménagement des ruelles du quartier a rassemblé plusieurs résidents. L'état actuel des ruelles (chaussée en mauvais état, manque d'éclairage, peu de verdure) et la possibilité de les améliorer ont été soulevés par un grand nombre. Le mandat du comité était de clarifier le statut juridique des ruelles, les titres de propriété, les servitudes existantes et le pouvoir de la Ville en cette matière; de réaliser un relevé de l'état actuel des ruelles et, finalement, de concevoir un programme expérimental de soutien financier à l'aménagement des ruelles.

La mobilisation de la population pour la formation de comités de ruelles s'est réalisée lors des réunions publiques du conseil, par le biais d'articles dans le journal de quartier et lors d'émissions radiophoniques. Un document conçu par le comité était remis aux personnes intéressées à discuter de la question avec leurs voisins. Deux comités de ruelles formés de propriétaires riverains ont présenté une proposition d'aménagement au conseil de quartier. Ce dernier a soumis cette proposition à la Ville, de même que les paramètres d'application d'un nouveau programme de subvention. La Ville a accordé le montant demandé et une équipe de fonctionnaires municipaux travaillent actuellement à l'élaboration du programme. La réalisation de ces projets devait se concrétiser à l'été 1995. Actuellement, cinq comités de ruelles ont déposé leur projet et un sixième comité est en voie de formation.

Le comité sur le patrimoine a été formé suite à la démolition d'une chapelle et d'une salle paroissiale pour permettre la construction de condominiums. Des résidents se sont mobilisés et ont fait part de leur déception au conseil de quartier. Un comité formé de citoyennes et citoyens, dont certains ont une expertise en histoire et en architecture, s'est donné comme mandat de sensibiliser les propriétaires et l'administration municipale à l'importance de préserver le patrimoine urbain du quartier et ce, même si le Vieux-Limoilou n'appartient pas à l'arrondissement historique de Québec. Un inventaire des bâtiments et des sites significatifs est en voie de réalisation. Comme le rappelle la responsable du dossier, «cet inventaire devrait être présenté en assemblée publique pour fins de validation, puis communiqué aux élus et aux différents services municipaux».

Le comité a convenu de critères pour le choix des édifices et des sites : l'âge, l'état de conservation, l'originalité, l'unicité et la signification pour le quartier. Plus de 108 édifices, sites ou ensembles ont été identifiés et catégorisés selon une typologie d'usage et de volumétrie. Des diapositives de chacun des bâtiments et sites répertoriés ont été prises en collaboration avec les étudiantes et étudiants du collège de Limoilou. Ces documents visuels ont servi lors de la consultation de la population à l'été 1995. Une initiative commune du collège de Limoilou et du conseil de quartier a permis la tenue d'une exposition photographique.

Finalement, le comité a formulé dix-huit recommandations, parmi celles-ci :

1. Sensibiliser les propriétaires à l'intérêt que représente leur immeuble pour le quartier et les informer spécifiquement des programmes d'aide à la conservation.

2. Aviser le conseil de quartier de toute demande de permis de démolition ou transformation importante de ces immeubles.

3. Ajuster les programmes d'aide à la rénovation résidentielle pour couvrir les travaux de «conservation», d'entretien ou de remplacement à l'identique des composantes architecturales suivantes : ouvertures, garde-corps, escaliers et galeries, corniches et parapets.

4. Soutenir et superviser l'entretien des arbres situés sur les terrains privés.

Le pouvoir d'initiative s'est aussi exercé à travers le dépôt de quatre mémoires, soumis dans le cadre d'audiences publiques. Un premier mémoire a été déposé au Bureau d'audiences publiques sur l'environnement (gouvernement du Québec). Celui-ci portait sur la venue d'un projet de «cogénération» (utilisation de la vapeur de l'incinérateur municipal à des fins de production d'électricité). Dans ce mémoire, le conseil de quartier exprimait plusieurs préoccupations des citoyennes et citoyens du Vieux-Limoilou : il expliquait comment l'environnement du quartier est déjà lourdement hypothéqué par la proximité d'une usine papetière et de l'incinérateur municipal. Le Bureau des audiences publiques a retenu plusieurs des recommandations du conseil de quartier. Le projet sera d'ailleurs déplacé plus à l'Est, pour en limiter les effets sur la qualité de vie de la population.

Finalement, trois autres mémoires ont été déposés à des audiences publiques tenues par la Ville de Québec : Plan directeur du réseau cyclable municipal; Commission consultative Femmes et Ville; Plan d'urbanisme des berges de la rivière Saint-Charles et schéma de réaménagement du parc Victoria (un grand parc urbain à vocations locale et régionale situé à proximité du quartier).

Dans un autre domaine, le conseil de quartier a usé de son pouvoir d'initiative afin de faciliter les échanges entre quelques citoyens et la Ville dans la résolution d'un problème local : l'étroitesse de la rue à un certain carrefour créait des problèmes de circulation. Tous les résidents de la rue et du secteur environnant ont été invités à une soirée de consultation. Suite à cette rencontre, à l'occasion de laquelle des pistes de solution ont été identifiées conjointement par la population et par les services municipaux, le problème a été résolu.

Plan de quartier
Par ailleurs, le conseil de quartier a été le premier interlocuteur du Service de l'urbanisme dans la révision du plan d'urbanisme du quartier. Un portrait général du quartier a été élaboré au regard des problématiques suivantes : environnement; transport et stationnement; sécurité; loisirs et vie communautaire; culture; patrimoine; habitation; design urbain; développement commercial et économique. Le plan de quartier propose un état de la situation. Il contient les grandes orientations ainsi que les objectifs qui s'y rattachent. Un plan d'action fut aussi développé en fonction des orientations du plan de quartier. Ce plan d'action inclut des moyens concrets pour atteindre les orientations ainsi que les délais et les coûts de réalisation.

Le plan de quartier, tout comme le plan d'action, a été élaboré à partir du travail conjoint de la population, des fonctionnaires municipaux et des membres du conseil de quartier qui ont organisé plusieurs ateliers de discussion ouverts à la population. Deux rencontres de consultation publique pour valider le nouveau plan de quartier et le plan d'action auprès des citoyens, avant de les soumettre au Conseil municipal, furent prévues pour l'automne 1995. Enfin, certaines citoyennes et certains citoyens actifs au sein des comités de travail souhaitent siéger au conseil de quartier tout comme certains des membres actuels s'apprêtent à poursuivre l'expérience. La continuité du projet semble donc être assurée.

SAINT-JEAN-BAPTISTE

Quelques caractéristiques du quartier
Le quartier Saint-Jean-Baptiste accueille l'Assemblée nationale du Québec. Des milliers de fonctionnaires viennent y travailler chaque matin, alors que depuis longtemps sa population est mobilisée pour défendre la fonction résidentielle du quartier. Situé à la limite ouest des fortifications du Vieux-Québec, le quartier Saint-Jean-Baptiste est l'un des plus anciens de la ville. Environ 9 500 personnes y résident. De ce nombre, à peine 9,3 % ont moins de dix-huit ans, alors que 45,5 % ont entre dix-huit et trente-neuf ans. Par ailleurs, 59 % de la population du quartier vit seule. C'est un peu le quartier latin de Québec. Au plan de la répartition des unités d'habitation, sur 5 630 logements, 82,3 % sont des logements locatifs (63,8 % appartiennent au secteur privé et 18,5 % sont détenus par des coopératives et des organismes sans but lucratif) alors que 17,7 % sont occupés par le ou la propriétaire du logement.

À l'origine formé par les faubourgs Saint-Jean et Saint-Louis, le quartier fut, dans les années 1960, littéralement coupé en deux par l'élargissement du boulevard Saint-Cyrille aujourd'hui nommé René-Lévesque. Au même moment, à l'Est, près des fortifications, la construction de l'autoroute Dufferin-Montmorency amputait le quartier d'une partie de son territoire tout en rendant périlleuses les liaisons piétonnes avec le Vieux-Québec. La construction du Centre des congrès et de grands édifices administratifs et hôteliers le long du boulevard René-Lévesque a marqué les décennies 1960 et 1970.

Au plan des fonctions, la partie Nord du quartier (le faubourg Saint-Jean) conserve son caractère résolument résidentiel et son aspect initial. Offrant une architecture diversifiée, la plus grande partie du parc de logements fut construite après l'incendie de 1881 et avant 1960. Alignées sur le trottoir, collées les unes sur les autres, des maisons de trois et quatre étages occupent l'espace. Ce type d'immeubles regroupe 77,6 % de tous les logements du quartier. À flanc de falaise, en dépit de leur étroitesse, les rues orientées dans l'axe sud/nord offrent des percées visuelles saisissantes sur la basse-ville et le massif des Laurentides. La plus grande partie des espaces verts est située dans les cours intérieures des résidences. Comme les bâtiments sont mitoyens, ces espaces verts ne sont pas visibles de la rue. Récemment rénovée, la rue Saint-Jean constitue l'artère commerciale de cette partie du quartier. Ses commerces servent les clientèles locale et régionale.

Inversement, dans sa partie Sud (le faubourg Saint-Louis), de l'autre côté du boulevard René-Lévesque, la fonction résidentielle coexiste avec les fonctions administrative et touristique omniprésentes. Cette partie du quartier est le coeur administratif de la capitale du Québec. La construction du Centre municipal des congrès et de grands édifices administratifs et hôteliers le long du boulevard René-Lévesque dans les années 1960-1970 a favorisé le développement de la fonction administrative et touristique de ce secteur. S'ajoutent de grandes conciergeries construites principalement durant cette période. Elles regroupent 19 % des logements du quartier et côtoient de grandes maisons cossues, d'inspiration victorienne, construites au début du siècle. À l'opposé de la partie nord du quartier, les maisons y sont distantes du trottoir. Un peu plus au Sud, la Grande Allée constitue l'artère commerciale. Les commerces visent prioritairement la clientèle touristique. De plus, on y trouve de vastes espaces verts publics dont celui du parc des Champs de bataille (les Plaines d'Abraham).

La construction de l'autoroute, l'élargissement du boulevard, la création de grands complexes hôteliers et administratifs dans les décennies 1960 et 1970, entraînèrent la démolition d'un grand nombre de logements et son corollaire, l'exode d'une bonne partie de la population. La population s'est mobilisée afin de renverser cette tendance et de redonner au citoyen le droit de cité dans son propre quartier. C'est également à cette époque que l'on observe l'arrivée d'une population plus jeune et plus scolarisée. Cette dernière participera à la création d'un comité de citoyennes et citoyens et à la mise sur pied de coopératives d'habitation.

L'ère des démolitions est aujourd'hui révolue. Le message de la population est passé et l'administration municipale privilégie maintenant une approche axée sur l'amélioration de la qualité de vie. Des programmes de subventions, notamment dans le domaine de la rénovation des maisons, viennent appuyer cette approche. C'est sur cette toile de fond que prend forme le Conseil de quartier Saint-Jean-Baptiste, constitué au printemps de 1993.

Pouvoir d'initiative
Outre son mandat de tenir des consultations publiques sur les demandes de modification au règlement de zonage et sur les autres questions reliées à l'aménagement du territoire, dès ses premiers mois d'activités, le conseil de quartier a organisé plusieurs assemblées publiques afin de déterminer les priorités d'action, faisant l'usage du pouvoir d'initiative. Les priorités retenues furent : l'aménagement du quartier, notamment l'intégration du nouveau Centre des congrès et le réaménagement du boulevard René-Lévesque et de l'autoroute Dufferin-Montmorency; la consolidation et le développement de la fonction résidentielle; l'amélioration de la sécurité; la mise en valeur et la protection du patrimoine. Par ailleurs, le conseil de quartier a invité la population à participer aux

comités de travail chargés de l'actualisation des priorités d'action. Outre les membres du conseil, une trentaine de personnes se sont jointes à l'un ou l'autre des comités.

Face au projet d'agrandissement du Centre des congrès, l'action du conseil de quartier vise l'intégration harmonieuse du projet, tant du point de vue architectural que de celui des mesures à prendre pour consolider la fonction résidentielle située à proximité. L'actuel Centre des congrès présente sa façade arrière aux résidents du quartier. Le projet d'agrandissement proposé tourne le dos au quartier et est fermé sur lui-même. Il n'offre aucun lien direct avec le quartier, ce qui empêche l'échange entre les congressistes et les commerces. Sans accès ni activité propice à créer une animation, la façade arrière ne concourt aucunement à améliorer la sécurité des résidents et des piétons. En outre, son architecture ne reflète en rien celle du quartier et ne propose aucune solution pour atténuer le caractère massif de cet immeuble de grande taille.

Dans ces circonstances, le conseil a demandé à la Ville de le soutenir dans ses démarches auprès du gouvernement du Québec et de la Société immobilière du Québec, responsables de la construction du Centre des congrès. Ces démarches réalisées en collaboration avec plusieurs organismes du quartier et le soutien des commerçants ont tantôt pris la forme de conférences de presse, de rencontres avec le ministre responsable du dossier ou avec la Société immobilière du Québec. Les actions du conseil de quartier ont amené la Société immobilière à réviser ses plans. Ainsi, la fenestration sera augmentée. Tous les objectifs n'ont pas été atteints mais le travail du conseil de quartier a permis une bonification et une meilleure intégration du projet d'agrandissement du Centre des congrès.

En ce qui a trait aux mesures visant à consolider la fonction résidentielle présente autour du Centre des congrès, la Ville a réservé une somme de 2 750 000 $ à cet effet. Le travail du conseil de quartier consistait à mobiliser la population du secteur dans le cadre de l'élaboration du plan d'aménagement, à faire connaître les orientations défendues par le quartier, à suivre l'évolution des travaux menant à l'élaboration du plan d'aménagement et, dans la phase finale, à tenir la consultation publique sur le projet définitif.

En ce qui a trait au réaménagement du boulevard René-Lévesque, l'enjeu consiste à rétrécir le boulevard, à rendre de nouveau possibles les communications Nord-Sud pour rétablir les liens naturels qui jadis avaient été coupés et finalement, à réaliser un aménagement susceptible de consolider la fonction résidentielle. Dans le dossier du réaménagement du boulevard René-Lévesque et de l'autoroute Dufferin-Montmorency, comme dans celui de la consolidation de la fonction résidentielle dans le pourtour du Centre des congrès, les opinions de la Ville et du quartier convergent. Tous les participants s'entendent pour éliminer le caractère autoroutier de ces voies de circulation et leur donner les attributs de boulevards urbains, c'est-à-dire faciliter les communications entre les parties du quartier et avec les quartiers voisins. Dans le cas du boulevard René-Lévesque, les enjeux concernent l'intégration d'une piste cyclable dans le nouvel aménagement et l'utilisation de la plus grande partie possible de l'espace récupéré sur la chaussée pour consolider la fonction résidentielle. En ce qui a trait à l'autoroute Dufferin-Montmorency, les enjeux se situent au niveau de la sécurité des traverses piétonnes et de l'utilisation de l'espace récupéré sur la chaussée.

Dans l'élaboration de son mémoire présenté aux audiences publiques sur le réaménagement de ces artères, le conseil de quartier a tenu une assemblée publique afin de discuter avec la population des principaux enjeux. Ce travail a permis au conseil de préciser son point de vue et de se présenter aux audiences publiques avec un mémoire dont les principales recommandations étaient inspirées de l'assemblée publique.

Pour ce qui est des résultats, le conseil a convaincu la Ville d'intégrer une piste cyclable au projet de réaménagement du boulevard René-Lévesque. Par contre, la demande de consacrer une plus grande partie de l'espace récupéré sur le boulevard René-Lévesque à la consolidation de la fonction résidentielle n'a pas été retenue. En ce qui a trait à l'autoroute Dufferin-Montmorency, la Ville a accepté la recommandation de plusieurs organismes du quartier de poursuivre l'étude du projet et de revenir en consultation publique avec une nouvelle proposition.

La révision du plan d'urbanisme du quartier, amorcée en 1994 par l'administration municipale, amène le conseil de quartier à consacrer une bonne partie de ses ressources pour poursuivre une vaste réflexion sur l'avenir résidentiel du quartier. Un comité est créé et organise un «Carrefour sur l'habitation» pendant l'hiver 1995. Plus de soixante-dix résidentes et résidents participent à cet événement pour dire comment ils vivent dans le quartier, comment ils s'y logent et ce qu'il représente pour eux.

Dans son rapport au conseil de quartier, le comité sur l'habitation suggère un ensemble de mesures visant à consolider et à développer la fonction résidentielle. Ces mesures ont trait à la réglementation municipale en matière de zonage et de circulation, au renforcement ou à la création de programmes pour attirer les familles dans le quartier, à la consolidation des parcs et des espaces verts et à la protection du caractère historique des édifices. Également, le comité insiste sur l'importance de penser le plan d'urbanisme de quartier en plaçant le piéton et le respect des résidents au centre des préoccupations. Si l'un des privilèges des gens du quartier est d'avoir accès à tous les services à pied, on observe que cette accessibilité est rendue difficile voire périlleuse par l'omniprésence des véhicules et des voies de transport et par la faiblesse des mesures favorisant le piéton.

Pour corriger cette situation, le comité demande que la Ville élabore une charte du piéton. Cette charte aurait l'avantage de guider la Ville dans l'élaboration des plans d'aménagement. En ce qui a trait au respect des résidents, le comité souligne que les participants au Carrefour ont l'impression que la Ville privilégie le développement de projets sans considérer la population en place. Ainsi, la consolidation de la fonction résidentielle ne veut rien dire si on autorise simultanément des projets qui par leur gabarit viennent diminuer la qualité de vie des résidents du quartier. En outre, les personnes participantes réclament une plus grande sensibilité et ouverture de la part des fonctionnaires municipaux. Le rapport du comité fut présenté et adopté en assemblée publique du conseil de quartier. Ce document constitue maintenant un outil important de référence dans l'élaboration du plan de quartier dont l'étude en assemblée publique fut prévue pour la première moitié de 1996.

À l'automne 1993, des citoyens et citoyennes se sont réunis dans le but d'améliorer la sécurité des résidents. C'est ainsi que le groupe OEIL est créé (Organisme d'entraide et d'intervention locale). Interpellé par ce groupe et par la population, plutôt que de dédoubler les actions en créant sa propre structure, le conseil de quartier travaille de concert avec OEIL et parraine une recommandation à la Ville à l'effet de reconnaître ce groupe comme expérience pilote et de lui accorder une subvention de fonctionnement ainsi qu'un local. À la fin du printemps 1995, la Ville répond favorablement aux demandes du groupe OEIL.

Ce groupe a concentré ses activités de l'été 1995 à la réappropriation par les résidents des parcs publics du quartier qui étaient monopolisés par quelques indésirables. OEIL organisa des activités se déroulant tantôt le jour, tantôt le soir : théâtre pour les enfants et présence des camions de pompiers le jour, volley-ball en soirée, improvisation au parc-école, soupers de poésie ont constitué le coeur des activités dans les parcs. Mission accomplie, outre le fait de participer, plusieurs ont pris l'habitude de fréquenter régulièrement les parcs. Également, OEIL suggéra des aménagements à l'un des parcs afin de le rendre plus visible de la rue, la nuit.

Dans le cadre de l'élaboration du plan de quartier, la Ville a fait réaliser une étude sur le patrimoine bâti de Saint-Jean-Baptiste. Suite à cette étude, la Ville a demandé au conseil de quartier de commenter la proposition d'un plan de conservation et de mise en valeur. Pour réaliser ce travail, un comité formé d'une dizaine de personnes résidentes, motivées par l'objectif de protéger et de développer le patrimoine du quartier, a été mis sur pied.

Dans un premier temps, la Ville présenta au comité l'étude sur le patrimoine. Par la suite, le comité entreprit l'analyse de la proposition. Dans son rapport au conseil de quartier, le comité indique «qu'il faut mettre en place des mesures qui permettent une amélioration de l'état d'authenticité de l'ensemble des édifices du quartier plutôt que de concentrer les ressources sur quelques édifices représentatifs du quartier. C'est la valeur d'ensemble du quartier qu'il faut sauvegarder».

Pour y parvenir, les programmes de rénovation et de construction doivent inclure des conditions ayant trait au respect de l'intégrité du patrimoine. Par ailleurs, le comité suggère que les propriétaires, tout comme les fonctionnaires qui administrent les programmes, soient sensibilisés au patrimoine du quartier. En outre, le comité recommande à la Ville de doter le quartier d'un statut particulier en matière d'architecture. Puisqu'il ne s'agit pas de figer le quartier dans le passé, ce statut particulier doit présenter les caractéristiques suivantes : offrir une certaine souplesse qui permette la créativité architecturale; favoriser l'autonomie et la responsabilisation des propriétaires et leur coopération avec la Ville; permettre une évolution harmonieuse du quartier et développer une approche incitative plutôt que coercitive.

ÉVALUATION

La façon de s'acquitter de leur mandat de consultation publique et de participer aux audiences publiques de la Ville est analogue dans chacune des deux expériences de conseil de quartier. Par contre, c'est dans l'utilisation du pouvoir d'initiative que les deux expériences se démarquent.

Dans le Vieux-Limoilou, le conseil de quartier s'est servi du pouvoir d'initiative pour animer la population. Au-delà de la mobilisation de la population, l'action du conseil de quartier a amené la Ville à inscrire dans ses priorités d'action l'aménagement de ruelles alors que le comité sur le patrimoine visait à la fois la sensibilisation de la population et de la Ville au patrimoine architectural du quartier. L'expérience du Vieux-Limoilou a permis de montrer que le conseil de quartier est un outil majeur permettant d'influencer la Ville en l'amenant à inscrire dans ses priorités des actions qui n'étaient pas prévues.

Dans Saint-Jean-Baptiste, l'usage du pouvoir d'initiative est défini par les grands enjeux de développement urbain qui y ont cours. Ainsi, la réfection du boulevard René-Lévesque, l'agrandissement du Centre des congrès et la mise en place d'un plan de secteur doté d'un budget substantiel afin de consolider l'habitation dans le pourtour du Centre des congrès ont mobilisé le conseil et ses comités.

Dans le cadre de l'évaluation de l'expérience des conseils de quartier, les membres des conseils de quartier soulignent que «les résultats obtenus montrent que le conseil de quartier a exercé une bonne influence sur les décisions de la Ville». Les expériences pilotes se sont terminées en juin 1995. L'administration municipale a demandé à son Service de la planification d'évaluer ces expériences. Il en ressort que :

1. Dans l'ensemble, les conseils de quartier se sont acquittés de leur mandat. Ils ont accompli de façon significative la plupart des activités pour lesquelles ils ont été créés. Leurs membres ont consacré de nombreuses heures bénévoles (le temps moyen mensuel consacré par chaque membre est de seize heures). Depuis le début de l'expérimentation en juin 1993, le Conseil de quartier Vieux-Limoilou a tenu vingt-cinq séances de travail et quatorze réunions publiques, alors que dans Saint-Jean-Baptiste trente-sept séances de travail et treize réunions publiques ont eu lieu. Dans Vieux-Limoilou, les réunions des différents comités se chiffrent à quatre-vingt-dix-neuf. Les autres activités du conseil s'élèvent à soixante-deux. Parmi ces activités, nous retrouvons principalement les invitations des différents organismes du milieu à siéger sur des comités conjoints, les colloques, les réunions d'information organisées par la Ville et les audiences publiques. On observe un volume comparable d'activités pour Saint-Jean-Baptiste.

   Interrogés sur leur tâche de travail, les membres ont noté une multiplicité de mandats; ils ont indiqué que les dossiers initiés par le conseil ont été nombreux. Certains membres ont suggéré de «diminuer le nombre de séances de travail et de réunions publiques, limiter le nombre de dossiers dans le plan d'action et d'établir des règles de durée des réunions».

   En outre, lors de l'évaluation de l'expérience, les membres notaient l'importance des comités de travail et de la participation de la population à ces comités. Chaque comité était composé de deux membres du conseil et de plusieurs citoyennes et citoyens. Ils ont affirmé que «le climat de confiance réciproque a permis le développement d'une méthode de travail efficace en comités de travail». Les membres ont aussi apprécié le caractère convivial du groupe et le sentiment d'appartenance à une équipe.

2. L'expérience des conseils de quartier démontre une participation constante et significative de la population des deux quartiers. Dans chacun des quartiers, la participation à chaque assemblée publique varie entre quarante et cinquante-cinq personnes. Au plan de la consultation publique, les conseils de quartier s'acquittent efficacement du mandat qui auparavant était confié aux comités consultatifs. La spécificité des conseils de quartier quant à la participation de la population réside dans la

tenue régulière d'assemblées publiques et l'élaboration d'un plan d'action axé sur les préoccupations du quartier. Certains souhaits sont formulés par les membres : «Augmenter la participation de la population aux différentes activités du conseil; assurer une meilleure diffusion des réalisations du conseil et alléger la procédure de la consultation publique afin de favoriser les échanges entre le public et les membres du conseil de quartier.»

3. L'influence qu'ont exercée les conseils de quartier sur la Ville est également mesurable. Tous les avis dressés au Comité exécutif et ayant fait l'objet d'une décision ont été retenus.

4. Par ailleurs, leur influence ne s'est pas limitée à des avis qui auraient été transmis, suite à des consultations publiques telles que les menaient les comités consultatifs. Ainsi, la spécificité des conseils de quartier a été relevée dans plusieurs dossiers qui n'auraient pas été mis de l'avant par des comités consultatifs. Notons le programme d'aménagement des ruelles, le projet de recyclage de la caserne dans le Vieux-Limoilou, les réflexions approfondies sur des dossiers majeurs et transmises lors du dépôt de mémoires à l'occasion d'audiences publiques. Les rapports d'audiences font état des demandes et des préoccupations des conseils de quartier et, dans plusieurs cas, on observe que les recommandations sont reprises par les commissaires.

Selon les membres, «le pouvoir d'initiative a été au-delà des attentes prévues : création de comités de travail, rédaction et dépôt de mémoires. Le pouvoir d'initiative est plus important qu'un pouvoir décisionnel». Par ailleurs, interrogés sur d'éventuels pouvoirs décisionnels qui pourraient leur être conférés, un des membres soulignait que «l'absence de pouvoir décisionnel permet d'éviter les pressions de la population». Les membres ne souhaitent pas de pouvoirs décisionnels. Ils sont unanimes : «Le conseil de quartier doit demeurer consultatif. Les décisions appartiennent à la Ville.»

D'une façon générale, les membres sont d'avis que la formule des conseils de quartier doit se poursuivre. Elle constitue un lieu non partisan dont l'objectif premier est de rassembler les énergies individuelles autour d'un objectif commun : un meilleur devenir pour leur quartier.

LA SUITE

En septembre 1995, le Conseil municipal annonçait son intention de rendre la formule des conseils de quartier disponible dans tous les quartiers de Québec. Des amendements à la *Charte de la Ville* devaient d'abord être obtenus de l'Assemblée nationale du Québec qui devait traiter la requête au printemps 1996.

Pour chaque quartier, une pétition de 300 noms devait d'abord être transmise au Conseil municipal et une assemblée de consultation devait confirmer la volonté de la population de se doter d'un conseil de quartier. En l'absence d'un conseil de quartier, les comités consultatifs demeureraient.

Les conseils de quartier constitueront désormais des entités juridiques autonomes, accréditées par le Conseil municipal. Ils recevront chacun une subvention de 10 000 $, un local, le matériel de bureau nécessaire et, finalement, le support financier et logistique du Bureau des consultations publiques pour l'organisation des activités prévues dans la Politique de consultation publique. Le Bureau des consultations publiques affectera une personne ressource par trois conseils de quartier. Ces derniers pourront compléter leur financement par d'autres revenus de source autonome (dons de fondation, subventions des gouvernements supérieurs, campagnes de levée de fonds). L'administration municipale souhaite ainsi soutenir de façon économique le fonctionnement de douze conseils de quartier sans multiplier indûment le nombre de fonctionnaires impliqués. Les conseils de quartier expérimentaux de Saint-Jean-Baptiste et du Vieux-Limoilou bénéficiaient chacun d'une ressource professionnelle en support. Leur budget de fonctionnement était entièrement administré par la Ville.

En donnant aux futurs conseils de quartier plus d'autonomie juridique et financière, l'administration municipale souhaite favoriser le développement et la consolidation du pouvoir d'initiative des conseils de quartier. Ces derniers pourraient devenir, si les attentes sont comblées, des acteurs significatifs dans le développement social et économique de la Ville. En effet, les attentes de la Ville par rapport aux futurs conseils de quartier sont doubles :

1. Mettre en oeuvre la politique de consultation publique à l'échelle des quartiers. À cet égard, il est de la responsabilité de la Ville de soutenir totalement les conseils de quartier dans l'accomplissement de leur mandat.

2. Développer le pouvoir d'initiative. À cet égard, la Ville a une responsabilité, particulièrement pour les dossiers qui sont de sa compétence. Il n'est pas interdit de penser cependant que les conseils de quartier interpelleront aussi les autres intervenants gouvernementaux et privés. Les conseils de quartier pourraient eux-même générer les ressources

nécessaires à la réalisation d'objectifs spécifiques. Ce qui est espéré ici, c'est que les membres des conseils de quartier sauront identifier les projets capables de consolider le tissu physique, économique, social ou culturel de leur quartier, et avec l'aide de la Ville, canaliser les ressources nécessaires à leur réalisation.

La consultation publique s'est avérée être une première étape quant à la participation de la population. L'exercice d'un réel pouvoir d'initiative par les conseils de quartier constitue un saut qualitatif sur lequel il est permis de fonder des espoirs. En une vingtaine d'années, nous serions ainsi passés du citoyen extérieur à son administration municipale et qui doit hausser le ton pour influer sur les décisions qui affectent son quartier, au citoyen consulté pour les dossiers jugés importants par l'administration pour en arriver, finalement, au citoyen acteur significatif dans l'identification et la mise en oeuvre des stratégies de développement de sa ville et de son quartier.

L'expérience est encore très jeune. Si on recense plusieurs types de conseils de quartier aux États-Unis et en Europe, ils sont encore plutôt rares au Canada. Il faudra observer l'implantation progressive des conseils de quartier et leur évolution avec le passage des ans avec le renouvellement des conseils municipaux.

Un consensus semble s'établir dans la culture politique locale autour de la nécessité et de l'utilité de développer la participation du public à la vie municipale, au sein même des quartiers. On peut espérer que les conseils de quartier sauront continuer à évoluer au-delà des débats et des stratégies politiques partisanes pour s'affirmer comme de véritables outils de développement aux mains des citoyens et des citoyennes.

Nous reprenons ici, en conclusion, les propos de M. André Beauchamp, spécialiste de la participation du public et ex-président du Bureau des audiences publiques en environnement. Nous lui avons demandé de réfléchir aux perspectives d'avenir des conseils de quartier. La citation que nous avons retenue résume le défi des conseils de quartier à Québec :

Par ailleurs, c'est autour du pouvoir d'initiative que la conscience du quartier pourra se construire. Si le conseil de quartier ne s'enlise pas dans la lutte politique partisane, il peut développer dans le quartier le sentiment d'appartenance et diffuser une conception renouvelée de la politique urbaine locale : définition des besoins et des attentes, dialogue sur les politiques, carrefour d'échanges et d'information, intervention auprès de tiers. Une lutte de représentativité peut surgir avec d'autres organismes du quartier. Mais il peut y avoir aussi symbiose, selon que le conseil de quartier saura ou non faire des alliances et instaurer la collaboration plutôt que la compétition.[1]

NOTE

1. André Beauchamp, «Analyse de la politique de consultation publique de la Ville de Québec» (Québec : Service des communications et des relations extérieures, 1995), p. 27.

6

Expanding the Frontiers of Public Participation: Public Involvement in Municipal Budgeting and Finance

W. Michael Fenn

A PUBLIC ROLE IN LOCAL DECISIONS

On any given Monday night in most communities across Canada, a citizen can address the municipal council, directly and in public, simply by reserving a place on the agenda. In contrast, appearing at the bar of the House of Commons or at a cabinet meeting and expecting to be heard would likely yield the citizen's unceremonious physical ejection. As a result, the notion of public participation in municipal decision-making has an entirely different meaning than it does in other areas of the public sector. Municipal government also has a long and extensive experience with the "direct democracy" measures, such as the plebiscites and binding petitions, which lately have become fashionable items on the political agenda for senior levels of government.

Another common characteristic of the Canadian municipal scene is that local decisions on environmental or land-use issues are usually the most contentious and most easily appealed beyond local elected bodies to the provincial government, or to one of its quasi-judicial tribunals, or to the courts. This adds another dimension to any generic discussion about public involvement in municipal decision-making.

When these institutional conditions are superimposed on a non-partisan, frequent, low-cost and easily accessible municipal electoral process, it may seem curious that there is so much concern for enhancing public participation in local decision-making. The answer probably lies in another feature of municipal decision-making: the decisions made by municipal councils may not be as costly or momentous as those of Hydro Quebec or Transport Canada, but they are highly visible to the average citizen, in both fiscal and physical terms. Local decisions affect people where they live, and the consequences of those decisions are often visible every day for a generation or more.

One could also speculate that the very accessibility of local government leads to heightened public expectation that it will reflect citizen preferences. Citizens often seem resigned to the fact that their governments in Ottawa or in the provincial capital will do things with which they disagree, citing competing interests or institutional arterial sclerosis. But when locally elected representatives make decisions that do not reflect the citizen's preference, the reaction is often quite vigorous. Excuses are not tolerated.

For all of these reasons, both legislation and practice have made municipal government very sensitive to the need for routine, direct and substantive involvement of the residents and interest groups within a community.

A History of Public Involvement in Local Decisions

The origin of the idea that there should be a "direct democracy" component in local decisions, even in a society with institutions of representative democracy, goes back to the time of Louis-Joseph Papineau and William Lyon Mackenzie. Traces of the "town-meeting" tradition of the American Loyalist immigrants remain evident in our modern municipal institutions. But the real institutionalization of public participation in municipal government dates from the early 1900s.

The first third of this century saw recurring municipal debt crises. The abuses of the turn-of-the-century railway-building period, machine politics in some major centres, and, ultimately, the Depression-era insolvency of many municipalities led to provincial laws requiring local referenda on capital works and bond issues. "Local improvement" legislation prescribed neighbourhood petitions for and against extensions of physical services in urban areas and for drainage works in rural areas.

Following World War II, with economic prosperity rising and memories of the debt crises of the 1930s fading, issues related to rapid urban growth gradually took precedence over issues of debt and tax rates on municipal government agendas. In the 1960s and 1970s, references to public participation in municipal decision-making were almost synonymous with public participation in the development process (land-use planning, traffic and urban redevelopment decisions). By the late 1970s, "the development process" also embraced municipal decisions affecting the natural environment and pollution issues.

During this time, the importance of public involvement in fiscal issues was substantially downgraded, both in law and practice. Legal requirements for approval by the electors for major capital works and municipal bond issues (debentures) were repealed or routinely waived by provincial authorities. Provincial approval or public endorsation for special-area taxation were gradually eliminated. Public infrastructure and building projects, formerly controlled by benefiting neighbourhoods through local improvement petitions and special-area taxation, were now financed through general taxation or were supported by development revenues, such as lot levies or subdivision agreements. By the mid-1980s, public involvement in municipal budgeting and fiscal issues had largely disappeared. Financial discussions in municipalities were generally confined to municipal councils, provincial agencies, and the development industry.

Nature and Impact of Public Involvement in Development

As public involvement in the fiscal process waned, it was more than replaced by public involvement in the development process. In fact, some have lately argued that the public-participation process went "too far" in the land-use and environmental fields. Certainly, few would deny that public-involvement processes, whether directly at the municipal level or through appeal mechanisms, added materially to the time, cost and litigiousness of the decision-making process on development issues. Protracted and unpredictable municipal public decision-making processes have had impacts on the cost of housing and commercial development, on the climate for business investment, and on construction employment. But, with the possible exception of those who believe in a wide-ranging veto over development rights, few would seriously argue that the public is disenfranchised any longer in the land-use decision-making process.

The nature of public involvement in the land-use and environmental decision-making processes did have one feature that distinguished it from the earlier mechanisms to involve the public in fiscal issues. Public participation in fiscal issues aimed to allow the collective good to prevail over the specific interest. Public involvement in land-use planning and environmental issues has been premised on the assumption that the property-owner and the neighbourhood should be protected from the "tyranny of the majority," if it affects the residents' continued enjoyment of their property and neighbourhood in its present circumstances. Legislation and practice on land-use planning and environmental issues allowed dissatisfied individuals, neighbourhoods or community interest groups to prevent or significantly retard proposals that might otherwise enjoy widespread public support and be endorsed by the municipal council elected by that broader community.

Reflecting their historical origins, however, fiscal referenda and local improvement petitions aimed to ensure that broader community interests ultimately prevailed over one or two disaffected property-owners standing in the way of the extension of local services or community facilities. They also put restraints on any "special interest" promoting a publicly financed project of questionable value or content.

CONTEMPORARY PUBLIC PARTICIPATION IN FINANCE ISSUES

In the early 1990s across most of Canada, the public agenda at the local level shifted from concern over development (or redevelopment in more mature cities) to a concern over taxes. With the residential real-estate market in the doldrums and with commercial development stalled by the effects of economic restructuring, proposals for good-quality new development were as rare as the bank financing for them. Municipal councils heard much more frequently from individual businesses and taxpayers, and later from organized groups (taxpayer coalitions, small business associations, etc.) demanding curbs on municipal and school-board spending and property-tax reductions.

To accommodate the demands for more public input on fiscal issues, municipal councils used the devices close at hand and with which they were most familiar. They provided these groups with a forum to be heard at municipal council meetings and responded to their detailed critiques of municipal and school-board spending, borrowing, and revenue-generation practices. In essence, municipal councils invited those with concerns about fiscal issues to address those issues using the same public-participation mechanisms that served public-participation in the development process.

It became obvious fairly quickly to municipal councils, however, that this approach to public involvement on fiscal issues was not serving the needs of either the aroused public or members of council, who had to make the final decisions. The existing laws and practices were designed for the development process, where individual and localized concerns had to be protected from the collectivity. In the case of fiscal issues, those appearing before municipal councils were claiming to represent the broader community against the special interest and against "business as usual." Frustrations and recriminations were starting to appear; a new format was needed.

Nature of the Challenge

In terms of substance, the criticisms from the taxpayers' coalitions and similar groups tended to revolve around too much spending and too much accommodation of special-interest groups. Local politicians, however, had their own concerns. As people who were very close to their electors, municipal council members and school-board trustees were not sure that the taxpayers' advocates had heard the anti-tax message clearly enough. To the council members, the message sounded more like "no new taxes" and "no cuts in services," rather than the version of the advocates, who often argued for tax *cuts* at the expense of programs and services. Both municipal councils and school boards were also quite convinced that the advocates of fiscal rectitude simply did not understand the complex and intractable budgetary, fiscal and labour-relations challenges that local government was facing.

BURLINGTON'S RESPONSE

As an illustration of the nature of the municipal response to demands for greater public involvement in fiscal and budgetary matters, consider the approach of the Burlington city council.

With the onset of the 1990 recession, the City of Burlington (an affluent suburban community of 132,000 residents, with several thousand businesses) saw the advent of taxpayer groups that were very active and that attracted considerable popular support and media profile. Burlington had an active public-participation program in connection with urban development, as one would expect in a rapidly growing centre between Hamilton and Toronto. But, by early 1990, the city was looking at alternative means to involve the public in fiscal issues.

Burlington's experiments fell into two categories: citizen budget review and community-attitude surveys.

– *Citizen Budget Review:* As a first step in involving the public in policy development, tax-restraint advocates were asked to join other stakeholders in a unique process. Council directed the city manager to use the "mediation model" to produce a consensus on a new regime for the development charges that finance new major municipal infrastructure. Following the unique success of this experiment, a cross-section of citizens, including representatives from taxpayer-advocacy groups, were invited to conduct a citizen budget review. The membership of the Citizens' Budget Advisory Committee was selected by the city council from among the most prominent advocacy groups, supplemented by individual citizens who were known to have an interest and expertise in this area and who reflected elements of the broader community. The Citizens' Budget Advisory Committee aimed to use public participation as a means to raise public awareness about the complexities and realities of municipal finance, while exposing municipal budgets to refreshing external scrutiny.

– *Community-Attitude Surveys:* Reflecting the concerns of many members of city council that the "real" public should be heard, not just the vocal public who attended meetings and sent letters to the editor, community-attitude surveys were conducted, in 1990 and again in 1993, on cost and servicing issues.

In public policy there is an old adage that "for every complex problem there is an answer that is simple, straightforward and wrong." Reflecting this, city council felt that the proposals it was hearing from tax-cut militants were simplistic. Believing that the solutions being proposed by taxpayers' advocates were impractical but journalistically persuasive, city council decided to draw a cross-section of the public, including taxpayers' advocates, into the policy-development process, so the public could see firsthand what policy options really were available.

The remainder of this chapter describes and evaluates these two innovations. Following the Burlington experience with community surveys, a similar approach has been used by the Regional Municipality of Hamilton-Wentworth. The two experiences will be contrasted.

CITIZENS' BUDGET ADVISORY COMMITTEE

The 1994 Ontario municipal and school-board elections were held in the depths of an economic recession. Regardless of past partisan affiliation, most successful candidates ran on platforms in which tax restraint featured very prominently. For his part, the newly elected mayor of Burlington proposed the creation of a citizens' committee to review the city's budget position and budgeting system. City council ultimately accepted this proposal, although not without a healthy debate about whose job it was to set municipal priorities and budgets, especially with a fresh electoral mandate.

In addition to the mayor and the council member who chaired the council's budget and strategic planning committee, city council appointed eight citizens to the "Citizens' Budget Advisory Committee." The appointees included the vice-president of the "Taxpayers Coalition"; the treasurer of the district labour council (and financial secretary of a large Canadian Auto Workers Local); a well-known local activist and environmentalist; a retired vice-president and comptroller of a major steel company; the president of a major Canadian security company; a professional researcher who was a prominent advocate on behalf of the local arts community; a former financial executive (and past chair of the library board); and the vice-president of a national development company with significant local holdings.[1]

The citizens' committee met throughout February to May 1992 and attended regular council budget meetings from late January to early March. Members reviewed the proposed current and capital budgets in detail, with assistance from city staff and politicians; they studied the budget process followed by the municipality; and they examined the budget process as it was understood by the general public, including the public information and involvement processes.

In the end, the citizens' committee produced an extensive array of recommendations that far exceeded even the expectations of its proponents. It challenged city council to adopt a commercial approach to budgeting, irrespective of the acknowledged political environment. Give firm "endpoint" budget directions to staff, the committee said, and then hold staff responsible for meeting those objectives. Gone were the days of staff coyly bringing in inflated budgets and leaving council members to pare them down to acceptable size (with the attendant public posturing).

The citizens' committee also criticized the budget's annual focus, noting the tendency to make short-term decisions and to ignore the interplay between this year's capital budget decisions and next year's current budget debt-service costs. The committee provided considerable incentive to adopting multiyear (three-year) current budgeting. The citizens' committee also criticized the lack of focus on product and service outputs, not a surprising finding for a committee dominated by the private sector. It proposed a program orientation in the presentation and, in particular, the evaluation of budgetary performance. The committee paid special attention to the capital budget and emphasized its linkage to the current budget on the multiyear basis that the committee was recommending.[2]

Recommendations on Citizen Involvement

In keeping with their role as representatives of the public, members of the citizens' committee went beyond its objective of introducing more of a private-sector orientation into the municipal budgeting process. Having sat through a number of regular budget meetings, the committee members noted that city-council committees were encouraging public participation by scheduling their meetings on weekday evenings, when they listened to many delegations appearing on budget and funding issues. The effect of accommodating the public in this fashion was, however, that debate and decisions on very significant issues were often being delayed until very late at night.

The citizens' committee argued the need for curfews, so that important financial decisions were not made under conditions of fatigue and declining alertness. It also argued for a different format for public meetings on budget matters, at a time and under conditions where the public, especially the commuter population, might be encouraged to attend and to comment. Ultimately, this led to a public meeting on Saturday morning and scheduling some evening meetings when no decisions were on the agenda.

Reaction to the Citizens' Committee

In all, fourteen concrete recommendations were received from the Citizens' Budget Advisory Committee. Whatever their initial misgivings, both staff and council members recognized that the decision to appoint the committee was an unqualified success. For their part, members of the citizens' committee concluded that the municipal budgeting process was quite open and rational, requiring significant changes but no major surgery. The recommendations of the citizens' committee were subsequently adopted, for the most part, and they proved to be very effective in improving the budget process during the difficult years of the Ontario Social Contract.[3]

An interesting aspect of the process proved to be its impact on the general public. The local media gave the process very positive coverage. This, in turn, reinforced the public's view that the municipality was open and well managed. As is often the case, the municipality had a positive story to tell, but it needed others to tell it.

Having completed this successful venture in public involvement, city council used the same model in a number of contentious areas, such as developing a group-homes policy. Ultimately, council even used a similar public-participation model to review public participation itself. In a series of workshop sessions in 1994, involving a cross-section of over fifty local residents and business representatives, city council was presented with a variety of useful suggestions under the headings of "bricks," "bouquets," and "public participation in the future."[4]

Of special significance is the fact that these useful experiments were not one-shot ventures. The citizens' committees frequently pointed out the need for more evaluation of results, not just planning for the future. This is certainly a valid criticism of much of the public sector. As part of its response to this direction, city staff brought forward detailed "report cards" on the progress made in meeting the Citizens' Budget Advisory Committee's recommendations (in September 1992, for the 1993 budget cycle)[5] and in meeting the Public Participation Review Working Group's recommendations (in February 1995).[6]

COMMUNITY-ATTITUDE SURVEYING: THE FIRST BURLINGTON EXPERIENCE

In the spring 1995 edition of CANADIAN PUBLIC ADMINISTRATION, Hari Das, Mallika Das and Francis McKenzie evaluated the experience of a Nova Scotia community with customer-attitude surveying.[7] This scholarly analysis outlined another model for a practice that has been growing rapidly in the municipal field for the past decade. In Canada, communities as far afield as Oakville, Ontario, Winnipeg, Manitoba, and St. Albert, Alberta[8] have used community-attitude surveys to develop strategic plans and budgetary priorities. The City of Burlington had used community-attitude surveys in connection with its 1990 preliminary work on its official plan, to guide the update of its strategic plan, and to respond to proposals for municipal restructuring within the "Greater Toronto Area."

The International City/County Management Association, based in Washington, D.C., has developed an extensive literature on the experience of dozens of U.S. municipalities with community-attitude surveying.[9] This material served as the basis for Burlington's 1990 experiment with community-attitude surveying, which posed questions to the residents and to the business community as separate "customer" populations. The questions ranged across development issues and fiscal issues. The surveys attempted to distinguish, on geographic and demographic bases, among major communities or population groups in the city. The results of these surveys helped to give council the confirmation they needed to accept suggestions from the community or from city staff; in other areas, the results allowed elected representatives to discount special-interest pleading, with the confidence that the community would likely support their leadership on a given issue.

Burlington's 1990 surveying experience was very useful, but it turned out to be flawed from a timing viewpoint. In early 1990, buoyed by the Ontario economic and development boom of the late 1980s, Burlington's affluent suburban residents had yet to feel the effect of a prolonged recession and middle-class layoffs. The municipality was enjoying continued financial support from senior levels of government, especially from an NDP government in Ontario, committed to the now-quaint notion of spending its way out of recession. Concerns over fiscal issues had yet to permeate the public mind, and the prevailing viewpoint was optimistic. Suggestions for reductions in the range, level and financial support for community services received very lukewarm support among those surveyed. Within a year, municipal officials knew intuitively and anecdotally that the public mood had dramatically altered.

SURVEYS IN A CHANGED ENVIRONMENT

As a matter of law and tradition, the municipal corporation has been seen to be "owned" by its resident and business taxpayers. They were seen as involuntary shareholders, to whom the board of directors (city council) was accountable through the electoral process. The emphasis was on good governance, on dealing with unhappy "shareholders," and on avoiding mistakes that would reflect poorly on the stewardship of the corporation and on the assets it was managing on the community's behalf. Since property taxes were secured with property assets and were viewed as constant in any economic climate, there were few practical restrictions on access to the funds of the "shareholders." Concerns about cost and efficiency were subservient to the priority of avoiding management errors that might yield unflattering journalism.

Municipalities were given very wide latitude in delivering services. The level of satisfaction of the customer and the client had only to meet the low test of the standard acceptable for a governmental bureaucracy or a monopoly service. In the 1970s and 1980s, business ratepayers and new investors in communities also learned the two laws of municipal electoral politics: the residents vote, but businesses don't, and only *current* residents, not future residents, vote.

By 1991, however, as telephone companies and cable-television firms were also to discover, it was not enough simply to keep the shareholders happy, even with a captive market for your service monopoly. Individual residents and businesses increasingly refused to accept a status as minority shareholders or purchasers without alternatives. Businesses and suppliers began to realize that they had options. They were not compelled to accept municipal services and business practices on the terms ordained by the municipal corporation.

In many older communities, business ratepayers began to "vote with their moving vans," threatening the tax base that supported a wide range of modestly priced or tax-subsidized urban community services. Residential ratepayers began to apply the tactics of consumer militancy, which were altering the retail and utility sectors, by demanding better quality, more choice, and greater value for the property-tax dollar and the user-fee. With the pressures of the recession, local businesses urged municipal councils to adopt more "business-like" processes. Business advocates sought such diverse reforms: more timely payment of accounts; avoiding municipal activities that competed with the private sector; more serious consideration of commercialization and privatization of municipal functions and facilities; and general deregulation of business-licensing obligations and fees.

The net effect of these changes was a radical transformation in the nature of the relationship between municipal governments and the people they were created to serve. Although the residents and businesses in the community remained simultaneously "owners" and "clients" of their municipal corporations, they increasingly saw themselves as "customers," not "shareholders," of municipal government. In some communities, municipal officials recognized and responded to this dramatic change in their operating environment. But, for the early part of the 1990s, most municipal authorities were so close to the events that they misdiagnosed them or failed to detect the fundamental character of the change they were seeing.

BURLINGTON'S RESPONSE

As a community in the heart of Ontario's hard-hit manufacturing heartland, Burlington's municipal officials were surrounded by evidence of the ongoing economic restructuring in the manufacturing and commercial/service sectors. It is perhaps not surprising, therefore, that Burlington's municipal government adopted the concept of "reinventing government" early and enthusiastically.

The process began with a fundamental change in attitude on the part of the management and council of the municipality. Municipal residents and businesses had traditionally been seen in public-sector terms: as voters and taxpayers and, in some circumstances, as clients. The challenges of the recession and the Ontario government's Social Contract policy caused a fundamental reconsideration of the nature and purpose of municipal government. While it retained many important governmental features, in areas such as commercial regulation and development control, the municipality began to place more emphasis on its role as a provider of products and services.

This transformation in attitude affected the approach both in delivering those products and services and in dealing with those who were receiving them. The products and services were seen as "consumer products," and the residents and businesses were seen as "customers." The municipality accepted the proposition that a happy consumer would be a satisfied shareholder and a supportive voter. The municipality also recognized that the municipal sector would now be in competition with other areas of the public sector for the increasingly scarce tax dollar. Without reliable community support, the taxpayers might well place a higher priority for their tax dollars in some other area of public expenditure, whether local, provincial or federal.

Restructuring to Serve the Customer

Making a fundamental adjustment in outlook early and fundamentally was only part of the task. With little experience in seeing itself in the customer-satisfaction business *per se*, the city considered ways in which it could turn its fine-sounding objectives into practice. City officials aimed to mirror the experience of its commercial sector during the recent period of economic restructuring. It would undertake its own three-phase "restructuring program."

Burlington staff reviewed the popular and scholarly literature on restructuring. It showed that relatively little had been done across Europe and North America to generate a customer-driven restructuring in a municipal governmental setting. In the United States, municipal governments had experienced the economic and fiscal impacts of Proposition 13 and the Reagan-era transfer-payment cuts throughout the 1980s, so it was assumed that there would have been many innovative responses to the challenge of reconciling lost revenues with the need to maintain basic community services and infrastructure. In practice, the responses had been fairly pedestrian, focusing on ways to reduce or to privatize municipal facilities and services or to cultivate new tax sources. Following considerable research, however, it was determined that the best examples of customer-centred restructuring were found in the City of Virginia Beach, Virginia, and in the City of Charlotte, North Carolina.[10] With further research, including a senior-management workshop that included a senior staff invitee from Charlotte, a modified version of the Charlotte methodology was recommended and accepted by the restructuring task force, established by city council.

In Phase One of its restructuring program, the city proposed to identify the principal products and services it provided to the community. Next, the city would use techniques drawn from the commercial marketplace to determine the demand for those products and services, the consumer acceptance of the price and quality of those services, and the willingness of the consumer to consider alternative "packaging" and cost structures for those services. The technique to be employed was to define in clear language the several dozen products and services offered by the municipality and then to use a consumer-products market-survey firm to test customer attitudes and to evaluate alternatives.

For Phase Two of the restructuring program, city council directed the city manager to reform the management practices of the administration and to organize the resources of the corporation around "core businesses" in a way that reflected the new, customer-driven priorities.

In the concluding Phase Three of the restructuring program, individual departments, under the direction of city council and senior management, would review and re-engineer their internal and external business processes to reduce cost and to improve customer satisfaction with the individual products and services. Another important feature of the third phase of the restructuring program was a direction to management to identify and develop "strategic alliances" and other opportunities to deliver municipal services in new ways, especially where the service was determined not to be a "core business" activity of the corporation, where the cost performance was poor or where cooperation with the private or non-profit sector could produce results that were superior to exclusive municipal delivery.

Restructuring, Phase I: What does the customer want?

The restructuring program began with a report by the mayor of Burlington in August 1993, following the imposition of the province's Social Contract legislation. In a departure from the direction being proposed by the provincial government (i.e., favouring days off without pay and selective closures of municipal facilities), the city adopted a "maintain-the-services" approach aimed at securing the loyalty of its customers. The mayor's report argued that the city was in the service business and that it should commit itself to maintaining those services for which the community demonstrated continuing interest. It advocated doing so without a tax increase, despite the reductions in transfer payments. The premise for this strategy was that municipal services could be restructured in a manner similar to the approach used in the commercial/service sector, where internal costs were reduced and delivery formats altered to produce a lower unit-cost, without a loss in quality or availability.

City council adopted the restructuring program strategy, which called for a three-year freeze on commercial and residential taxation, while continuing to offer the range, quality and level of those services for which the community demonstrated a continuing support or requirement.

Following council approval, a cross-section of senior city staff was asked to identify those services that the city delivered to the community that were not services to the city organization itself (e.g., tax collection, computer systems, purchasing, council secretariat). This process yielded a list of thirty-two municipal services, ranging from snow clearance and removal to public transit. Each of the thirty-two services were then summarized in a single-page format, using a freelance copyeditor to overcome the use of jargon.

A firm with expertise in consumer-products market testing was engaged. In consultation with staff and council members, the firm developed a questionnaire for delivery to a cross-section of three thousand households in the community. The same questionnaire was also to be administered separately and on a voluntary basis to the seventeen members of city council, and again separately to thirty-five senior staff. At the direction of the restructuring task force, a fourth survey population was added: two hundred randomly selected members of the city's workforce, below the senior-management level.

In 1990, the community-attitude survey included the business community as a separate population. The experience with that process was that the results were unreliable. It was unclear who spoke for the particular business responding, and that choice had a great impact on the reply for that firm. More significantly, many business respondents replied in a fashion that made it clear they were responding as residential ratepayers, not as business ratepayers. For these reasons, the 1994 survey methodology did not include a separate business population.

Consumer Preferences Surveyed

The survey questionnaire had to pose questions on thirty-two municipal services, so it was decided that the questionnaire format would not lend itself to conventional telephone polling. The cost of in-home, personal-interview surveying was also determined to be prohibitive, if the survey size was to be sufficiently large to produce solid, statistically reliable results. Consequently, a multipage, self-administered questionnaire format was selected.

The use of a long, written questionnaire was open to some debate, based on experience with consumer-products surveys in the Greater Toronto Area. The response rate for consumer-products surveys was traditionally low, in the five-to-ten per cent range, even with inducements. There was also the problem of uneven results from a population made up of diverse income, age and cultural profiles. Burlington's previous experience proved useful in answering these methodological concerns. History demonstrated that people were more interested in questionnaires that might give them a say in the future of their municipal government than they were in questionnaires about toothpaste or laundry soap. A higher-than-average response was a reasonable expectation. Burlington also had a generally well-educated and culturally homogeneous population, so barriers of understanding and language were fewer. But it was decided to include a "respondent profile" section in the questionnaire, so the survey firm could control for overrepresentation by age, income or local geography.

Learning from the experience in Charlotte, North Carolina, the questionnaire excluded reference to the cost or staffing of a particular service.

The exclusion of staffing and gross-cost data was based on the premise that the customer is an "expert" on the quality and importance of the service and may have informed opinions on the appropriate unit-cost of the service. However, few members of the public would know the gross cost of a service or its global staffing requirements, so providing information on these items might even skew the results on the basic questions for which straightforward opinions were being sought.

The questionnaire was divided into five sections. In the first two sections, the respondent was asked to rate each of thirty-two services, first according to priority, and then according to quality or how well it is delivered. Next, the respondent was asked his or her opinion on alternative-delivery options, raging from "no change," through higher user-fees, to contracting-out, privatization, community-control, or discontinuation. In keeping with a "customer" survey, the respondent was asked the obvious question: do you use the service, and if so, how much? Finally, the respondent was asked to give some basic information about himself or herself, on income, geographic location, age and similar demographic data.

To keep costs down, the questionnaires were delivered along well-identified "postal walks," for which Statistics Canada and municipal assessment data could be used to ensure that an appropriate cross-section of the community would be exposed to the survey. To promote a good return on such "householder" mail, the mayor was asked to do a number of radio "spots," just prior to the mail drop, emphasizing the importance of the task to those selected and assuring the anonymity of the survey responses.

Survey Results

The level of response exceeded all expectations, with over seven hundred and fifty respondents from the general population, far in excess of the projected three-to-four hundred respondents. This guaranteed the statistical reliability of the survey results and also largely dispelled concerns over demographic anomalies.

The survey firm grouped the thirty-two services into four tiers, reflecting a series of response clusters, with the highest priority services in Tier One and the lowest in Tier Four. Services related to public security and transportation rated highly, whereas support for cultural activities and recreation were ranked as having a lower priority. The ranking was then paralleled with the responses to the question related to customer satisfaction, thereby correlating importance and satisfaction. In general, high-priority services were perceived as being well delivered, while the level of satisfaction with lower-priority services seemed to reflect a lower expectation. In several key areas, however, there was a striking lack of correlation between the rating for the importance of the service and the perceived quality in delivery.[11] The firm developed a statistical correlation that it termed a "pressure-valve index" to demonstrate areas where the municipality was perceived as either doing a bad job in delivering an important service or, conversely, putting too much effort and expense into a low-priority service.

The information on alternative-delivery formats demonstrated that the public was open to new options, although the level of understanding of existing organizational arrangements made service-by-service conclusions less reliable. These concerns were reinforced by the responses to questions related to the respondent's frequency of use of the service. There were, however, three intriguing findings in this area. Despite the assumption that the public sees the private sector as more efficient and economical than the public sector, the community was not as enthusiastic about privatization as one might have assumed, especially for "core" services. In addition, response to the question on delivery format showed a greater willingness to consider alternative delivery formats, as long as they did not lead to additional taxation in another guise. Finally, public receptiveness to seeing municipal government becoming more entrepreneurial also rose in those areas that were identified by the respondents as being of relatively lower priority, although very few respondents gave support for municipal government abandoning any of the thirty-two identified services.

Another area of interest was the differences among respondent populations. A city council elected by ward is always interested in localized results, so a subsequent analysis was undertaken of citizen respondents by district. Interestingly, the differences among the populations were relatively minor and fairly easily explained by localized factors, such as lack of recreation facilities or greater development pressures in some areas.

The survey also demonstrated a curious correlation that generated some humorous but illuminating insights. Senior management and city council were surveyed as two separate populations, but their responses were remarkably close (although city council generally saw every service as a higher priority than any other surveyed population). The response rate among general city staff, who were surveyed separately on a voluntary basis, ran to over fifty per cent. Refreshingly, their answers closely mirrored the responses from the broader community they serve. The real irony, however, was that there was a significant discrepancy between the views of city council and senior management, on one hand, and the views of the broader community and the cross-section of city staff. This result is perhaps even more surprising, given that the survey was conducted soon after a municipal election. It is probably best explained by the tendency of the city council and the senior staff to form their opinions about priorities and effectiveness, based on unrepresentative and anecdotal information, reinforced by media coverage and public delegations at council meetings. Concern about the role of special-interest pleading was, after all, the point of departure for the entire exercise.

Acting on the Results

The survey findings provided both momentum and substance for Phase Two of the restructuring program: the city manager's reorganization plan. The staff organization was downsized by a further five per cent and re-focused on customer priorities, with special attention being given to areas the public identified as either being neglected or over-resourced. Environmental programs were given new focus at the senior-management level, and the economic-development field underwent a significant restructuring, with increased community involvement. Outside maintenance activities were consolidated (e.g., roads, parks, drainage systems, public facilities, cemeteries), facilitating the process of moving resources according to service priority and overcoming the "silo" effect of separate departments. Public transit remained a department of the municipal corporation and was given control over traffic and parking, in order to improve traffic flow and to promote transit use.

In keeping with the invitation to consider alternative ways to deliver public services, the reorganization plan gave priority to an entrepreneurial approach and a customer-service focus in the design and delivery of municipal services. A policy and process for establishing strategic alliances was subsequently adopted by city council, facilitating the creation of service partnerships with the community and commercialization, where opportunities presented themselves.

By late 1994, the customer-focused restructuring program in Burlington had developed to the point where it was widely seen as one of the more successful experiments to appear on the Ontario municipal scene during the 1990s. Both the business community and the media were very positive in their comments on the restructuring program and its results, including two successive modest tax reductions. Perhaps most telling, many members of the council who had initiated the program featured it prominently in their successful election campaigns. The unsuccessful challenger for mayor felt it necessary to claim that the program was not exclusively the handiwork of the incumbent mayor.

COMMUNITY-ATTITUDE SURVEYING IN HAMILTON-WENTWORTH

In mid-1995, the neighbouring Regional Municipality of Hamilton-Wentworth initiated a similar survey process. The regional municipality, which serves a population of 450,000 in six local municipalities centred on the City of Hamilton, was looking to adopt a customer-driven model for the review of its services, in order to deal with declining transfer payments,[12] slow taxable assessment growth, and the challenges of revitalizing the economy and infrastructure of a mature community.

Under the leadership of a regional chairman with a direct electoral mandate from the region's 450,000 residents, the regional council's Chairman's Budget Steering Committee initiated its own restructuring program. The dimensions of the restructuring program included a "market survey" of the regional community's municipal "customers"; a proposed limit on tax increases; a reorganization of the regional bureaucracy to focus on service priorities; and a broad program of business-process review and re-engineering.

The effort corresponded with a period in which the new Ontario government was taking a fundamental look at the much-maligned system of regional municipalities, whose public acceptance and customer sensitivity has long been an issue. It also corresponded to a period of unprecedented reductions to municipal transfer payments, in which regional municipalities were by far the most affected of all municipalities.

Surveying Hamilton-Wentworth: Unique Features

The services offered or funded by Ontario regional municipalities are generally different from those of area (or local) municipalities, with the directly or indirectly elected councils of the regions usually being responsible for delivering services such as water and waste-water, public health, social welfare, police, major transportation, transit, and solid-waste disposal.

The Regional Municipality of Hamilton-Wentworth began its process of service definition by identifying some thirty-two specific "external" services, some of which it delivers directly, some of which it delivers jointly or by contract through an area municipality, and some of which it simply funds, such as police and flood-control. Hamilton-Wentworth region is also a trend-setter in public–private partnerships and the privatization of municipal facilities. In addition to privatization ventures for its interurban bus system and the Hamilton Airport, the regional municipality recently concluded North America's largest contract for the management and operation of its water purification and waste-water treatment facilities with the Philip Utilities Management Corporation. The municipality is also heavily involved in public–private partnerships in the waste-disposal and resource-recovery fields. These unique organizational factors add interesting variables to the municipal "customer-survey" process, since the public is often unaware of these varied and frequently complex administrative arrangements.

The Hamilton-Wentworth questionnaire also reflected several methodological refinements. In developing the description of regional services for the questionnaire, municipal staff decided that the service description should have two additional features. Based on the service-outcome orientation favoured by David Osborne and Ted Gaebler,[13] among others, the service descriptions cited the anticipated benefit of the program or service, thus sharpening the basis on which the public would form its conclusion about the priority, effectiveness and delivery-mode of the individual services. The per-household annual cost of the individual service was also calculated and displayed.

Anticipating an imbalance in response between the 320,000 residents in the central City of Hamilton and the 130,000 residents in its five neighbouring area municipalities, the questionnaire flagged the location of respondents. It further distinguished opinion within the central city, by dividing Hamilton's older "lower city" section of approximately 186,000 residents from the 134,000 residents on the Hamilton Mountain, above the Niagara Escarpment. This allowed the region to identify consumer demands that often become submerged in area-municipality groupings.

The Burlington questionnaire made an attempt to determine whether the respondent had an informed opinion on an individual service by asking whether the respondent had used the service in the past year. This type of question, drawn directly from the consumer-products field, was not especially helpful in determining the awareness of a respondent about municipal services. Few residents have had first-hand experience with municipal fire services, for example, and it is equally difficult to determine whether you have "used" community planning in the past year, unless you are a developer or your neighbourhood had a re-zoning. In the Hamilton-Wentworth questionnaire, the burden was placed on the respondents to say whether they knew what they were talking about, by asking them simply to rate their level of familiarity with each service under discussion.

Another departure in the survey methodology reflected the more heterogeneous nature of the regional community and that the institutions of local government were known to be under active review (the region was undergoing a locally initiated local government review, conducted by a citizens body known as the Constituent Assembly). Since the Constituent Assembly process was being financed jointly by the province and the regional municipality, consideration was given to ensuring that survey work being undertaken by that group did not duplicate or interfere with the customer-attitude survey being undertaken by the regional municipality. The decision to use a written survey in the Hamilton-Wentworth community also required that the survey materials clearly indicate that the survey firm (Decima Research) would offer assistance to those with language or other barriers to completing the questionnaire, including a telephone interview for those with literacy or perceptual problems or translation services for someone unfamiliar with English.

Refinements in the Hamilton-Wentworth survey included an effort to identify business owners/operators, individually addressed questionnaires, more radio advertising to boost response rates, and a significant re-working of the alternative service-delivery options.

Building a Customer Base

One additional dimension of the restructuring program in Hamilton-Wentworth relates to the political environment within which Ontario regional municipalities have operated since their inception in the late 1960s and early 1970s. The Ontario public has generally responded to "regional government" with a combination of benign neglect and open hostility. Reporting in January 1996, the provincial task force on the future of local government in the neighbouring Greater Toronto Area, under the direction of Dr. Anne Golden, reflected that attitude in its recommendations to dissolve the five Toronto-area regional governments in favour of a Greater Toronto structure giving prominence to local rather than regional municipal governments.

The primary objective of the customer-attitude survey in Hamilton-Wentworth was to form a customer basis for restructuring service delivery across the regional community. However, the exercise also generated an improvement in the level of awareness of the regional community about the importance and quality of regional services and, correspondingly, about regional municipal structure that provides them.

The province and local communities are looking to restructure municipal government and municipal service delivery. For the continuation of a regional focus for municipal service delivery, it is important to go beyond the simple logic of engineering and finance as the justification for the efficiencies of delivering community services on a region-wide basis. Without customers who identify with regional services, who experience good, responsive customer service from regional employees, regional councillors who, in the specific case of Hamilton-Wentworth, are indirectly elected will continue to have strong "first loyalties" to their area municipalities, occasionally even at the expense of the best solution to region-wide servicing issues. If, however, the public understands the quality and importance of regional services and projects that support the organization providing them, elected representatives can be expected to respond positively to the regional demands and priorities of their constituents. The provincial government will also have the confidence to do likewise.

The response rate for the customer-attitude survey[14] in Hamilton-Wentworth was somewhat lower in percentage terms than in the Burlington case (581 responses, or 14.5-per-cent return). It was, however, well within the parameters of statistical reliability (±4.2 per cent, 19 times out of 20), and it afforded the first clear picture on public attitudes towards regional services. As *The Globe and Mail* predicted in its article on municipal funding cuts, the ability of Hamilton-Wentworth to know what its residents value and where they want their money spent, and whether residents are willing to accept service reductions, user-fees or commercialization, proved to be powerful tools in the hands of regional council members who were coping with very significant transfer-payment reductions.[15] Once again, the community's priorities were in policing, in water and environmental quality, and in transportation, while support for arts and culture, tourism and special events lagged.

Perhaps the most significant impact of the customer-survey process was felt through the Management Action Plan, adopted in early March 1996.[16] The Management Action Plan promised that the Hamilton-Wentworth regional government would become "smaller, more flexible and more 'customer-driven.'" This is to be achieved by combining some sixteen organizational departments and sections into four "core business units" (bolstered with corporate support resources) and by producing a fifteen-per-cent improvement in organizational productivity, to offset the impact of a planned fifteen-per-cent reduction in staffing levels over the next two years.[17] The customer-survey results, and council's response to them, contributed to the rationale and direction for the Management Action Plan, as well as for the 1996 multiyear budget plans.

There are significant differences between the city council in Burlington and the regional council in Hamilton-Wentworth. These may influence the degree to which the Hamilton-Wentworth council members are willing to embrace this essentially private-sector approach to setting public priorities. Hamilton is a community with a strong labour tradition and where civic politics have a traditional approach that is well established. But there are signs that the customer-attitude survey approach will have a significant effect. For example, consider the response of the arts community, which fared poorly in terms of community support on the survey questionnaire. The arts community initiated an effort to demonstrate their *economic* value to the community and voluntarily proposed a ten-per-cent funding reduction in the regional municipality's grant to arts organizations.

Especially at a time when municipal governments are under fiscal and political pressure to restructure, one of the most interesting elements of the Hamilton-Wentworth survey results, is the surprising degree of alignment in the responses, across various demographic groups and among various local municipalities within the region. While support for programs aiding the disadvantaged and the arts was marginally stronger in the urban core and concern about development and good highways was somewhat greater in suburban areas, the anticipated wide divergence of views did not emerge. Views on what is important and what is unimportant, what is well delivered and what can be spun-off to others, reflect a remarkable degree of community consensus on budgetary priorities. This finding should materially assist municipal decision-makers as they struggle with budget reductions over the next several years and reinforce the need to lend support to "core" municipal businesses in the face of representations from special interests. When the regional municipality's senior management employed the services of the computerized "decision laboratory" at a local college to set 1997 budgetary priorities, the results of the survey process certainly aided in the development of analytical "criteria" for priority-ranking.

CONCLUSION

Municipal finance and budgeting have long been in the background of public attention, in relation to more high-profile issues in community planning, community services, traffic and transportation. As the fiscal and economic situation of Canada changes, however, considerations of finance and budgeting, and the prudent, targeted use of resources, are coming to have significant political and organizational impacts on the quality of life and economic vitality of our communities.

Recent efforts in Burlington and Hamilton-Wentworth to involve the public in setting budgetary and service priorities and to give the public a substantive role in designing public policy in areas affected by finance, suggest that public participation has a new and different frontier in municipal government. But new roles require new tools. Municipalities cannot simply employ public-participation vehicles designed for the development process. The differing response of Hamilton-Wentworth and Burlington municipal councils to similar results is also worth noting. The lessons drawn from the findings can be significantly influenced, both in emphasis and impact, by the political culture and the local media within the municipality and by the communities they both serve.

Perhaps most significantly, municipalities must also be wary of the notion that involving the public will simply allow municipalities to enlist public support for existing arrangements by getting the municipality's point across more clearly. Public participation often leads to challenges of that municipal viewpoint and to demands for reform. For example, Burlington's Citizens' Budget Advisory Committee argued the need for curfews and for a different format of public meetings on budget matters. Likewise, the customer-attitude survey in Burlington demonstrated the uncomfortable fact that there was a significant discrepancy between the views of city council and senior management, on one hand, and the views of the broader community and the cross-section of city staff, on the other. In Hamilton-Wentworth, the relatively similar results from dissimilar demographic and geographic groupings across the region put in doubt the conventional wisdom about widely differing attitudes among residents of various local municipalities within the region and among residents of different parts of its central city, Hamilton. This has clear implications for issues like the structural reform of local government.

Some implications of the findings are quite clear. Municipalities must recognize that, as in the development process, involving the public in finance and service delivery may lead public policy and public institutions in directions that were not anticipated. As in the development process, the intensity of feelings of classes of ratepayers is not always equal. Those most materially affected by change will always be more energetic and more determined than the broader public. Attitude surveying may, however, suggest that there is support in the broader community for decisions that may appear unacceptable in the face of delegations at council meetings. With luck, this balance of interests will encourage political decision-makers to show leadership on issues rather than merely accommodating the aggrieved or the vested interest. Municipal officials must remain flexible and open to the opportunities that broad-based public participation will afford, because the "consumer revolution" will prove as compelling in the public sector as it has been in the retail and commercial sectors. Public participation in finance and service delivery is a process where leadership can lend order and greater predictability in turbulent times. It is not, however, a process whose results can be predetermined; nor can it be ignored without political and institutional consequences.

NOTES

1 Elizabeth Patton, "Ordinary taxpayers tackle the budget," *The Hamilton Spectator* 5 March 1992, p. B1.

2 City of Burlington, "Recommendations from the citizens' budget advisory committee," Report BAC-1/92, 19 May 1992.
3 City of Burlington, "Budget process enhancements," Report F-45/92, 26 May 1992.
4 City of Burlington, "Recommendations from the public participation committee," Report CS-15/94, 3 June 1994.
5 City of Burlington, "Budget process enhancements: implementation status," Report F-64/92, 16 September 1992.
6 City of Burlington, "Public participation review committee recommendations," Report Cl-11/95, 1 February 1995.
7 Hari Das, Mallika Das, and Francis McKenzie, "Assessing the 'will of the people': an investigation into town service delivery satisfaction," CANADIAN PUBLIC ADMINISTRATION 38, no. 1 (Spring 1995), pp. 77–93.
8 Earl Berger Ltd. and Environics Research, *St. Albert Community Attitude Survey* (Edmonton: City of St. Albert [Alberta] 1990).
9 Harry P. Hatry et al., *How effective are your community services?* (Washington, D.C.: International City/County Management Association, 1992), p. 284.
10 O.W. Whyte, P. Syfert and D. Cooke, "Rightsizing in Charlotte, North Carolina," *Municipal Monitor* (Mississauga: Association of Municipal Clerks and Treasurers, April/May 1995).
11 City of Burlington, *Services optimization study for the City of Burlington* (Toronto: Inter-Link Research, 1994).
12 Ken Peters, "Region to use survey in cutting costs," *The Hamilton Spectator* 25 August 1995, p. B2.
13 David Osborne and Ted Gaebler, *Reinventing Government: How the Entrepreneurial Spirit is Transforming the Public Sector From Schoolhouse to State House, City Hall to Pentagon* (Reading, Mass.: Addison-Wesley, 1992).
14 Decimal Research, "A Decima research report to the Regional Municipality of Hamilton Wentworth" (Toronto: Decima Research, 1995), p. 63.
15 Jane Gadd, "Municipalities scramble to replace provincial grants," *The Globe and Mail* (Toronto) 24 August 1995, p. A8.
16 Regional Municipality of Hamilton-Wentworth, *Mastering the Challenge: A Management Action Plan* (Hamilton: Office of the Chief Administrative Officer, 1996), p. 43.
17 Ken Peters, "350 regional jobs on the chopping block," *The Hamilton Spectator* 5 March 1996, p. B1.

7

Public Participation in the Budgeting Process: Edmonton's Ongoing Experiment

Edward C. LeSage Jr.

INTRODUCTION

This chapter investigates and analyses the practices and effects of public participation on Edmonton's budget-preparation process. Budgeting is an important topic to investigate in reference to public-participation initiatives, because setting the budget is the most significant, regular policy decision made by a local government. The significance of the budget is revealed by using any number of criteria: the amount of time devoted to budget preparation; the resources expended to frame the budget; the scope of organization participation; and the heat of debate surrounding budget proposals. Budgeting is also worthy of consideration, since, historically, governments have not invited public participation. This is certainly true at the federal and provincial levels but also true at the local level, including, until recently, Edmonton.

Pressures on municipal budgets are certain to increase, given federal and provincial government cutbacks and downloading and general citizen resistance to tax increases. This will lead to increased pressure for local governments to account for their expenditures and to maintain their legitimacy. These requirements point to pressure for greater public input and transparency in the civic-budget process.

In 1991, Edmonton's city council approved a formal process for public input into budget framing after a detailed review revealed its budget process had failed the municipality. Sufficient time has now passed to systematically analyse the public-input initiative.

Edmonton is one of Canada's largest municipal corporations, although, at slightly over 800,000, the population of its metropolitan region is decidedly smaller than that of Toronto, Montreal or Vancouver. The 1994 population of the City of Edmonton was 632,000.[1] The municipality's 1995 budget, excluding city-owned enterprises, boards and agencies, exceeded $1.14 billion, with $868 million budgeted for operating expenditures. Budgeted full-time equivalents for the 1994 staff complement were 9,051.[2]

The city is organized on a modified city-manager plan, which makes Edmonton one of the largest North American municipalities operating under this system. The thirteen-member council consists of the mayor, elected at large, plus twelve councillors, also referred to as aldermen in this chapter, elected two to a ward in a six-ward system.[3]

The budgeting pressures faced by Edmonton and other Alberta municipalities as a result of provincial cutbacks heralded what municipalities in other provinces would soon experience. The fiscal-restraint program undertaken by Alberta's Progressive Conservative government, however, was more radical than those implemented to date by other provinces and included the following extraordinary measures:[4]

– extensive reductions to and elimination of the provincial transfers to municipal governments;

– assumption of total control over local taxation for schools with potential effects on municipal tax base;

– introduction of a new system of assessment evaluation and the privatization of real property assessments; and

– passage of a new municipal government act that provides for a much more wide-open system of municipal government and also one with stronger public-input provisions.

Premier Ralph Klein and his municipal affairs minister have used their "bully pulpits" to argue forcefully for fiscal restraint at the local government level. They claim that local governments can and should effect considerable efficiencies and economies – that local governments should follow the lead of the provincial government. Under these circumstances, it is reasonable to view Alberta as a harbinger of late 1990s–style government cutbacks. Consequently, the dynamics and fate of public participation is of special interest.

The Research Question

The central research question of this chapter is, does public participation improve the quality of budget-making? The study focuses on public participation that occurs through channels specifically developed to obtain feedback on budget-related matters. The question of whether public input acquired through these channels is the only public input into the budget process, or even the most significant input, will be addressed in concluding remarks.

Five basic values of public participation will serve as criteria for testing the research question. These criteria evaluate public participation according to whether it

- provides more and better quality information;

- generates greater diversity in representation;

- enhances accountability from administration and council;

- builds the community and community institutions; and

- strengthens governmental institutions.

It is clear from the introductory chapter in this volume that public participation can contribute to better decision-making. It is also true that public participation does not necessarily lead to better decision-making. As suggested by Katherine Graham and Susan Phillips, some policy decisions simply do not lend themselves to public participation, and the positive effects of participation can be obviated if governments are not prepared to devote sufficient time and resources to citizen participation. Moreover, as Georgia Persons' review of the literature reveals, citizen participation initiatives often produce few results, especially when the purpose is to draw those other than conservative business interests into local policy-making.[5]

Little has been written on public participation in local government budget-framing. Much of what does exist tends to be technical and procedural in nature. For example, some of the most recent writing focuses on the use of surveys to determine expenditure priorities[6] and on the procedures municipalities can adopt to harness public input into the budget process.[7] These accounts are of interest in that they provide insight into methods that local governments can use, and they indicate cautions concerning their application and more generally concerning the efficacy of public participation. One important caution is that surveys must be carefully designed to be useful.[8]

Another stream of the literature examines variables that influence the budget policy process and budgets. According to one American study, public opinion influences U.S. county administrators' calculations when framing budgets, but media opinion and interest-group lobbies have little apparent influence.[9] A longitudinal study of urban local government budget-making reveals that administrators (with the implicit understanding of politicians) consistently "fudge" budget estimates to protect themselves and politicians against public criticism.[10] Moreover, this fudging is not particularly influenced by external variables such as elections, public pressures, or tax increases. The biggest contributing factor tends to be fiscal distress, which forces more realistic budget estimates.[11] While this literature does not directly address the effect of public participation in the budget-framing process, it nevertheless raises some interesting questions. For example, if public participation is viewed by budget framers as a means to obtain a better understanding of public opinion, then it may very well influence their budget decisions. Alternatively, if budget framers largely dismiss interest-group input, and the public participation process essentially serves as additional conduits for group representation, a likely result will be that little serious attention is paid to the participation process.

This chapter proceeds by laying out the context in which the City of Edmonton inaugurated public input into the budget. It provides an account of how the program developed to its present state and evaluates the city's efforts. The conclusion makes several proposals for improving the existing approach.

THE CONTEXT

A measure of opportunity for public input has long existed in Edmonton's budget process. Private representations can be made to council members and administrators before and during council's budget debates. Citizens have long been able to communicate their views through Edmonton's Citizen Action Centre (especially through a phone-in suggestion/complaint service, called the Citizen Action Line), whose employees record and forward messages to departments or aldermen. Public input at the corporate level is effected through Edmonton's many agencies, boards and advisory bodies, which are populated by citizens appointed by council. Moreover, as will be discussed in greater detail below, administrative departments have long involved the public in matters that bear directly on budget allocations through consultations, surveys, focus groups, and close working groups with many collectivities within the city.

And yet, for all these opportunities, up until 1991, the corporate budget-setting process was essentially a closed and largely secretive process. Budget deliberations were held in-camera, between the administration and the budget committee of council. The budget was tabled at council, and the budget debate was conducted among aldermen. No formal provision was made for general public input before or during the budget debate.

Two factors converged to change traditional practice. First, Edmonton city council experienced considerable difficulties in setting its budget – the press and council members spoke of a budget "crisis." Throughout the late 1980s and into 1990, the administration produced budget proposals that routinely required large mill-rate and tax increases. Council's budget committee sat for months investigating budget line items and making proposals for adjustments, economies and efficiencies. Council itself would then enter the fray in what was invariably a long, fractious budget debate. The result more often than not was to reject the budget committee's recommendations, which sent the proposed budget back to the administration for reforming. Departments, which had carefully constructed their budgets, were required to conduct major eleventh-hour surgery on their proposals. Careful budget plans were frequently traded for near-midnight adjustments, which were not nearly as well thought out or rationalized with other proposals. Moreover, after the debate and into the new year, the council would put money back into the budget, as interest groups and citizens pressed their case. Clearly, the approach did not work.

The second factor was that tax increases were a matter of growing concern to many ratepayers, especially to the local business community. Consequently, when the budget committee's 1991 proposal was made public, the Edmonton chamber of commerce labelled it "alarming" and "excessive."[12] So incensed was the chamber over the size of the proposed mill-rate increase that it staged its own budget forum in which members of the public were invited to vent their dissatisfaction with council's "tax-and-spend" approach. A central complaint levelled by the chamber was that there was little meaningful public input into the budget process. Speaking at the forum, chamber of commerce president Fred Windwick made this pointed criticism:

In almost everything the city does there is an increasing demand for public input into decision making. Yet, on the biggest decision-making process the city faces in any given year we're all handed a budget proposal and we're given three weeks to respond to it. ... Court challenges have been fought and won on the simple point that there was too much information to digest in too short a period ... [T]here's one certainty: the public is going to demand more input into the process.[13]

Faced with obvious problems with its budget-formulation process and harsh public criticism headed by the city's most powerful business association, city council established a task force on 11 September 1990 to examine what might be done to improve the budget process. A key concern expressed by council was that "there should be a process to allow some form of public input and reaction to the budget."[14]

Council received, debated, and approved the bulk of the task force report at its 14 May 1991 meeting. A newly defined budget process would operate in three principal phases: direction-setting, priority-setting and decision-making.[15] The public-participation section of the task force report was not approved, since it generated some controversy in council. Council referred the matter to the city manager who reported to council on 23 September 1991, offering a succinct statement of the rationale for public participation:

The need for the Corporation to ensure that both the Administration and Council have the most up-to-date and accurate information possible, coupled with a growing national trend of taxpayers toward an interest in meaningful involvement in decisions that impact their lives, gave rise to the examination and development of the public process. This process provides an opportunity for both individuals and special interest groups to input into the corporate budget process prior to decisions being made.[16]

The city manager, Richard Picherack, proposed a scheme in which the principal opportunities for public input would occur during the direction-setting phase. First, he recommended that a June public forum be hosted by city council. Second, a triennial market-research survey was envisioned as an ambitious customers' needs survey to ascertain the public's "broad global" views on corporate service priorities. According to the manager, "data collected will be used by the administration as one part of the information in establishing long term direction. City council will also have this information available to them in their consideration of the Administration's recommendations."[17] Third, an opportunity was envisioned for

broad based registered associations and special interest groups to share and explain their strategic plans to the Corporation. This opportunity would occur annually each fall. This would provide additional insight into the communities' programs and priorities to be utilized in the direction setting phase by both Administration and City Council.[18]

This event was to satisfy a specified requirement that interest groups be included in the process, although, as will be documented, there were also other motives behind the proposal.

City council approved a public-input plan at its 3 December 1991 meeting that made provisions for these three elements. Council approved $60,000 to implement the public-input process beginning in 1992 in preparation for the 1993 budget. Significantly, the amount was roughly half of that proposed by the administration to implement the scheme.

WHAT HAPPENED

Implementation of this public-input process can be summarized as follows. First, the public-participation initiative got off to a rocky start, because council approved the program late in 1991 and allotted a budget that was roughly half of what the administration requested. The late start in 1992 necessarily resulted in piecing together an alternative strategy for public input into 1993 budget-planning. This strategy involved dropping the June public forum and substituting it with a public call for written submissions and a November forum that permitted the general citizenry to make direct representation to council on the administration's proposed budget before council debated it.

This alternative approach, initially adopted on the grounds of expediency, became standard practice. General-public input into the budget would subsequently occur after the administration announced its budget (i.e., during the decision-making phase) and not during the direction-setting or priority-setting phases. The exception to this pattern was a 1995 focus group initiative in which citizens were consulted during the priority-setting phase. A companion open-house, held in May 1995, also sought public input during the direction-setting phase and comes the closest to realizing the original vision of the June public forum. However, the 1995 open-house was largely dedicated to providing focus-group participants with feedback on the information collected by the consultant, and few elected officials attended the event.

Budget stringencies led to postponing the market-research initiative, for three years, and the adoption of the "focus-group" approach, when a market-research venture was finally attempted in 1995. The focus-group thrust deserves special consideration, since it is a recent development and sufficed as the foundation of Edmonton's 1995 public-consultation program. Three objectives were defined for the focus-group exercise:

1. receive budget input from a balanced number of Edmonton residents throughout the six electoral wards before the administration developed its recommended 1996 budget;

2. focus the sessions exclusively on the *average* Edmontonian rather than

encourage presentations from "special-interest groups" who, in the words of the consultant retained to orchestrate the exercise, "are sufficiently well organized to have more opportunity to express their positions through other administrative channels"[19]; and

3. organize the session so that members of council can attend, "to give them an opportunity to hear how their constituents view the city's priorities and budgetary efforts, and to hear these views in a somewhat less formal setting than traditional public open house or ward meetings."[20] Council members played no active role in any of the discussions.

Focus-group participants were chosen at random within a sampling design that defined participants by ward cohorts, reflecting age and gender balances within each.[21] Each session plumbed participant opinions on matters such as likes and dislikes about Edmonton; service priorities for a core list of seventeen services; the relative importance and allocation of financial resources to these seventeen services; and capital priorities.

The facilitator walked the participants through the session, with budget office officials on hand to provide an introduction to selected sections and to provide technical answers to participant queries that emerged during the sessions.

One component in the public-participation process – the "presentation opportunity" – was implemented as proposed. This was the city manager's initiative and has been routinely conducted during the mid-months of the year and during the priority-setting phase of the budget process. The 1992 and 1993 efforts were criticized by certain councillors as being too representative of civic business interests. City manager Richard Picherack responded by greatly expanding the invitation list in 1994 and by holding three separate opportunities to accommodate the twenty-six interest groups that responded to the invitation. The 1995 event was less well attended and involved two sessions. It is appropriate to note that while the first two presentation opportunities were attended by nearly the whole of the city's senior management cohort, attendance by general managers dropped precipitously and coincidentally with the increase in sessions. The presentations became largely the city manager's affair.

Far from attempting to curtail the process, it should be noted that the city implemented several innovations to aid public participation that were not part of the December 1991 proposal. These included requests for written submissions, invitations for citizens to register their responses to the proposed budget on the Citizen Action Line and publication of information materials, such as the *Budget-in-Brief* and *Budget Highlights* documents. The most recent innovation, placing the approved budget on the

Edmonton Free-Net, is a significant development in providing the public with budget information.[22] It provides citizens with access to the whole budget, including the operating and capital budgets, corporate summaries, and thirty-two budget centres. Before this documentation was available online, citizens needed to visit the public library to access this information.

Finally, it is appropriate to note that the city council elected on 16 October 1995 decided to make one of its first actions the cancellation of the scheduled October public forum. The rationale for this decision was not fully described in the press, but its essence was that council members felt they had a solid understanding of public needs, as a result of their recent election campaigns and public consultations through the focus groups, and that past forums had been dominated by undefined "special-interest groups."

In short, while the City of Edmonton has undertaken new approaches in obtaining public input in its budgeting process, some elements of the 1991 plan were never implemented, others were modified or dropped and alternative techniques were put in place. This suggests the influence of politics and bureaucratic sensibilities on the course of public participation in municipal budgeting.

EVALUATION

Regardless of the specific course of events in the Edmonton case, it is important to ask whether public participation improves the quality of budget-making? What follows is a systematic analysis of this question. Each of the criterion outlined earlier is reviewed in the context of Edmonton and by using evidence collected in interviews of interest-group representatives, administrators and council members.

More and Better Quality Information

Evidence reveals that the administration and council received more information as a result of Edmonton's public-input initiative. Greater input was received from interest groups and from the general public, because the public-input initiative provided new communication channels. Interest groups, in particular, have enjoyed increased opportunity for providing information and for making their views known through presentation opportunities, written submissions, and the public forum. The general public has also gained new opportunities through solicitation of written submissions, the public forum and, more recently, the focus groups and the open house. Edmonton's Citizen Action Line functions as an avenue for budget-related comment, and, since citizens are invited to call with comments on the budget, it too can be considered a "new" channel.

The criterion of "better-quality" information is somewhat problematic, however. For present purposes, we accept that there is better-quality information, if the public-input process brings "new" information into the budget-making process and if at least some of this new information can be used by the administration or council members. Senior and central administration clearly gains new information from stakeholders through the input process. The presentation opportunities allow the city manager and budget officials to glimpse interest-group priorities and to gauge initial reactions to the evolving budget policy. They also provide forums for many interest groups to communicate unalloyed messages directly to the city manager and senior management. Since the pattern has been to invite new groups to presentation opportunities, they offer sources of new information insofar as many groups lack other opportunities to speak to the city manager and budget officials. New information is also gained through the written submissions that, in recent years, have been solicited after the administration's proposed budget is released.

How much of this information truly informs budget-framing is another question. Theoretically, the presentation opportunity, which occurs months in advance of the administration finalizing the budget, provides timely interest-group input into budget policy-making. City manager Picherack provided examples of information gained in the presentation opportunities that has stimulated administration action; for example, formation of the Edmonton arts council evolved from a presentation-opportunity exchange. Picherack also observes, however, that the budget is largely fixed and that it is affected by the pull and tug of many forces.

Many, but not all, interest-group spokespersons interviewed stated that, although the administration clearly hears and understands their representations, their organizations see no evidence that their representations are accommodated in the budget. A few spokespersons argue that the administration is simply closed to their representations. But, the fact that representations are not reflected in the budget does not obviate the "usable" character of the information. Presenters and receivers, however, may assign quite different utilities to the same communication. These differences may turn on the specific content of the message and on the agreement or disagreement with it, or they may rest on the distinct uses that the parties see for the information.

The city manager's comments suggest that the administration views the presentation opportunity as an event that supplies him with "intelligence" on the mood of and salient issues affecting interest groups. This information is solicited in anticipation of representations that will be made to council. It is difficult to judge whether this is the primary use of information received at the session. To the extent that so few stakeholders see their representations in the budget, it may well be so. The city manager also admits that some information acquired at the sessions cannot be put to immediate use but indicates that it informs the administration's longer view of policy issues. Some interest-group members will be pleased to hear this, since their participation is based on the belief that there will be some form of longer-term "educational" effect.

Written submissions and presentations to the public forum also have some utility for the administration. Since this input is provided after the administration's proposed budget is made public, however, its utility rests in proving or disproving the administration's assumptions concerning the positions these organizations will take on various budget proposals. In addition, stakeholder-group input at the council venues can reveal the power and influence that these groups exert within the council chamber.

Input by the general public is another source of new information for the administration. Written submissions, invited Citizen Action Line (CAL) calls, presentations at the public forum, and the 1995 focus groups are all new channels for citizen communications. The CAL produces a comparative flood of comments on budget matters, and this may be the most important channel for eliciting comments from the general public. However, no ready information exists that permits a comparison between the number of calls logged before and after the advertised invitations to comment.

The quality and utility of information culled from the general public through the channels is more difficult to assess. Written submissions and CAL feedback supply the administration with a sense of the public mood on specific budgetary issues. These issues are often ones that are excited by media reports on the budget – reports that are sometimes false and often incomplete. Moreover, much of the public input collected from the CAL and written submissions is of dubious representativeness. Many calling the CAL are certain to be repeaters, and it is by no means clear if they represent the range of opinion found in the broader public. The same thing can be said about written submissions.

Citizen Action Line communications are necessarily "flattened" and "distorted" by officials who summarize and categorize them for reporting purposes. As a result, in budget-related and other complex matters, messages may become so oversimplified that their utility is significantly reduced. The same observations apply to written submissions if they are summarized for distribution within the administration. Summarizing written submissions, in fact, can be more difficult and more subject to misinterpretation than CAL communications. Emotional public responses undoubtedly provide administrators with material that informs public-policy making in some respect. However, the administration is left to interpret the context of the remarks, the intensity of the views expressed, and their meaning within a larger scheme of priorities and trade-offs.

Although the evidence collected on this point is scant, presentations by private citizens at the public forum appear to be less useful to the administration than those made by stakeholder groups. Presenting anything but the most cursory exposition of an idea or complaint is difficult, given the format of the public forum and its necessary time constraints. While the same limitations apply to interest groups, the administration has a context for their arguments and ideas. Citizen inputs are not so readily contextualized.

Much of what has been stated about the amount and quality of information gained by the administration also applies to council. It is less obvious that the public input is viewed with the same utility by administration and council. For example, while interest-group spokespersons are especially keen on the value of written submissions, a number made it clear that the value depended on these being processed by the administration and being read into the public record. Several spokespersons voluntarily distinguished between the administration's and council's dealings with written submissions. The prevailing view is that someone in the administration reads submissions, while it is considered less likely that council members do so – perhaps because budget time is a busy one for councillors.

Councillors are in a much better position than administrators to put information gained at the public forum to immediate use. This is because public forums have been held on the cusp of the budget debate and because of the existence of a million-dollar "mad money" allotment. This is a recent innovation by which council can freely devote money to issues that emerge at the eleventh hour. Under these circumstances public input at the forum, and through submissions and CAL calls, is undoubtedly of considerable saliency for councillors. Council is able to appear beneficent and responsive by distributing the money in the direction of prevailing political winds.

Another factor that heightens the utility of citizen input for council is the shear abstractness of the budget exercise. Democratic politics places a premium on elected officials "connecting" with the citizenry – something that generally cannot be said of bureaucratic life. Most who are successful in big-city politics understand the need for this connectedness, and they thrive on it. Council's public forum provides opportunity (no matter how limited) for achieving this connectedness through exchanges between citizens and councillors. The enormity and abstractness of the budget is rendered to a human scale in the interaction between a private citizen and the body of councillors. This probably contributes to council members' disdain of the increasing domination of the public forum by "special-interest groups."

The utility of focus-group data for council members is impossible to gauge since no evidence is yet available on how they use it. Aldermen interviewed were enthusiastic about the exercise, and one spoke positively about how the information will provide council with improved capacity to set budget directions and priorities and restrict elements of the administration from advancing their priorities. However, the utility of the focus-group data for aldermen may have more to do with the ability to evoke "scientific" proof in defence of a particular point of view than anything else. Experience will tell whether council members are careful consumers of focus-group input. Early signs are that they will not be.

It is reasonable to deduce from the evidence that public input promotes the injection of new and useful information into the budget-making process. The utility of the information may differ in the eyes of the administration and council members. But these differences are to be expected, given the distinct concerns and charges of administrators and politicians.

Increased Diversity of Representation

A key principle in the city's participation initiative is to ensure that all parties with a stake in the civic budget have an opportunity to participate.[23] A diverse cohort of interest groups has been drawn into budget discussions, and the general pattern has been to expand the mix. For example, invitations to the inaugural 24 June 1992 presentation opportunity went to representatives from the following sectors: manufacturing; construction; transportation; wholesale/retail; finance/insurance/real estate; business/community/personal services; tourism; aboriginal community; multicultural community; arts/cultural groups; environmental groups; organized labour; community leagues; social-services groups; disabled persons; development industry; and business groups. The business sector was well represented, but, despite the range of invitations, other sectors were less well represented in presentation opportunities in the first two years. The mayor and some council members were critical of this perceived imbalance. This resulted in the administration putting additional energy into drafting expanded invitation lists and proactively seeking a better balance of interests. Undoubtedly, the most significant feature of this redoubled effort was the administration's decision to send invitations to small and issue-oriented interest groups. Prior to this invitation, many of these marginal groups had no opportunity to effect an exchange with the senior administration on budget matters. It is clear that they welcomed the opportunity to be involved in an exchange of views with the city manager, even though several reported that they did not believe their input had much effect on city-budget policy.

City manager Picherack's effort to seek interest-group input at the presentation opportunity reached an apogee of sorts in 1994. While the "big tent" invitation philosophy was practised in 1995, the number of interest-group representatives in attendance dwindled: twenty-six attended the 1994 presentation opportunities, while only nineteen representatives attended the 1995 presentation opportunity. Although the city manager stated that what amounts to a standing invitation exists for all interest groups, at least one spokesperson claims that her organization was dropped from the 1995 invitation list.

Council's public forum has also provided interest groups with new opportunities to participate in the budget-framing process, and, indeed, interest groups not involved in the presentation opportunities have used this venue to make their case. One of the consequences of the new council's 1995 decision to cancel the public forum was to deny interest groups not otherwise involved in the budget-framing process access to council to make their case. Effectively this means that council and the administration now hear from whom they wish to hear. The new council's complaint that the public forum had been captured by organized interest groups appears to be disingenuous in the light of the standing policy of accommodating all who have a stake in the budget process.

It is less apparent that a greater diversity of citizens has been engaged in the budget process. No data exist to substantiate the possibility that written submissions and the public forum draw citizens who would not otherwise have had a voice except through direct representations to individual aldermen or through the CAL.

It is clear that some members of council were unhappy with the diversity and amount of representation obtained from the general citizenry. The specific nature of councillors' concerns differed according to the political position of the council member. Self-described "progressive" councillors were concerned that the inattentiveness and occasional hostility of conservative aldermen at the public forums made representations by progressive citizens a moot exercise. Thus, even though a forum for a diversity of views existed, the principle of diversity was not being honoured. For their part, conservative councillors viewed the public forums as being increasingly the preserve of "special-interest groups," which ostensibly pushed average citizens off the agenda. While it is difficult to understand how citizens would have been pushed off the agenda by organized interests, the fact remains that the number of private citizens participating in the public forums dwindled and, more generally, that the forums tended to serve as a venue for a minuscule number of citizens.

Council members pressed for a focus-group initiative directed towards the "average citizen," in large part because of the lack of diversity evident at the public forums and the indeterminate character of representations made through other available public channels. There was, in fact, a lack of representativeness in the initial focus-group exercise. No better evidence of this is found than the consultant's report, in which it is observed that even though an effort was made to achieve representativeness using gender and age criteria, "it is not possible to control exactly who will attend even after a commitment has been made through the recruiting process."[24] A review of the age and gender demographics of focus-group participants reveals that the under-thirty age-cohort was not well represented, even though Edmonton is demographically a young city. Similarly, males represented fifty-eight per cent of participants. Participants were selected from a proprietary list that the consultant had developed over the years to conduct market surveys. It seems likely that some form of systematic bias is found in this list, since it is constructed on a willingness to participate in market research. In addition, the timing of the events and physical location of the venues were certain to provide barriers to some types of participants. Some of the sessions ended late in the evening, since two were scheduled for each evening. Moreover, residents of some wards had to travel considerable distance to attend the sessions. Other criticisms can be raised, but the important point to observe is that the most systematic attempt to collect input from a diverse general population falls short on several counts.

In sum, the evidence reveals that a greater diversity of stakeholder groups is participating in the budget exercise. Opening the budget process to the general citizenry and actively soliciting input undoubtedly results in greater diversity, but who is included and who is left out remain unanswered questions.

Greater Accountability

An argument can be made that the public-input process has resulted in greater administrative and council accountability in budgeting. Certainly, the system is more open, and with this comes a greater potential for accountability. The public forum is a venue where citizens directly confront council on its priorities and performance, with the media present. Recall that prior to the budget-participation initiative, the Edmonton chamber of commerce held its own public meeting to rail against council's budget in the absence of a council forum. The public forum institutionalizes the chamber's initiative and has placed council front and centre each year in order to entertain two days of "beefs" and "bouquets."

Written submissions and Citizen Action Line representations share some of the advantages of the public forum in that they provide any citizen with the opportunity to make an unfettered representation directly to the administration and council. However, for reasons discussed above, submissions communicated through these avenues tend to be summarized and flattened, leaving the message open for interpretation by the final consumer. This weakens the accountability–communication exchange.

Focus groups are a less certain and less direct means of effecting accountability. They provide council and administration with an understanding of citizen-service priorities and, for that matter, with any issue of significance that the city might raise. There is an opportunity for participants to hold the consultant accountable for accurate reporting of focus-group concerns, if the precedent of an accompanying "open house" is maintained. Moreover, if an acceptable level of reliability and validity of focus-group results is achieved, and if these results are published widely, they might come to be regarded by citizens, administrators, and council as a public declaration on selected budget priorities and issues. The same would be true of a full-blown market survey. It is difficult, however, to imagine council members surrendering their political discretion to focus-group or polling results. Accountability is enhanced only to the extent that councils consistently ignoring polling results can be called to account. But, in themselves, focus-groups and consumer surveys do not provide an avenue for effecting accountability. These must be sought elsewhere.

The city manager's presentation opportunity is also of dubious value as an avenue for effecting accountability, although it is not completely devoid of value. The invitation list and agenda are controlled, thereby influencing opportunities to discuss the administration's and the council's performance. Sessions are held in-camera, and the administration prepares the summary of proceedings, two features that further diminish the ability to hold the administration to account. The administration is not obligated to act on participant comments and criticisms, and it seems that a number of interest groups have simply stopped coming to the sessions because the administration promises nothing.

Making the budget generally available, especially through a medium such as the Edmonton Free-Net, means that a portion of the public can easily access, retrieve, and manipulate budget data and information. For Free-Net users, access is much easier when compared to the alternative of viewing hard copies of the budget at the public library. The computer link enhances the citizenry's ability to educate itself on the budget and, over time, to become expert. Obtaining budget information and statistics is the first step in citizen education, and this education itself provides a basis for holding the council and administration accountable for budget decisions.

Four additional cautionary notes must be sounded, lest the argument for increased accountability be made to sound too good. First, the 1995 cancellation of the public forum represents a step back from accountability, since it eliminates the one event in which the public (general or organized) can make direct representations to and engage policy-makers, with a large audience and the press in attendance. The public forum may have been mostly theatre, but the same can be said about any legislature's Question Period. What counts *is* the theatre, since arguments are stated sharply and publicly, there is exchange, and there is a potential for embarrassment and dramatic concessions. Accountability is thus brought closer to the surface.

Second, the bulk of comments on the proposed budget must be formulated and articulated within the brief period between the release of the proposed budget and the beginning of the budget debate. Edmonton largely abandoned its original plan to consult heavily during the priority-setting phase and has never seriously contemplated involving the public in broad direction-setting. To be sure, the 1996 focus-group initiative did involve citizens in priority-setting, but this exercise was flawed. In general, there has simply been too much information to digest in too short a period. Holding council and administration accountable under these conditions is difficult.

Third, and more broadly, there is an inherent problem in making Edmonton city council accountable, since local politics is non-partisan. As a consequence, there is less opportunity than at other levels of government to focus criticism in the election process. The lack of parties and party discipline means that a civic politician votes according to his or her best judgement, which can be informed by hard-held beliefs, tight and dispassionate reasoning, calculations of expediency, and good old political "log-rolling."[25] A few interest-group representatives observe that this makes any effort to hold aldermen accountable very difficult: "It's like trying to nail jelly to the wall."

Finally, despite the greater availability of the approved budgets on the Free-Net, budget research is not an easy matter. The documentation is dispersed and sometimes hard to obtain. Moreover, holding council and administration accountable is difficult, given the absence of a uniform exposition of business plans within the budget documentation. This is compounded by the absence of any published performance indicators.

Suffice it to say that business plans and performance indicators, publicly declared in an easy-to-read fashion, greatly increase the prospect of the public holding the administration and council accountable.

Does public input, as it exists in Edmonton, increase administrative and council accountability in budgeting? The answer is a tentative "yes." New avenues provide citizens and interest groups with opportunities to challenge council, and budget information is more readily available. However, a variety of factors weigh against these challenges being effective, and the information remains difficult to acquire and organize.

Building Community and Community Institutions

In theory, public participation builds community by creating more open communications that bring citizens and the principal government actors closer to one another. Scholarly analysis of American cities that have extended avenues for budget input to the neighbourhood level – such as Dayton, Washington and Portland – suggest this.[26] Resulting interactions foster discourse, understanding and action, and this presumably results in an enhancement of the community. Community institutions develop from the success of these interactions and the "willingness" of parties to contribute to or abide by the regime.

It is difficult to draw any conclusion about whether Edmonton's civic "community" is enhanced as a result of the budget-participation initiative. First, there are difficulties in properly defining "community" at the city-wide level. Simply, it is not clear what constitutes "the community." There are difficulties in determining the independent effects of budget input on the city-wide "community." The budget-participation process has *not* contributed to building local communities (i.e., neighbourhoods), at least not in any consistent way. This is because the process does not formally reach down to the neighbourhood level and is not organized to solicit and systematically incorporate neighbourhood input.

Some neighbourhood associations have used the budget-participation process to voice concerns and needs. Millwoods' area council (an agglomeration of community leagues and cultural organizations) has routinely used the public forum as a venue for communicating its neighbourhood concerns and aspirations to council. In the main, however, few communities have used the process, and, with the exception of the Millwoods area council, most representations have been issue-focused.

The process is very new, so, in the strictest sense, it is premature to speak of institutions being developed. To date, however, it appears that the process itself has not become institutionalized and may very well not become so. The most compelling evidence of this is city council's cancellation of the centrepiece public forum in 1995. Little public criticism attended the cancellation, and the new council does not appear to be enthusiastic about the prospect of other forums. City manager Picherack's presentation opportunities are appreciated and disparaged by the interest groups that have participated, thereby making it difficult to assess the desire to continue them. In the final analysis, the presentation opportunity is the city manager's show and is conducted largely so that the administration can obtain information for its own purposes. It will be interesting to see if the practice outlasts the city manager's tenure.[27]

Strengthening Governmental Institutions

The city government received accolades from spokespersons for local organizations and focus-group participants when the public-input process was inaugurated. This does not, however, provide evidence *per se* that governmental institutions are strengthened in the public mind. Since the initiative was launched, the input process has been criticized in the press and by many of those who participated in it. The leading newspaper's civic affairs columnist contends that the public forum amounts to patronizing "a grateful populace." This is perhaps too severe an indictment, but it raises the prospect that the city's stock, in fact, has been reduced by the effort. A number of interest-group spokespersons became equally caustic about the city government's efforts to facilitate citizen input. In surprisingly candid conversations, they echoed a common theme – that the open process was more "show" than anything else.

From an internal perspective, Edmonton's administration appears to benefit from input gained through the presentation opportunities. A principal benefit appears to be reconnaissance on interest-group views and arguments, which alerts the administration to the character of representations that will be made to council and in public forums. For the city manager in particular, the opportunities provide personal contact and insights into interest groups' relations with the departmental administrations.

Council–administration relations may also be strengthened by the public-participation initiative. Perhaps the greatest benefit of the participation initiative is to place council and senior administration in the same information stream. This is a precondition, but not a guarantee, that they will develop common understandings of issues, problems and opportunities. There are also some problems. The low quality of information received and the timing of the significant input opportunities do not do much to bind council and administration. Data of questionable quality leaves much to individual interpretation and can even promote acrimony between principals who hold different views. Timing of input, which has been concentrated in the decision-making phase of the budget process tends to separate council and administration, since most general citizen input comes as a criticism of the administration's proposed budget.

The contribution of the budget-consultation initiative in strengthening government institutions is mixed. Support by citizens, interest groups, and the media for the participation process appeared to be ambivalent prior to cancellation of the 1995 public forum. Cancellation likely did the process damage, even though the forum itself had become a devalued venue for public input. The focus-group initiative is well regarded by participants, and perhaps this points to a positive future for the participation initiative. On-line budget details, the Citizen Action Line, and submission opportunities offer important avenues for public edification and comment. Indeed, to the extent that there are opportunities for edification and comment, governmental institutions are probably strengthened, but this must be taken as an article of faith, since proof is hard to objectify.

CONCLUSION

There is uneven support for the research proposition that public input improves the quality of budget-making. However, an obvious and compelling subsidiary question is *how much* does it improve the quality of budget-making? The answer, in a nutshell, is that the quality of budget-making *is not greatly enhanced* by Edmonton's public-input initiative. This argument is supported by several observations:

1. The quality of much of the general public's information is open to question, since it is sparse, unrepresentative, emotive, often based on false or partial facts, offered without context, and often highly processed by the administration.

2. The bulk of citizen input on the budget is collected far too late to make any significant difference in directions or priorities.

3. Council members heavily discount interest-group inputs and, for that matter, citizen contributions that are not consistent with their own closely held views.

4. The city's practices in disseminating budget information to the public limit the potential for accountability.

It should also be noted that direct public input into the budget occurs in the context of a much larger, well-established, and ongoing process of citizen and organized-interest representation. The results of this ongoing process form the basis for the administration's proposed budget and are not subject to much alteration by public input occasioned through the budget process – at least not in an immediate way. For example, a recently initiated water-quality task force that includes representation from environmental groups attending the presentation opportunity provides council and the administration with important direction-setting information on this key policy issue, which if followed, will directly inform budget-framing activity. The same is true of a massive review of the city's transportation masterplan in which considerable public input has been sought.[28]

There is considerable consultation at the neighbourhood level, especially related to neighbourhood redevelopment and service-improvement activities. The Urban Development Institute complains that this consultation has simply gotten out of hand, with community "agitators" dominating public forums and furthering their personal agendas.[29] The results of these consultations are fed into departmental budgets and are sent to council for expenditure approval. Moreover, Edmonton's numerous boards, commissions and agencies involve representatives from the general public. These bodies are institutionally tied into the city's budget process, and citizen input from their public members flows through these channels.

There is also considerable representation through advisory committees and institutionalized meetings on which influential interest organizations sit at the invitation of departments and council. For instance, there is an annual meeting between council and the Edmonton chamber of commerce; quarterly meetings between the Road Builder's Association and senior officials in the transportation and planning departments; and consultations between Federation of Community League executives and civic officials. These consultations inform budget matters, and the results of these consultations are invested into the preparation of branch and departmental budgets. In short, while the public-input process may improve the quality of budget-making, its contribution must be kept in perspective.

To finish on a positive note, three improvements are proposed for the public-input process. These proposals do not exhaust the improvements that can be made to the process; rather, they are offered to point the way.

Conduct a Citizen Survey

A citizen-"marketing" survey should be commissioned on a regular basis. The City of Edmonton budget task force's proposal for a three-year cycle seems a good place to start, even though an annual survey would be more valuable. A general survey is needed to establish a base of data that can be analysed using advanced statistical methods, that can provide a foundation for longitudinal analyses, and that is representative. Arguments that there is not enough money in the budget or that the initiative is simply not of high priority are difficult to accept. The more likely reasons for a survey not being inaugurated are tied to administrative and political concerns over the results (and the use of the results). While there are good reasons to be concerned, much depends on the definition and administration of the survey and on the analysis and exposition of results. Suffice it to say that other municipalities have used surveys to assist them in their budget-framing and so should Edmonton.[30] Importantly, a general survey allows the administration and council to obtain public input that can inform them during the direction-setting and priority-setting phases of the budget process. Public input in these phases has been especially thin, and the survey would help address the problem.

Develop Business Plans and Performance "Report Cards"

The development and promulgation of multiyear business plans and companion performance-to-plan report cards will improve the quality of public information on the budget. It will also increase the ease with which the public can hold council and administration accountable. Annual business-plan "report cards" would make budget priorities and decisions comprehensible to the public and would increase the citizens' ability to comment on budget results. Such report cards should contain a standardized reporting format and report directly and clearly on the achievement (or lack of achievement) of stated objectives, as well as on changes to priorities and objectives.

This observer is not naïve and does not underestimate the difficulties involved in implementing such innovations. Defining business plans is difficult, and it is an initiative that must be directed centrally. To get off the ground, there must be considerable political and administrative will. Finding this will in municipal government presents a significant problem, owing to the "loose-fish" voting behaviour of councils – it is difficult to define and hold a political course. Providing an accurate report card may be even more difficult. While Edmonton city council has shown leadership in creating the position of auditor general, the post and activities of the officer have at times been controversial. The auditor general can and has embarrassed the administration and council during the faithful execution of his legal responsibilities. Whoever is charged with producing the report card on the business plans will inherit the same controversy as that experienced by the auditor general. Nevertheless, the idea can improve public input into the budget process.

Create a Permanent Civic Deliberative Congress

Even with the focus groups and a general survey, Edmonton would lack a forum in which civic issues can be discussed and debated in an informed way. An ongoing congress of stakeholders and interested parties is needed. An intriguing and successful model for such a congress is the continuing Thursday Morning Roundtable in Syracuse, New York. This congress of community leaders has run continuously for thirty years and has become a community institution. The roundtable's monthly meetings explore issues of concern to civic leaders. The cumulative effect of the discussions is reputedly a high level of common understanding among a broad base of civic leaders regarding problems that confront the municipality and area. It should be added that Mr. Picherack's presentation opportunity is a distant relation to the Syracuse roundtable in that both venues provide opportunities for civic leaders to exchange ideas. The difference is that in Edmonton the events are held behind closed doors and occur once a year. Edmonton's stakeholder groups are involved for half a day. In contrast, Syracuse's congress meeting monthly Thursday mornings for several months of the year involves scores of citizens in a continuing dialogue and has the added advantage of being orchestrated by a major university located in the city.

NOTES

1 City of Edmonton, *The City of Edmonton Reports to You: 1994–95* (Edmonton: Corporate Communications Office, n.d.), p. 1.
2 Ibid.
3 The "alderman" title was officially used in addition to that of "councillor" until 25 October 1995. See Jim Farrell, "Symbols hot item at city hall," *The Edmonton Journal* 24 October 1995, p. B1.
4 For a discussion of this program, see Trevor Harrison and Gordon Laxer, *The Trojan Horse* (Montreal: Black Rose Books, 1995).
5 See Georgia A. Persons, "Defining the Public Interest: Citizen Participation in Metropolitan and State Policy Making," *National Civic Review* 79, no. 2 (March 1990), p. 121, for a list of counts on which public participation disappoints. An informative review of the literature is found in William Simonsen, Nancy Johnston and Russell Barnett, "Attempting Non-Incremental Budget Change in Oregon: An Exercise in Policy Sharing," *American Review of Public Administration* 26, no. 2 (June 1996), pp. 231–50. I thank Dr. Simonsen for his generosity in forwarding his draft paper and reports detailing the 1992 public surveys conducted in Eugene, Oregon.
6 See Mark A. Glaser and John W. Bardo, "A Five-Stage Approach for Improved

Use of Citizen Surveys in Public Investment Decisions," *State and Local Government Review* 26, no. 3 (Fall 1994), pp. 161–72; L.A. Wilson II, "Surveying the Populace: How to Do It and Why It Helps," *National Civic Review* 76, no. 2 (March/April 1987), pp. 151–55.

7 See Paul D. Epstein, "How Citizen Participation Spruces Up Performance," *National Civic Review* 76, no. 2 (March/April 1987), pp. 147–51; Steven Falk, "When Budgeting Focuses on Value: Nine Strategies for Value Basing," *Public Management* 76, no. 5 (May 1994), pp. 20–3. For an unorthodox approach, see Doyle Buckwater, Robert Parsons and Norman Wright, "Citizen Participation in Local Government: The Use of Incentives and Rewards," *Public Management* 75 no. 9 (September 1993), pp. 11–15.

8 William Simonsen, "Citizen Preferences and Budget Policy." A paper presented at Shaping the Urban Future: International Perspectives and Exchanges [an international seminar jointly organized by Urban Affairs Association, the School for Advanced Urban Studies, University of Bristol and the Department of City and Regional Planning, University of Wales College of Cardiff], Cardiff, Wales, U.K., 10–13 July 1994.

9 Sydney Duncombe, William Duncombe and Richard Kinney, "Factors Influencing the Politics and Process of County Government Budgeting," *State and Local Government Review* 24, no. 1 (Winter 1992), p. 22.

10 Patrick D. Larkey and Richard A. Smith, "Bias in the Formulation of Local Government Budget Problems," *Policy Sciences* 22, no. 2 (May 1989), pp. 123–67.

11 A study that appears to confirm this finding is Susan A. MacManus, "Budget Battles: Strategies of Local Government Officers During Recession," *Journal of Urban Affairs* 15, no. 3 (Fall, 1993), pp. 293–307. MacManus reports that strategies adopted during periods of recession vary from those adopted following more permanent, statute-imposed shortfalls. Expenditure reductions are far more common than revenue-raising strategies. Across-the-board cuts are more popular than deep programmatic cuts or abolishments, reflecting the perception that cuts during a recession do not have to be as deep, because the shortfalls are temporary.

12 Scott McKeen, "Chamber invites public to beef about budget: It's a phoney tax revolt – Mason," *The Edmonton Journal* 20 November 1990, p. B3.

13 Rod Ziegler, "Can you budget a city like a business?" *The Edmonton Journal*, 27 November 1990, p. D7.

14 City of Edmonton, Budget Task Force, *Report*, 14 May 1991, p. 3.

15 During the direction-setting phase, it was proposed that council provide the administration with guidelines concerning tax increases and communicate its general program and service-area priorities. During the priority-setting phase, the administration would prepare a budget with attention to council's priorities. The particulars of the administration's proposed budget would be estab-

lished through a meeting of the general managers and the city manager to "horse trade" and determine the programs and activities of highest priority. Finally, council would confirm or amend the administration's program in light of its original intentions and new exigencies at the decision-making phase.

16 City of Edmonton, City Manager, "Report to City Council." 23 September 1991.
17 Ibid., p. 1.
18 Ibid., p. 2.
19 HarGroup Management Consultants, "A Report on 1996 Municipal Budget Priorities Expanded Focus Group Sessions." [draft] Edmonton, June 1995, p. 2.
20 Ibid., p. 3.
21 Participant lists were generated from a proprietary list that the consultant had developed over the years in order to conduct market surveys. The list contained names of persons who had previously been successfully contacted by the firm when it was conducting market research. Names were randomly drawn from the list to create three lists of fifty. Prospective participants were screened according to age and gender so that the actual distribution of the ward pairings could be closely reflected. The consultant observed that the final attendance may have been skewed away from actual population distributions since it is not possible to control exactly who attends, even if a commitment is made by the participant during the recruiting process. Each participant received a modest cash honorarium.
22 The address for the budget "gopher" site: is gopher://freenet.edmonton.ab.ca:70/11/i/edmbudgt
23 See Budget Task Force, *Report*, 14 May 1991.
24 HarGroup Management Consultants, "A Report on 1996 Municipal Budget Priorities," p. 6.
25 A good example of such behaviour is found in a story from *The Edmonton Journal*: Mike Sadava, "'Fiery' fight heating up over tax hike: Aldermen want rollback to 6.5%," *The Edmonton Journal* 10 May 1991, p. B1. The essence of the story is that Alderman McKay was convinced to support a mill-rate increase of 6.7 per cent, after Alderman Campbell agreed to support McKay's efforts to have council reconsider its policy on dedicating one per cent of civic buildings to art.
26 For discussion of the Eugene, Oregon, process see Edward C. Weeks and William Simonsen, *Eugene Decisions: Results of Citizen Input* (Eugene, Ore.: City of Eugene, [January] 1992); and Edward C. Weeks and Susan Weeks, *Eugene Decisions: Results of Citizen Input* (Eugene, Ore.: City of Eugene, [July] 1992).
27 At the time of publication, Mr. Picherack had stepped down as city manager at the end of his contract, and a new manager had not yet been appointed.
28 According to *The Edmonton Journal* the city's transportation masterplan is being devised by a broad-based citizen's advisory committee that is "made up

of more than 20 individuals from all areas of the city who also represent a wide range of interests from truckers to cyclists." Andy Ogle, "Traffic problems won't end with Keillor vote," *The Edmonton Journal* 15 October 1995, p. B1.

29 See Mike Sadava, "'Community Agitators' Dominate Planning," *The Edmonton Journal* 5 March 1994, p. B2.

30 See the chapter by Michael Fenn in this volume.

8

Negotiating, Arbitrating, Legislating: Where was the Public in London's Boundary Adjustment?[1]

Andrew Sancton

Until the creation of Toronto's "mega-city" in 1997, the City of London was Ontario's most populous single-tier municipality. Because of a huge annexation in 1961, London escaped two-tier regional government in the late 1960s and early 1970s. Because of an even larger annexation in 1993, the city can now itself be considered a form of single-tier region. What role did the people of the area play in shaping London's distinct form of municipal organization? Did public participation help shape a more satisfactory outcome? Answering these questions is the major objective of this chapter.

The introductory section of this chapter involves a brief examination of the 1961 annexation. This is important for two reasons: 1) it provides an important part of the historical context for the 1993 annexation; and 2) the main decisions were made by the Ontario Municipal Board (OMB). The OMB was not a factor in the 1993 annexation. Knowing how the OMB worked with respect to the 1961 annexation makes it easier to understand the significance of the different procedures used between 1988 and 1993.

The main body of the chapter involves a review of each of three distinct procedural phases related to the 1993 annexation. The first – between 1988 and January 1992 – involved the attempted implementation in London of the Municipal Boundary Negotiations Act, 1981.[2] The second phase, the most crucial, lasted only from February to April, 1992. It involved "arbitration" of the annexation dispute by a provincially appointed "arbitrator" who was charged with conducting public hearings prior to making his decisions. The third and final phase – from April to December, 1992 – was the legislative process at Queen's Park. Although legislative approval was originally supposed to be a kind of automatic outcome of the arbitration, in reality it took on its own quite distinct characteristics. For each of the three phases, the emphasis will be on analysing the process for public

163

participation. The first phase deliberately precluded such participation; the second encouraged it but only for details, not principles; the third involved no more and no less public participation than is usually associated with the provincial legislative process.

THE ONTARIO MUNICIPAL BOARD AND THE 1961 ANNEXATION

Like most Canadian cities, London's boundaries prior to 1961 were shaped by a long series of incremental annexations of populated suburban areas (some of which were themselves incorporated as towns or villages) and of areas in adjacent rural townships that were ripe for urban development. Between 1840 and 1959, the largest annexation took place in 1912, comprising 877 hectares. In 1958, however, the London city council approved a by-law calling for the annexation of 24,000 hectares from four adjoining townships; about one-sixth of this land had already been developed. Because the city at the time only comprised 3,140 hectares, this was a proposed annexation of truly massive proportions. Its main aim was to prevent the rural townships – especially the townships of London to the north and Westminster to the south – from continuing to function as the main locations for new urban growth. Between 1941 and 1959 the population of the city had only increased from 78,134 to 102,542 while the combined populations of the two townships went from 18,429 to 65,108.[3]

In accordance with the province's legal requirements for municipal annexation, the 1958 by-law was referred to the OMB. A three-member panel held hearings on the matter in London for seven full weeks at various times between April and December, 1959. Ten different lawyers representing fourteen different organizations and individuals were given formal standing. In May 1960, the panel released its thirty-eight-page decision in which it awarded the city 12,220 hectares, or about half what it had asked for, all from the townships of London and Westminster. The annexation was ordered to take effect on 1 January 1961. While the city had requested sufficient land to enable it to plan the outward expansion of the urban area over a period of twenty-five years, the OMB allowed an amount that "contains all the present development which is a part of the London community as well as lands adjacent or proximate where the further development envisaged in this decision can be expected to take place within a reasonable time in the future."[4]

The members of the OMB panel clearly believed that their function was to determine the structural arrangements that promoted "the greatest common good." They explicitly rejected the view that municipalities themselves had interests that merited consideration:

Many opinions expressed as to desirable municipal boundaries seem based on a hypothesis that a municipal corporation is much the same as a mercantile corporation. Indeed, many submissions made at the hearing and particularly many of those made in opposition to annexation seem to assume that municipal corporations possess certain vested interests and rights which they are entitled to assert and retain against the whole world, as it were. The Board is of the respectful opinion that any claim of this nature made by a municipal corporation must be regarded only in the light of the best interests of all the inhabitants of and other ratepayers in the whole area in question.[5]

As far as participation by interested members of the public is concerned, the OMB decision makes reference only to "[a] very large number of petitions," all of which expressed a fear that annexation would cause an increase in taxes.[6] Board members were obviously sceptical about the petitions, because they note that "it was impossible to determine the circumstances under which a great many if not most of the names were obtained. ... [I]t is not surprising to find a substantial and even spirited response to any petition circulated for the purpose of keeping taxes down."[7] The decision also notes that there were no expressed objections "by petition or otherwise" from any ratepayer within the city and that the board "has neither the duty nor the right to permit the wishes of a part only of those concerned to outweigh its findings of what is clearly in the best interests of all the inhabitants and ratepayers in the whole area."[8] There can be no doubt that OMB panel members were effectively saying that their job was to represent the interests of the silent majority. This is as close as they came to being concerned with the role of the public in a process that was otherwise dominated by lawyers, experts and developers.

There is a brief passage in the decision relating to the position of the local federation of agriculture. Federation members objected to having their farms placed under the jurisdiction of a municipal government concerned with urban, rather than rural, administration. They were especially concerned about high levels of urban taxation. By not granting the city's full territorial demands, the board effectively agreed with the federation's position. In a position contrary to that adopted by the arbitrator and by the provincial government in 1992, the board stated that "[n]o farmlands should be included except those within the area of the present urban development and those that will be so developed within a reasonable time." It then wryly predicted that owners of such land would not object, because "they will very probably be able to sell their land for subdivision before long in any event."[9]

The 1960 OMB decision on London's annexation is a well-reasoned, comprehensive document. In retrospect, it served the city well. Had the annexation not taken place in 1961, London almost certainly would have had imposed on it a two-tier regional system of the kind implemented a few years later in Ottawa-Carleton. But the virtues of the process involved in the 1960 decision are less obvious. Even the OMB panel members themselves refer to the hearings on the London annexation as "lengthy, very costly and dislocating."[10] By the late 1970s, there had been many other examples – notably in Barrie – of protracted OMB hearings on annexation. Perhaps because it was clear by this time that no new regional governments would be established, the issue of improving boundary-adjustment procedures had become a priority. In 1979, the Ontario Ministry of Intergovernmental Affairs established a pilot project in the City of Brantford and the County of Brant to settle a local boundary dispute through negotiation rather than by quasi-judicial hearings conducted by the OMB. The experiment was successful. It resulted in the passage of the Municipal Boundary Negotiations Act, 1981, a law designed to reduce drastically the role of the OMB in annexation proceedings and to replicate the Brant experience in other parts of the province.

NEGOTIATIONS, 1988–91

By 1979, annexation was once again on London's political agenda. The mayor claimed that there was no longer sufficient industrial land within the city to accommodate manufacturers requiring lot-sizes of over eighty hectares. The city's economic-development commissioner predicted that between 1990 and 1995 the city's supply of industrial land would be totally exhausted.[11] Despite various studies, speeches, threats, and committee meetings, nothing really happened until 1988. On 18 November, the city informed the Ministry of Municipal Affairs that it wished to "proceed as expeditiously as possible under the provisions of the *Municipal Boundary Negotiations Act, 1981*" to annex "certain lands from the Township of London and the Town of Westminster."[12] The detailed proposal called for the annexation of 4,339 hectares from London township and 2,792 hectares from Westminster. Since the last annexation, Westminster had aggressively pursued industrial development on its lands near Highways 401 and 402 and had changed its status from township to town. It was clearly the city's most difficult annexation opponent. In its proposal, London offered to provide water and sewer services to 1,498 hectares in Westminster's industrial and commercial area adjoining the city's southern boundary. The area's development had been restricted due to the town's limited servicing capacity.[13]

There was absolutely no public involvement in the development of the city's proposal, nor was there any evidence that there had been consultation with those most directly affected. Indeed, there was good reason for the city not to consult privately: inside information about where the new boundaries might be located could be of great potential value to land speculators. It was abundantly clear, however, that the development industry in general was a major force favouring the principle of annexation. Although individual developers could not be expected to agree with each other about ideal boundaries, they did share an obvious interest in opening up new serviced land beyond the existing city limits. At this early stage in the process no one else seemed interested.

In January 1988, city council formally approved an annexation by-law, but the actual area under consideration was never made public. Mayor Tom Gosnell justified the secrecy by saying "This is a matter of negotiation and we don't intend to negotiate in public."[14] On 20 June, city council met in closed session for four hours to discuss its annexation strategy.[15] The 18 November proposal that officially launched the negotiations was not made public until it appeared as a city advertisement in *The London Free Press* on 10 December 1988. Because it did involve the servicing agreement with Westminster and did not involve annexing land from the adjacent townships of Lobo and West Nissouri, it was clearly a different proposal from what council had been discussing earlier in the year.[16] Explanations of how and why city council changed its strategy during 1988 are not on the public record.

Incredibly, this entire period corresponded with a municipal election campaign in which annexation was scarcely an issue. Newly elected councillors were invited to a closed meeting of the old council on 28 November so that they could be brought up to date on annexation developments. One of the new councillors was quoted as saying he "didn't even know [the issue] was coming up." The official proposal was not mailed to the affected townships until a day before it was published in the newspaper, a full three weeks after it had been submitted to the provincial government.[17] It is hard to imagine a policy-making process that could be any less public or more secretive. It is obvious that special efforts were taken to prevent annexation from becoming an election issue. By not releasing any clear proposal prior to the municipal election in early November, there could be nothing for anyone to criticize. But before the new council actually met, the proposal had already been sent to the provincial authorities.

According to Section 4(1) of the Municipal Boundary Negotiations Act, 1981, the next step rests with the minister of municipal affairs, who

> may determine and inquire into the issues raised by the application, determine the party municipalities, obtain the opinion of any local board that the Minister

considers is affected by the application, and send to the clerk of each party municipality a report setting out the issues, the party municipalities and such other matters as the Minister considers appropriate.

In this case the minister appointed a ministry official as a "fact-finder." The first meeting in May 1989 of the fact-finding "steering committee" involved the fact-finder herself, and representatives of the City of London, the County of Middlesex, the Town of Westminster and the Township of London. Despite the requests of representatives of the non-city municipalities, meetings of the steering committee were not open to the public. The fact-finder was quoted as saying "We just find that closed meetings work better."[18] Members of the Middlesex board of education were incensed that they were not included, pointing out that any significant annexation would drastically affect their financial position and could lead to the loss of some of their schools to the city board.[19] By the time of the third meeting in late September, the board had been given permission to send an observer.[20] In late December, the ministry announced a "development freeze" in Westminster and London township, affecting any development proposal requiring provincial approval. The move was an obvious effort by the province to force the county and the two municipalities to become more cooperative.[21]

The fact-finder's report was sent to the affected municipalities on 25 April 1990. It laboriously reports the "issues presented" by each of the parties to the discussions. Probably the most significant finding was that, after the building of a planned sewage system, "Westminster will have no additional debt capacity [as defined by the OMB] to undertake any future projects."[22] Until the very last page, there is no reference to any municipality other than those involved in the fact-finding discussions. The conclusion, however, recommends that the next stage in the process involve a negotiating committee that would also include representatives from the adjoining townships of West Nissouri, North Dorchester, and Delaware.[23] In short, the fact-finder's conclusion does not match the facts that were found.

The conclusion makes sense only when it is related to the minister's covering letter in which he states the following:

As a result of the fact-finding process, I have concluded that the lands proposed for annexation by the City, the joint servicing proposal and the City's decision to defer annexation proceedings with the Townships of West Nissouri and North Dorchester were not in the best interest of the area. Consequently, the area affected is much more extensive than identified by the City in its proposal and the issues must be approached in a more comprehensive manner.[24]

This ministerial declaration, made in what would be the last few months of the provincial Liberal administration, was probably the most significant decision made in the entire annexation process. It was totally unrelated to any "facts" discovered by the ministerial "fact-finder." It did not reflect the official positions of any of the participants in the fact-finding process. It was arrived at on the basis of absolutely no public hearings or participation and in the complete absence of any known studies or reports that advocated increased comprehensiveness.

In the same letter, the minister announced that, in accordance with Section 6(1)c of the act, he was accepting the fact-finder's recommendation concerning the negotiating committee. Chaired by the ministry's "chief negotiator," Don Taylor, the committee first met in June 1990. Once again, the talks were held in private, "at the province's demand, a move to prevent land speculation and political grandstanding."[25] Notwithstanding the private status of the committee's work, it was not hard for interested parties to find out about what was going on. The city's revised annexation proposal, which had been the subject of a two-hour closed session of city council on 10 September, was leaked by somebody involved in the process and published on the front page of *The London Free Press* a few days later. The leaked proposal called for complete absorption of Westminster into the city, as well as large annexations from the three townships. Within a few weeks, Westminster's plan for a two-tier regional government in the area and the county's proposal for a joint city–county commission were also leaked to the press.[26]

Meanwhile, a London city councillor (who would soon be seeking the federal Liberal nomination for a constituency covering much of the area the city proposed to annex) tried to get city council to agree formally to make public its position and to hold public hearings. The mayor responded that everything had to be kept secret because of provincial requirements.[27] Although the province clearly wanted the actual negotiations to be confidential, it could not possibly have prevented a city council from publicly debating its own position. Mayor Gosnell's response was, at best, an exaggeration.

The councillor's initiative proceeded no further, although he remained a constant critic of the annexation process. On 22 September, the councils of Westminster and London township published in *The London Free Press* a joint, open letter to Premier-elect Bob Rae in which they asked "Why can not the process be open, so that all affected ratepayers in the London-Middlesex area can be made aware of the financial aspects, the alternatives, and the real costs and impact both now and in the future, of the various proposals?"[28]

The last formal session of the negotiating committee was held in early

April 1991. The ministerial deadline for local agreement expired on 26 April. Nevertheless, sporadic meetings and negotiations were conducted for much of the rest of the year, with a brief break for another round of municipal elections in November. The City of London and London township actually reached a compromise agreement: the township agreed to a modest annexation in return for the extension of the city's sewer and water services to two nearby hamlets that were to remain outside the city borders.[29]

Again, annexation was not a significant election issue within the City of London. In Westminster, it was. The incumbent mayor – a fervent opponent of annexation and proponent of regional government – chose to retire. Of the three mayoral candidates, two supported the position of the incumbent. But it was the third – a candidate without prior municipal experience, who thought regional government would be too expensive – who was elected. The new mayor was obviously more open to compromise than his predecessor.

The chief negotiator submitted his final report to the minister in January 1992. In it he was highly critical of the "deals" made between the city and London township and those contemplated for other townships. He claimed that they "do not serve Provincial interests because of their lack of comprehensiveness. They do not bring about the most effective and efficient delivery of services because they leave duplication over a single community of interest in place."[30] He then went on to outline very briefly twenty-one separate items that were considered to be provincial interests and principles. With respect to two-tier government for the county and the city, the chief negotiator explicitly declared that it was not in the provincial interest. Three possible structural solutions were proposed: 1) a gigantic "City of Middlesex" to include all of the city and county; 2) a very large "City of the Greater London Area" to include the city and all of its adjacent municipalities; and 3) "Annexation to the City" – a plan that corresponded very closely to the London's 1991 proposal. The recommendations to the minister were that a process leading to draft legislation should be started as soon as possible and that such a process "should allow for input from a wide range of interests." The process was to have terms of reference that "should articulate Provincial interests up-front to guarantee emergence of acceptable product."[31] Only later did it become clear what this inelegantly worded report really meant: the necessity for a large annexation had already been determined. The only role of the public was to help determine how large it was going to be.

ARBITRATION, 1992

On 30 January 1992, the NDP minister of municipal affairs, Dave Cooke, came to London to announce that he was appointing John Brant, a London businessperson, as an arbitrator of the London boundary dispute. Cooke called the appointment "a first in Ontario" and said that, if successful "it could be a model for resolving future disputes, and produce changes in boundaries legislation."[32] Brant was given until the end of March to produce a solution. After that date, Cooke said, "I will implement the arbitrator's report."[33]

Brant was instructed to consult "a broad range of interested parties, agencies and elected people in the London/Middlesex area" and to challenge consulted parties "to consider and make suggestions reflecting provincial interests." The most crucial section of the Terms of Reference came under the heading of "Provincial Interests" and the subheading "Growth." One of the essential principles that must be reflected in the solution emerging from the arbitration process was

[t]hat there be a government structure comprised of [sic] elected people and based on the principle of representation by population, with responsibility for at least planning and servicing to cover the area reasonably anticipated to be within the City of London's area of major influence for at least twenty years, including:
- future urban areas dependent upon London-centred infrastructure
- London Airport
- sufficient lands adjacent to the Highway 401/402 corridor.[34]

In an awkward "Note" in this section, the terms of reference also declared that "'Regional Government' for the current County of Middlesex and City of London is not a preferred option due to the availability of other growth management options, and the City's dominance when the principle of representation by population is applied."[35]

A few days later, Brant announced the dates and locations of eleven evening public meetings to be followed by a final all-day Saturday session on 14 March. He stated in a media interview, "I have no intention to have any closed-door meetings."[36] This statement seemed to imply that he would be operating on principles roughly equivalent to those used by the Ontario Municipal Board, that is, all presentations to him would have to be made in public. In fact, by his own admission, not all meetings were held in public. In his own letter transmitting his report to the minister, he refers to having met "with a wide variety of experts including concerned citizens, engineering and business consultants, employees of municipal and provincial governments, both local and provincial elected officials, and members of the University of Western Ontario faculty."[37] Since the time and place of such meetings were never publicly announced, it would seem that they were, indeed, "closed-door meetings."[38] There was certainly no mechanism worked out whereby interested parties were informed of what had transpired.

Another disturbing practice was that Brant received about seven hundred written submissions outside the public hearings. Notification of such submissions – even the most obviously important ones – was not circulated to interested parties. For instance, on 10 March, the city stated in its public brief to Brant that it required 1,594 hectares for industrial development between 1992 and 2026. But in a letter to Brant dated nine days later, the city's economic-development manager claimed that the correct figure was 4,742 hectares.[39] There was no way that any one other than Brant could have known about this important change in the data being used to support the city's position. Brant himself also made reference to having "received much private correspondence outlining developer concerns."[40]

The public-hearing process seemed to be an enormous success. Meetings were well attended and well reported in the local media. Over three hundred people made oral submissions.[41] Many obviously had put a great deal of work into their presentations. Brant went to great pains to have everyone feel relaxed, and he seemed genuinely open to all the ideas presented, especially if they came from "ordinary citizens." Herein lay a major problem: Brant's terms of reference did not allow him to be open to all ideas, especially to those expressed by the vast majority of participating citizens who wanted to keep things more or less as they were. At every public meeting he referred to his terms of reference, but only rarely did he point out to citizens that it was not possible for him to accept what they wanted. More typical were the kind of comments he made at the final public meeting, when he stated that "the opportunity to look out for the little guy is as important as to look out for the big guy" and that he "was struck by the strong emotional response from county residents" and "would take [it] into account."[42]

Brant's report was delivered to the minister on 30 March 1992 and publicly released four days later. The report contained twenty-one discrete recommendations, but Brant stated that they "can only be considered in their entirety: they are completely interrelated and balanced to provide an optimal opportunity for the entire area. They must be implemented as though they were one."[43]

On the crucial subject of the city boundaries, Brant allocated to London 26,000 hectares from the four adjoining municipalities – almost all of what it asked for. The Town of Westminster was to be eliminated, with most of its territory transferred to the city. Deciding Westminster's fate "was the hardest single part of the decision."[44] But the difficulty apparently derived from assessing Westminster's financial viability rather than from any attempt to weigh the expressed wishes of residents against the provincial terms of reference.

In a newspaper interview a few weeks later, Brant reflected on the arbitration process. When asked if he was surprised about the overwhelmingly negative public response to his report, he stated,

> There was a large number of people who were anxious that London not expand or that London's expansion be minimized. Those people had hoped to persuade me to break my mandate. ... People are coming back to me and saying 'you didn't hear us, you didn't listen.' The truth of the matter is that they didn't read the terms of reference. ... The nice thing about the process was that the terms of reference were always clear. ... I never really challenged the terms of reference. ... I didn't have any problem with the terms of reference.[45]

Brant was also asked about the relative importance of what he heard at the public hearings, compared to "the material ... received outside the public process." His answer: "If I had to pick a number, it would be a 50–50 impact. It's all in the public forum now, by the way. All a person has to is go and look at it at the [London Public] library."[46]

What exactly was this so-called "arbitration" process all about? This turned out to be not just an academic question. On 21 May 1992, the County of Middlesex launched a legal action aimed at quashing everything that had happened since the first report of the chief negotiator. The grounds for the action were that "the Minister failed to follow the procedures set out in the [Municipal Boundary Negotiations] Act, and that the Arbitrator adopted a procedure which violated the principles of natural justice or fairness."[47] Legal arguments were heard before a three-judge panel of the Divisional Court in Toronto on 17 and 18 June, but the court's decision was not made public until 4 August 1992. The aspects of the decision relating to whether the minister followed the correct procedures under the act are not especially relevant to the main concerns of this paper. In essence, the court ruled that the act provided the minister with enough authority to do more or less what he wished, including to appoint an arbitrator.

The court's discussion of the "Arbitrator's duty to act fairly" is much more interesting. It merits lengthy direct quotation:

> In his capacity as a purported arbitrator, Brant was acting in a manner which approached a judicial form of decision-making for the simple reason that the Minister indicated that Brant's conclusions would be implemented. ... In our opinion Brant had a duty to act fairly; the more pressing issue involves a determination of whether that particular duty was breached in the circumstances of this case.[48]

This aspect of the decision is by itself highly significant. During the arbitration process there was not the slightest hint from anyone that Brant was in any way restrained in his actions due to the quasi-judicial nature of his position. Indeed, the common belief was precisely the opposite: because the issue was not being determined by the OMB, the process was not quasi-judicial.

The court held that

in the context, fairness did not require Brant to conduct a trial or a public hearing with notice to all participants of all the submissions and evidence he considered in arriving at his conclusions.
Brant's process might have departed from the ordinary approach used in other types of arbitration ... but we are not convinced that the applicants were treated unfairly in the particular circumstances of this case.[49]

Lawyers for the County of Middlesex paid considerable attention to the letter dated 19 March from the city's economic-development manager. They argued that this letter "unfairly influenced the arbitrator." The court did not agree, pointing out that the city's position on how much land it wanted was not changed in any way by the letter and said, "It is not apparent to us what influence, if any, Gallagher's letter had upon Brant's recommendations."[50]

John Brant's report survived its judicial process unscathed. The legislative process, however, was another matter. When the report was made public on 3 April 1992, the minister of municipal affairs announced that legislation would be introduced to implement the report and that the new boundaries would be in place by 1 January 1993. He also stated that "[t]he lobbying and manoeuvring are over."[51] Two weeks later, in response to the question "Is there any opportunity for more public hearings, anything like that?" he answered, "No, the public hearings – that was the arbitration process."[52] For Cooke, however, the difficult part of the political process – complete with more public involvement – had just begun.

LEGISLATION

Under the terms of the Section 14 of the Municipal Boundary Negotiations Act, 1981, the minister has the authority, if there is local agreement or if local disagreements have been settled by the OMB, to implement new boundaries by order-in-council. In other words, no new legislation is needed. In London's case, however, there was no local agreement, and the OMB was not involved. Legislation was required if Brant's decisions were to be implemented.

Dave Cooke's most obvious legislative obstacle was the NDP member for Middlesex, Irene Mathyssen. Her constituency included much of the area slated for annexation, and she was not happy. Other NDP members from rural areas near large cities shared her concerns. On 7 May, when Cooke announced that the cabinet had "accepted in principle" the Brant report, he also said that there would be more public hearings on the report's details. He pointed out that cabinet approval "does not mean every part of the Brant report will be in the legislation." He specifically alluded to "outstanding issues," some of which were raised by Irene Mathyssen.[53]

On 12 May, Middlesex county council learned that, contrary to one of Brant's decisions, the county would not be required to restructure itself prior to 1 September 1993.[54] Two weeks later, at a meeting of area Ontario municipal councillors at the University of Western Ontario, John Brant claimed that he would "speak out against annexation legislation" if it did not include compulsory county restructuring. He reiterated his argument that "his plan only works in total."[55]

The real evidence that the Brant report was in trouble came on 5 June. Cooke stated publicly that he was "willing to consider" a plan devised by Irene Mathyssen that would see most of Westminster's rural land go to neighbouring townships rather than to the city. Instead of London's area tripling, it would merely double; Westminster would still be eliminated; the stipulations in Brant's terms of reference would not be violated. Brant was obviously furious. He claimed that, if the Mathyssen plan was adopted, "you might as well tear the whole thing apart ... you can throw the whole report out the window ... I cannot believe that [Cooke] would even consider it. I talked to him [yesterday] and he gave no indication of anything like this."[56] This was the point at which it was clear to all concerned that the Brant report was now just one factor among many in a complex, ongoing, highly political process.

In an interview with the press, the warden of Middlesex County, Frank Gare, claimed to know little about the Mathyssen plan. Nevertheless, he called it "a promising start to dismantling Brant's plan ... the break we have been looking for."[57] However, on the day before his remarks were printed, he wrote the following in a letter to Mathyssen:

I cannot accept your offer to alter the boundaries in the proposed annexation legislation. ... I cannot unilaterally make decisions which affect the townships. ... [T]he decision must be theirs. ... The County and the townships are currently preparing an alternative package of proposals on annexation which deal with the concerns we have identified.[58]

In a letter to Cooke dated 12 June, Gare stated:

I am concerned that the refusal by these townships [presumably North Dorchester and Delaware] to accept this proposal will be interpreted as a refusal by the County to discuss with you an alternative package or proposal on annexation. The County wants to ensure that the annexation agreement is beneficial to both the residents of the City and the County and believes that alternatives or amendment's to Brant's report warrant discussion.[59]

The townships apparently could not accept the Mathyssen plan, because it appeared likely that the costs of absorbing the rural parts of Westminster outweighed the benefits. This is precisely why Brant had assigned the area to the city in the first place.

Just as it appeared the annexation issue was lurching out of control, Cooke came to London on 12 June to announce that he had rejected the Mathyssen plan and that he still believed the Brant report held "a workable solution to this long-standing complex, emotionally charged debate." Admitting that he had "lost a lot of sleep over this," he made it clear that a major difficulty with the Mathyssen plan was that it did not have the support of the affected townships or of the county.[60] Had he accepted it, he presumably would have gained peace within his own party, but he still would not have satisfied key local politicians. Furthermore, he would be seen by many – including John Brant – to have completely undermined the Brant report, a document that would have to remain as the major justification for what would still be a very significant annexation.

For the County of Middlesex and the townships, Cooke's decision on the Mathyssen plan was quite acceptable. There was no particular reason for them to help Mathyssen extract herself from a very difficult political spot. The county was only marginally better off under her plan than under Brant's; the townships were probably worse off. In the circumstances, it is not surprising that Cooke returned to the relative safety of the Brant boundaries.

In the legislature, Cooke ran into numerous delays and difficulties. The bill did not receive first reading until 23 June. Cooke's plan to have second reading completed prior to the summer recess was blocked by opposition parties. This meant that the legislature's committee dealing with the bill could not hold public hearings in London during the recess, as Cooke had originally planned. It also meant that there was more general uncertainty and more time for opponents to mobilize. Local politicians in rural municipalities throughout the province had become so upset about the London situation that on 8 June Cooke sent an "open letter to all municipal councils" in which he pointed out London's unique characteristics and offered his "personal assurance that no other area in the Province will experience the scope and size of the annexation that was necessary in London."[61] When John Brant was first appointed as arbitrator, Cooke had hoped that the arbitration process in London could serve as a model for use elsewhere. Now he was doing everything possible to argue that London's experience would not be a model.

On 10 July, the county sent Cooke its alternative plan, which called for an annexation to the city of only 9,760 hectares and the continued existence of the Town of Westminster.[62] The new proposal did not comply with the province's requirements as stated in Brant's terms of reference. It is not surprising in the circumstances that the proposal seems not to have been given consideration as a serious alternative to the position taken by John Brant.

Because a legislative committee had no authority at this stage to hold hearings in London, Cooke arranged his own. On 24 and 25 September, he personally listened to about sixty briefs over thirteen hours. Annexation opponents orchestrated demonstrations outside the county building in which the hearings were held. One enterprising farmer brought along a cow, complete with a placard declaring "I'm a county cow, not a city cow."[63] Few of the presentations contained anything that had not been heard many times before. But the hearings were significant, because they were the first occasion that county residents actually had the chance to address someone in public who had the authority – unlike John Brant – to devise a solution with which they might be able to agree.

During the hearings, Cooke slowly jettisoned a few more parts of Brant's integrated package of recommendations. He talked, for example, about possible changes to the compensation package for affected municipalities and transitional arrangements concerning representation for the annexed areas on London city council – both matters that Brant had carefully considered. Most importantly, he explicitly countermanded Brant's decision that the city's landfill site located in the Town of Westminster would "be made available to all municipalities in the region, not just those in Middlesex County."[64] Cooke's hearings in London made it abundantly clear that Cooke was himself making the decisions; he was not simply implementing what Brant had already decided. Indeed, John Brant never spoke again in public on the annexation issue in London. He now lives in the United States.

During October 1992, the legislature concluded the second-reading debate on the annexation legislation. The most significant contribution was made by Irene Mathyssen. Her speech was focused on the issue of intermunicipal servicing agreements. She pointed out that both the previous Liberal minister and Dave Cooke claimed that such agreements do not work. She noted, however, that even John Brant advocated servicing agreements for two hamlets beyond the new northern boundaries of the city: "If such agreements are possible, then why annexation? If such agreements are possible now and were possible in 1988, why on earth such an extensive annexation?"[65]

She went on to contradict data contained in the 1990 fact-finder's report concerning Westminster's debt capacity and to conclude that there is sufficient financial capacity "to expand service areas as needed."[66]

In response to attacks on Dave Cooke from the opposition parties, Mathyssen responded as follows: "The Minister of Municipal Affairs did accept a compromise I proposed last June. It was a compromise that was my second choice, and the county of Middlesex rejected that. So I don't think it's at all fair to paint him as the bad person in all this."[67] Nevertheless, the next day, Mathyssen joined the Liberals in voting against the bill, on second reading, the only NDP member to do so. Seven Progressive Conservatives voted against the bill while three, including Dianne Cunningham (PC-London North), the only conservative MPP in the London area, voted for it.[68]

The legislature's standing committee on finance and economic affairs considered the bill on four separate days, between 29 October and 19 November. In addition to presentations from the Ministry of Municipal Affairs, nineteen delegations from the London-Middlesex area had one last chance to make their views known.[69] The county formally presented its alternative plan but was told that it did not have sufficient local support and that its proposed boundaries were not sufficiently comprehensive. Both the county and the Town of Westminster declared that they could now support the city's 1988 annexation proposal, but it was obvious that, at this late stage, nobody else was interested in turning the clock back to 1988.[70] The committee approved the bill, and it received third reading in the legislature on 10 December. On 1 January 1993, the Town of Westminster ceased to exist.

PUBLIC PARTICIPATION AND MUNICIPAL BOUNDARIES

It is not unheard of for all participants in a particular decision-making process to be dissatisfied with the outcome. Usually such dissatisfaction results from the adoption of a compromise that is no one's first choice. What is peculiar about the outcome of the London annexation process is that the final result went beyond what the original proponent of annexation was actually seeking. In short, no one in the London area was advocating annexation on the scale that eventually resulted. On the surface it appears that the City of London changed its position part way through – and, in a formal sense, it did. But, as the city administrator acknowledged just before his retirement, "It was really the province that pushed us into it."[71] The province's key strategic decisions were taken not only in the absence of any form of public participation but also in the absence of concern for the original stated positions of the affected municipalities. In one sense the City of London was the victor – but only in the sense that its original objective (a relatively small-scale annexation) could more easily be adapted to meet the province's policy of comprehensiveness than could the objectives of any of the other key players, especially the Town of Westminster and the County of Middlesex.

Perhaps, however, the province was acting to reflect the opinion of the "silent majority" in the area, people whose views were somehow not being reflected in the positions taken by municipal politicians. To examine such a hypothesis we need, at a minimum, some reliable survey data. Two public-opinion surveys were carried out in mid-1992. Nordex Research, a local London company, asked questions of 505 respondents, from 23–28 April. Because the Nordex survey instrument focused on a side issue – the future of London's Public Utilities Commission – that is of only dubious relevance to annexation, the results are not wholly reflective of people's views on municipal boundaries. Nevertheless, thirty-four per cent of the respondents were "very satisfied" or "somewhat satisfied," while forty-three per cent were "not so satisfied" or "not satisfied at all" with the way in which the provincial government handled the London-Middlesex annexation issue. For respondents living within the City of London, equivalent figures were thirty-nine per cent and thirty-five per cent, respectively.[72] In mid-1993, Londoners learned that the provincial government had commissioned Decima Research to poll area residents during the summer of 1992. Respondents' attitudes concerning support or opposition to Brant's proposed boundaries were almost identical to the Nordex results, both for area residents as a whole and for those living within the city.[73] Whatever might be said about these data, they clearly do not indicate overwhelming support for the provincial government's position.

Neither the Liberals nor the NDP came to office pledging to expand the boundaries of urban municipalities – either for Ontario generally or for London in particular. Even within the London area, the issue was not a factor in the 1990 provincial election. The evidence points to only one plausible conclusion: the main proponents of a large annexation in the London area were civil servants within the Ministry of Municipal Affairs. Their concerns were the determining factors in convincing the Liberal minister of municipal affairs to insist on a more comprehensive solution and the NDP minister to formulate Brant's terms of reference such that a large annexation was the only possible result.

As long as cabinet documents remain unavailable, it is extremely difficult in a parliamentary system of government to determine the policy-making role performed by civil servants. For the details of the London case, the evidence, of necessity, is mainly circumstantial. But there can be no doubt that the general "ministry view" in Municipal Affairs is that there are too many municipalities in Ontario; that intermunicipal service agreements are problems, not solutions; and that special-purpose bodies should be eliminated. In the absence of any firm political direction to the contrary, these are the positions that the minister of municipal affairs, of whatever party, will likely advocate. Provincial decision-making on municipal issues can only be understood if the importance of this "ministry view" is recognized. Local governments must realize – if they do not already – that civil servants are just as active in trying to influence a minister to a particular point of view as local governments are. The main difference is that the civil servants usually have better access. This is especially important when ministers are overworked and have little apparent interest in the subject-matter of their ministries. When Dave Cooke was the NDP minister during the height of the London controversy, these conditions certainly applied.

The importance of the "ministry view" in determining the outcome of the London annexation controversy forces us to consider not just the failure of the public hearings associated with the Brant arbitration but also the failure of more traditional mechanisms designed to insure that the views of ordinary citizens are considered during the policy-making process. These traditional mechanisms involve municipal councils and local MPPs expressing local views and transmitting them to the relevant minister. In making his or her decision, the minister and the cabinet then balance such views with expert advice received from civil servants in determining the outcome. But in this case there is precious little evidence that either the Liberal or the NDP minister was paying attention to local elected politicians at either the provincial or municipal levels. Only towards the very end did Dave Cooke show any signs of relying on Irene Mathyssen, and, by this time, it was far too late.

Because of the strict provisions of John Brant's terms of reference, the seemingly more innovative mechanisms for direct public involvement in the arbitration process could never be a substitute for the traditional indirect mechanisms. At the beginning of the process, nobody pointed out publicly exactly what the terms of reference meant. For London's politicians favouring a large annexation, it would have been counterproductive to proclaim their victory before Brant's work had begun. For the municipal councillors in Westminster who favoured a form of regional government, the terms of reference seemed to hold open the possibility of creating an intermunicipal planning and servicing commission – as long as such a commission was not called a regional government. But most potential participants simply did not pay much attention to the terms of reference, and, if they did, they assumed that Brant could be convinced to ignore their most objectionable provisions. In any event, someone at the very beginning could have focused attention on the terms of reference. Nobody did. The result for many who participated in Brant's hearings was a sense of complete betrayal. For these people, the concept of public participation in local decision-making became nothing more than a cruel joke.

CONCLUSION

The conclusion from all this is not that public hearings never make a difference. The point is that public hearings are always conducted within certain terms of reference. If the terms of reference are narrow – as they were in London – then all the enthusiasm, research, and passion that is directed at obtaining a result contrary to the terms of reference is not going to make any difference. Better to boycott the hearings than to legitimize them by participating. If the terms of reference are broad, then it is likely that the individual or group conducting the hearings is acting in a purely advisory capacity. No government minister is going to delegate broad decision-making authority to any appointed commission. When participating in hearings conducted by this type of advisory body, the prudent strategy would be to plan a follow-up campaign to influence the minister as well.

If drawing municipal boundaries is a highly technical subject for which there is a demonstrable optimal solution, there is nothing wrong with having civil servants make the real decisions. We allow it all the time for such matters as deciding appropriate standards for the presence of bacteria in food. The point, of course, is that for such matters we generally do not hold widely advertised public hearings in which we encourage lay people to participate. We assume that members of the public are simply not qualified to make useful judgements.

For most people, debates about municipal debt capacities and policies for financing sewer systems are about as technical and obscure as anything can possibly be. If these are the key factors in the proper determination of municipal boundaries, then there is no need for public participation. Important insiders in the London annexation controversy believe that such matters are exactly what the issue was all about. Not until one knows the differences among development charges, front-end financing, and municipal debenturing is one really qualified to join the discussion. Within this framework, everything in the London controversy hinged on

Westminster's financial capability to extend its water-supply and sewage systems. Westminster's own advocacy of a regional government system in which the city's tax base would be used to finance such services outside its borders indicates that town politicians themselves realized the importance of this issue.

Technical issues of this kind can suitably be determined by the Ontario Municipal Board, by intermunicipal negotiation, or by ministers of the Crown introducing legislation based on advice from expert public servants. Specialists in local government can debate which of these procedures is best in any given set of circumstances. The important point, however, is that none of these processes – all of which were employed in London at one time or another during its past two major annexations – is well-suited for public participation.

The problem, of course, is that the drawing of municipal boundaries also involves the delineation of territorially based groups of people for purposes of self-government. The real experts on the subject of communities are the people themselves. Sometimes groups of rich people want to create their own municipalities to avoid having to subsidize poorer people in adjoining areas. Most Canadian provinces have been fairly successful in preventing (or ameliorating) this form of class-based municipal fragmentation. They have been less successful in taking account of genuine community desires to protect local institutions and practices that local citizens consider important to preserve their identity and autonomy in the face of massive centralizing pressures.

Balancing the sometimes conflicting imperatives of technical and community factors is not easy. Unfortunately, John Brant's arbitration process did not succeed. The technical considerations were firmly entrenched in the terms of reference. The hearings, however, were joyfully participatory: there were no legalistic rules, no partisan politics, no concluding votes, in which one side loses and the other side wins. Everyone could go home feeling that they had made their pitch to a man of obvious integrity who was not just a mere adviser. He was the man who was going to make the decision. But when the report came out, it was obvious that the important decisions had been made before the hearings had even begun. Later, it became apparent that, even though Brant had adhered rigorously to his terms of reference, the minister still could not avoid picking and choosing among Brant's various "decisions."

If John Brant had had no limiting terms of reference, if he had been guided in making his decisions by what most people had told him in the public meetings and if the minister had fully implemented his report, then the whole process would arguably been a great victory for direct public participation. Unfortunately, however, it would have been a victory not over the evil forces of corrupt politicians, expensive lawyers, monopoly capitalists, or rapacious land developers. It would have been a victory over Ontario's system of representative parliamentary democracy, a system which, when working properly, does provide for indirect participation through local municipal councils and MPPs. The idea was that a complex political problem in a democratic society could be completely resolved in eight weeks by a non-partisan arbitrator who followed his terms of reference and who listened to people. It was simply too good to be true.

NOTES

1 I gratefully acknowledge helpful comments on an earlier draft from Chip Martin of *The London Free Press*; my colleague, Michael Keating; and Susan Phillips and Katherine Graham.
2 Municipal Boundary Negotiations Act R.S.O. 1990, c. M-49.
3 Ontario Municipal Board, "In the Matter of ... [London annexation by-law]," P.F.M. 7054, 9 May 1960, pp. 1–8.
4 Ibid., p. 37.
5 Ibid., p. 11.
6 Ibid., pp. 25–6.
7 Ibid., pp. 31–2.
8 Ibid., p. 32.
9 Ibid., p. 36.
10 Ibid., p. 7.
11 n.a., "Gleeson says annexation can't be avoided," and n.a., "The basic conflict in annexation attitudes" [editorial], *The London Free Press*, 11 and 17 September, 1979, p. C1 and p. A6, respectively.
12 City of London, Office of the City Administrator, "Proposal for Boundary Adjustments" [letter of transmittal] 18 November 1988.
13 Ibid., Section 4.
14 Tony Hodgkinson and Joe Matyas, "Annexation details withheld as part of London strategy," and Don Murray, "Secrecy no surprise to reeves," *The London Free Press*, 20 January 1988, p. B1–B2 and p. B1–B2, respectively.
15 n.a., "London council reviews annexation proposals," *The London Free Press* 21 June 1988, p. B2.
16 For a general account of what the city was originally seeking, see Joe Matyas, "'Enough land for a decade or two'"; Don Murray and Joe Matyas, "'The gauntlet has been thrown down and we are prepared to pick it up'"; Don Murray, "They're ready for a fight in Westminster," *The London Free Press* 30 January 1988, p. B1.
17 Greg van Moorsel, "Rookie aldermen 'in' on annex plans"; Howard Burns,

"Proposal a relief to two townships"; Marianne Fedunkiw, "'Leave us alone,' 'Been waiting,' among reactions to annexation," *The London Free Press* 12 December 1988, pp. B1, B2 and B2, respectively.
18 Greg van Moorsel, "Talks shrouded in secrecy," *The London Free Press* 7 September 1989, pp. B1–B2.
19 Debora van Brenk, "Middlesex trustees 'incensed' over not being included in talks," *The London Free Press* 6 June 1989, p. B2.
20 *The London Free Press* 21 September 1989.
21 Greg van Moorsel, "Development freeze stirs tempers," *The London Free Press* 30 December 1989, pp. C1–C2.
22 Ontario, Ministry of Municipal Affairs, Municipal Boundaries Branch, *The Fact Finding Report on the City of London Boundary Issues* (Toronto, Queen's Printer, 1990), p. iii.
23 Ibid., p. 80.
24 John Sweeney, minister of municipal affairs to M.C. Engels, city administrator, City of London [letter] 25 April 1990.
25 Greg van Moorsel, "Quick deal unlikely in bid for more land," *The London Free Press* 30 June 1990, p. C1.
26 Greg van Moorsel, "New plan to annex vast area possible" and "Sally Ann plans high-rise condos"; and n.a., "Apartment dwellers lose recycling bid," *The London Free Press* 11 September 1990, p. B1, p. B7 and p. B9, respectively; Lynn Marchildon, "St. Thomas stance could stymie talks," *FreePress* 20 September 1990, pp. B1–B2; Greg van Moorsel, "County plan puts squeeze on London"; and n.a., "Middlesex proposal," "Political reaction," "Chronology," *Free Press* 19 October 1990, p. A1 and p. A2, respectively. Concerning Westminster's proposal for regional government, the reader should be aware that I was retained as a consultant by the City of London to write a paper outlining why two-tier regional government was not an appropriate structural arrangement for the London area. The assignment was completed by the end of November 1990, and I did not act again in such a capacity for any of the participants in the annexation process.
27 n.a., "Annexation proposals defy fast solution"; and Greg van Moorsel, "Secrecy of annexation comes under attack," *The London Free Press* 18 September 1990, p. A6 and p. B3, respectively.
28 Open letter titled, "Equity Needed in Annexation Process: An Open Letter to Premier Elect Rae," *The London Free Press* 22 September 1990, p. A5. See also Hank Daniszewski and Don Murray, "Neighbours slam London attempt at annexation," *Free Press* 24 Septermber 1990, p. B1.
29 Ontario, Ministry of Municipal Affairs, Municipal Boundaries Branch, *Chief Negotiator's Report to the Minister of Municipal Affairs on the London/Middlesex Committee Negotiations* (Toronto: Queen's Printer, 1992).
30 Ibid.

31 Ibid.
32 Chip Martin, "10-year battle of boundaries nearing an end," *The London Free Press* 31 January 1992, p. B1.
33 In a subsequent legal challenge to the arbitration process, this statement was of considerable importance. All parties to the dispute agree that it was made. *Middlesex (County)* v. *Ontario (Minister of Municipal Affairs)*, [1993] O.R., Third series, 10 at 7.
34 Ontario, Ministry of Municipal Affairs, Greater London Area Arbitrator, *Co-opportunity: Success Through Co-operative Independence* (Toronto: Queen's Printer, 1992), Appendix 1.
35 Ibid.
36 Chip Martin, "Arbitration process in boundary dispute to be totally public," *The London Free Press* 6 February 1992, p. B3.
37 Letter of transmittal from John Brant to Dave Cooke, dated 30 March 1992.
38 Along with other academic colleagues interested in urban issues, I participated in one such meeting held at the University of Western Ontario. I urged Brant to recommend an annexation smaller than that apparently permitted by his terms of reference.
39 I discovered the letter during a search of Brant's arbitration papers, which he presented to the London public library shortly after his work was completed. I transmitted it to *The London Free Press* in late April 1992. Reporter Chip Martin referred to it in an interview with John Brant, the transcript of which was published on 27 April 1992 ("Brant answers his 'bashers,'" pp. A1–A2). In response to a question involving the letter, Brant replied: "I can't honestly say that any particular piece of information had specific impact." During and immediately after the Brant arbitration, I wrote a number of opinion pieces for *The London Free Press*. One that referred specifically to the letter was published on 22 May 1992.
40 Chip Martin, "Westminster crowd hits views of city developers," *The London Free Press* 13 March 1992, p. B2.
41 I made a public submission on 10 March 1992. Its contents were briefly reported in *The London Free Press* the next day. See Chip Martin, "School board flunks boundary questions," *Free Press* 11 March 1992, p. B4.
42 Chip Martin, "Feelings important in finding solution," *The London Free Press* 16 March 1992, p. B3.
43 Ministry of Municipal Affairs, Greater London Area Arbitrator, *Co-opportunity*, p. 1.
44 Ibid., p. 5.
45 Chip Martin, "Brant answers his 'bashers,'" *The London Free Press* 27 April 1992, pp. A1–A2.
46 Ibid.
47 Corporation of the County of Middlesex and the Corporation of the Town of

Westminster to the Minister of Municipal Affairs, "Notice of Application for Judicial Review," 21 May 1992, p. 12.
48 *Middlesex (County)* v. *Ontario (Minister of Municipal Affairs)*, [1993] O.R. Third Series 10 at 17.
49 Ibid.
50 Ibid., at 17–18
51 Chip Martin, "Irate county officials told time for talking is over," *The London Free Press* 4 April 1992, p. A1.
52 Greg van Moorsel, "Annexation a done deal, says Cooke," *The London Free Press* 16 April 1992, p. A1.
53 Greg van Moorsel, "Cooke plans to let public comment on boundary law," *The London Free Press* 8 May 1992, p. B2.
54 Chip Martin, "Province eases restructuring order to county," *The London Free Press* 13 May 1992, p. B2.
55 Chip Martin, "County must restructure, annexation author says," *The London Free Press* 28 May 1992, p. B5. I was the main organizer of this meeting.
56 Hank Daniszewski and Alison Uncles, "London expansion could be slashed," *The London Free Press* 6 June 1992, pp. A1, A3.
57 Ibid.
58 Frank Gare to Irene Mathyssen [letter] 5 June 1992.
59 Frank Gare to Dave Cooke [letter] 12 June 1992.
60 Chip Martin, "London set to triple in size," *The London Free Press* 13 June 1995, pp. A1, A3.
61 Dave Cooke to all municipal councils ["open" letter] 8 July 1992.
62 Warden Frank Gare to Dave Cooke [letter] 10 July 1992.
63 Chip Martin, "Cooke caught in anti-annexation wave," *The London Free Press* 25 September 1992, p. B7.
64 Ministry of Municipal Affairs, Greater London Area Arbitrator, *Co-opportunity*, p. 21. For the report of Cooke's decision not to accept Brant's decision on this point, see Ibid.
65 Ontario, Legislative Assembly, *Official Report of Debates (Hansard)*. 35th Parliament, 2nd Session. 20 October 1992 (Toronto: Queen's Printer, 1992), p. 2814.
66 Ibid.
67 Ibid., p. 2817.
68 Ibid., p. 2835.
69 I made a presentation to the committee. See Ontario, Legislative Assembly, Standing Committee on Finance and Economic Affairs, *Official Report of Debates (Hansard)*, "London-Middlesex Act, 1992." 35th Parliament, 2nd Session. 19 November 1992 (Toronto: Queen's Printer, 1992), pp. F245-9. Contrary to what is implied by the way the Hansard was edited, I was not speaking on behalf of the University of Western Ontario.
70 Ibid., 29 October and 15 November, pp. F166-73, F175-5 and F206-11. I was

involved as a member of a small group of local elected officials and other interested people who were trying to resurrect the city's 1988 annexation proposal as a last-minute compromise. See Chip Martin, "Coalition dusts off 1988 proposal," *The London Free Press* 29 October 1992, pp. B1, B10.
71 Hank Daniszewski, "Working the Engels: The tight-lipped man who shaped the city," *The London Free Press* 30 June 1992, p. 137.
72 Nordex Research, "Media Backgrounder," May 1992, p. 9.
73 Greg van Moorsel, "Opposition strongest in Westminster, Middlesex," *The London Free Press* 31 July 1993, p. C7.

9

Public Participation in Restructuring Local Government to Create the City of Miramichi

John C. Robison

INTRODUCTION

Restructuring of municipalities within a region almost invariably produces conflict. Wealthier municipalities are concerned about sharing their tax bases with their poorer neighbours. People fear losing their sense of community. Almost everyone wants to ensure local control over how restructuring takes place and is fearful that a resolution will be imposed by the provincial government. Restructuring of local government for the communities at the mouth of the Miramichi River illustrates some of the tensions involved in amalgamation and shows the critical importance of an open and consultative process.

While sharing a common economy and essentially common goals and aspirations, restructuring government for the communities of the Miramichi to create one strong local government was slow to materialize. Since the turn of the century, uniting the communities with one strong local government was seen as a vehicle for dealing effectively with area problems. Economic ups and downs, community rivalries, duplicated services, disparities in the relative ability of municipal governments to serve residents, and the need for strong united leadership were often cited as reasons for considering an amalgamation.

One of the seven significant urban-centred regions in New Brunswick, the Miramichi area was identified in the 1992 provincial government discussion paper *Strengthening Municipal Government in New Brunswick Urban Centres* as one that could benefit from restructuring. It was selected, along with the Moncton urban community, as the subject of a feasibility study into local government restructuring in June 1993.

The primary objective of the study was to examine the feasibility of amalgamation of communities, annexation or the "regionalization" of local government services. Secondary objectives were to make recommendations on how existing boards, commissions and agencies might offer services on a regional basis, if such was not already the case; to make recommendations regarding the management structure of such bodies; and to make recommendations regarding accountability for such services to elected municipal officials and, thereby, to the community served.

The study was conducted by John Robison, city administrator, Fredericton; Leo Burns, New Brunswick Telephone district manager; and Tim McCarthy, former Newcastle town councillor and erstwhile president of the New Brunswick Federation of Labour.

THE MIRAMICHI

The Miramichi study-area comprised two towns, three villages, and six unincorporated areas, with an approximate population of 22,000. As such it is the fourth largest urban area in New Brunswick, surpassed only by the cities of Saint John, Moncton and Fredericton. No boundary restructuring had taken place since 1967, when a major municipal reform program, commonly referred to as the Program for Equal Opportunity, was implemented by the provincial government. At that time, three of the area's five incorporated municipalities came into existence, with the creation of the villages of Douglastown, Loggieville and Nelson-Miramichi. Regardless of the relatively recent incorporation of several of the municipalities comprising the Miramichi urban community, many of the communities had existed as separate district communities for over two centuries, and the towns of Chatham and Newcastle were incorporated in 1896 and 1899, respectively. Community rivalries were prevalent and, indeed, a way of life. This was much like many Canadian communities separated by rivers, other natural boundaries, or railway tracks. But in addition, polarization existed, with rivalries in commerce, religion, sports, government and politics.

In undertaking the restructuring-feasibility study, the provincial government predetermined that the process would require community consultation and that public participation was vital. To this end, the initial step was to appoint the Miramichi Community Advisory Committee. Comprising political, business and community leaders, the committee was to be instrumental in determining the approach and in making recommendations and suggestions regarding all aspects of the study.

While the actual appointment of the committee fell to the minister of municipalities, culture and housing, all members were selected from among nominees provided by the various elected municipal councils and community groups. Considerable effort and care was taken to ensure that a good cross-section of the community was represented on the Community Advisory Committee. While it was a requirement of the study-team to prepare the final report and recommendations, the Community Advisory Committee was to have an active and meaningful role in shaping the recommendations. It assisted the study-team in its deliberations by providing a forum through which it would review findings and test options, gauge support or opposition, and advise on matters pertaining to the study. The committee acted essentially as a focus group or sounding board reflecting the views and concerns of the study-area communities. Throughout the study, the Community Advisory Committee took a strong leadership role.

As is often the case with amalgamation studies in Canada, the threat of the province taking unilateral action and imposing a solution was not one that was regarded with much favour by Miramichiers. The desire of local community leaders to take control of their destiny was apparent throughout the study.

The Miramichi area is one of wide-ranging differences. On a per capita basis, it included the highest-spending municipality in New Brunswick, the Town of Newcastle. But it also included one of the lowest-spending municipalities, the Village of Loggieville. The recent decision by Repap, a major Canadian paper producer to construct a multimillion-dollar upgrade to its Newcastle mill provided a large increase in that community's property-assessment base. With approximately one-quarter of the study-area population, the Town of Newcastle had almost one-half of the area's total property-assessment base. Based on property assessment, the region included one of the wealthiest communities in the province and some of the poorest. Some were struggling to provide even the most basic of services. To others, raising revenue for services presented no difficulty at all. The area included one large employer, Miramichi Pulp and Paper Inc., which employs directly in excess of twenty per cent of the area's workforce. This one employer had a property assessment of approximately $120 million, being one-eighth of the overall assessment base of $1 billion for the entire region.

From its very beginning, the restructuring exercise was community driven. Previous attempts to join municipalities politically had failed, but a bond existed among residents of the area, and their pride in the Miramichi River and the culture centred around it prevailed. Consolidation or amalgamation of the communities at the mouth of the Miramichi River remained, however, the dream of many. Yet, on the surface, at least, more attention seemed to be paid to those issues and characteristics that divided the community rather than those that united it. Dating back to lumber-baron rivalries, "northsiders" were the natural opponents of the "southsiders." Protestants had their differences with Catholics, with those of Irish ancestry dominating the community. Sports teams from the two sides of the river created rivalries, which had been in existence for decades. Long-time residents stated that about the only time it seemed that locals recognized the oneness of their community was when they travelled beyond the area to outside communities or to other provinces. At such times, area residents would gladly and proudly proclaim, "I'm from the Miramichi." And while differences and rivalries existed over the decades, the pride in being from "the Miramichi," with its proud and colourful history, was always paramount.

While differences tended to accent the community, a number of common approaches to issues, problems and services had been developed over the past three decades. However, one might conclude that such common approaches were the product of adversity. For many years, the Miramichi community was the base of operations for the Roman Catholic diocese in New Brunswick. It also was home to St. Thomas University. It was a bitter blow to the area when the headquarters for the church were relocated to Saint John, while St. Thomas University was transferred to Fredericton. While the loss of these institutions took place three decades earlier, an even greater threat was looming with the potential closure of Canadian Forces Base Chatham, a major influence on the employment and economy of the area.

By the time the restructuring study got under way, the Miramichi area was showing signs of recovery from the serious recession of the mid-1980s. The recession had affected the Miramichi community hard because of its strong reliance on resource-based industries, especially mining and forestry. Community leaders had worked together in the search for ways and means to strengthen local government, which was seen as only one opportunity for strengthening the community as a whole. By this time, one chamber of commerce had been created to promote the business interests of the greater community. A regional economic-development commission had been established to promote employment creation and job retention. A common land-use planning effort was being undertaken, as well as a united approach to pollution-control and solid-waste management. As well, one common weekly newspaper, the *Miramichi Leader*, served the entire community. Committed to the betterment of the broader community, the newspaper served as a catalyst for change. With its broadly based readership, it was a vehicle for public participation, encouraging debate and expressions of opinion. Editorial positions regarding community development encouraged the various communities to work together for the common good. It had promoted amalgamation of the various communities as a means of providing greater power in economic development. Further, it promoted amalgamation as a means for the larger community to obtain a better share of the benefits resulting from senior governments decisions.

THE RESTRUCTURING EXERCISE

It was apparent that, in many respects, people of the area were pulling together and seeking solutions, as they worked to shape the future of the community they held so dear. Indeed, the timing was appropriate to examine the feasibility of political amalgamation.

While earlier attempts had failed, there was a strong feeling among many community leaders and residents that continuing to exist as separate municipal units was holding the community back. They wanted to shape the future of the whole community and to speak with one voice in promoting the area. They also sought to have their community take its rightful role among the larger urban centres in New Brunswick, by being recognized as an economic driver of the province.

With two large population centres, Chatham and Newcastle, on either side of the Miramichi River, some thought was given to establishing two consolidated municipalities, divided by the river. This approach was rejected in that the north–south rivalry separated by the river was seen as an obstacle to overcome, not to enhance. Two-tier regionalization was seriously considered, as it could provide a vehicle for greater cooperation but, at the same time, allow communities to retain their rich and valued community identities. In the end, this option was rejected, because it did not provide for neat, direct accountable government without duplication and community rivalries. Regionalization was also viewed by the Community Advisory Committee as a means of delaying the inevitable community amalgamation. Many were of the view that, if the opportunity was not seized now, the community would not have a second chance for some time. Regionalization would only delay that opportunity.

While the study-team reviewed various options for community realignment, amalgamation became the preferred option. It was seen as the best option for implementing a vision for the future of the community, to plan and promote economic development, and to provide a higher level and quality of local services throughout the community. It was also viewed as the best opportunity for sharing resources in an equitable fashion, with a government accountable to the whole community.

Supported by intensive research and led by public support, amalgamation of the eleven communities into one City of Miramichi was recommended. Shortly thereafter, the Government of New Brunswick adopted the recommendation, and the City of Miramichi came into existence on 1 January 1995.

PUBLIC DELIBERATION AND DEBATE

Committed to a very public process, as had been mandated by the Government of New Brunswick, the study-team took a number of initiatives to ensure a publicly driven study. Two of the three study-team members were highly respected members of the Miramichi community, with an extensive history of community service and involvement. While the third member was from outside the area, he brought to the table a history of municipal experience. His opinion was sought and respected, as the various issues concerning amalgamation were considered. Working directly with the study-team was the twenty-one-member Community Advisory Committee, all volunteering as significant stakeholders in the community. The committee not only monitored the work of the study-team but provided continuous liaison with residents and interest groups throughout the area. The study-team leaders were committed early in the process to respecting the wishes and collective recommendations of the Community Advisory Committee. As such, the committee liaised with the study-team in an atmosphere of mutual respect.

With amalgamation having been a community issue for some time, many civic and community leaders had already committed their views on the desirability of amalgamation. Others were hesitant, awaiting the findings of the feasibility study and expressions of public opinion. Yet, the fact that some had already expressed their views in favour of amalgamation gave the study a momentum. It also countered resistance to change, which is so often prevalent in governmental restructuring studies.

In an earlier plebiscite, a question had been placed on the municipal election ballot on the issue of amalgamation. Although the results had demonstrated strong public support in favour of amalgamation, no provincial government action had been taken on this earlier ballot. The debate continued on the various benefits and shortcomings of amalgamation.

Some people thought that, since the study was provincially mandated, the effective decision in favour of amalgamation had already been made. This was not so, however. The constructive participation demonstrated by local leaders helped to allay fears of a predetermined outcome in some quarters. Nonetheless, some scepticism in this regard continued throughout the course of the study. The perceived threat of unilateral provincial action served as the most consistent distraction to a community-driven solution to local government restructuring.

A decision was taken by the study-group at the very beginning that any individual or organization, public or private, who wished to be heard or to ask questions would be given that opportunity. Numerous groups and individuals did so. Public input was solicited, and all identifiable community organizations were invited to give their views, orally or in writing. All those expressing an interest in meeting with the study-group were given that opportunity, and all requests were honoured. Organizations that had not responded to the invitation to make a submission or meet with the study-team were contacted with an offer by the team to meet with them, regardless. Some organizations responded positively to this direct solicitation.

Recognizing that many individuals would prefer not to make a formal submission but yet present a point of view or express a concern, letters were invited from the public. As well, a telephone-voice mailbox was established to accommodate those who wished to use this medium, offering an opportunity to leave a message, anonymously or not. While not heavily used, the initiative seemed to be appreciated.

Among individuals directly affected were politicians who had been elected from the various communities in the study-area. Meetings between the study-team and all elected municipal councils were held, even though all municipalities were represented on the Community Advisory Committee. It was recognized that the various municipal councils had interests and concerns they wished to express on behalf of their respective municipalities. They also had a very real personal interest in their future and wished to be kept informed. There were thirty-three elected politicians on existing municipal councils and twenty-four local advisory committee members serving the unincorporated communities. Many of them recognized the likelihood that amalgamation would reduce the total number of municipal politicians who would sit at an amalgamated council table. Yet, many, if not most, perceived the amalgamation option as the best course of action in the community's best interests. Four of the five municipal governments favoured amalgamation. The council of the Town of Newcastle, while split, opposed amalgamation primarily because of the potential dilution of its comparatively stronger tax base. Of the municipal governments, the Town of Newcastle expressed the greatest opposition of all of the incorporated municipalities. While not organized in such a manner as to allow a vote, most local advisory committees that served the unincorporated communities within the study-area similarly favoured amalgamation. Throughout the study, individual councillors maintained a keen interest and took advantage of opportunities to share their thoughts and ideas.

Similarly, meetings were held with local members of the provincial legislative assembly and the federal member of Parliament. This liaison was pursued so that all provincial and federal elected members would be informed of study progress and of issues that were being raised. It also provided an opportunity for the study-team to gain feedback on matters respecting the study identified by constituents to the elected members.

Public submissions overwhelmingly supported amalgamation, notwithstanding concerns regarding financial impact, potential loss of community identity, and the loss of well-established volunteer services. The need for a governance model that would provide fair consideration of local issues was also a key area of concern. Regardless of relative size, no community wanted to be lost or left out by a future municipal council, which would favour the larger communities.

The Miramichi chamber of commerce organized two public meetings for all area residents. The first such meeting was held early in the study-process, while the second was scheduled as the study neared its conclusion. The leadership demonstrated by the chamber in keeping the issues before residents, as well as its members, was apparent throughout the study.

Five open-house sessions were arranged in various locations throughout the Miramichi area. Open-houses provided the opportunity for the study-team to share results of their research, along with the various options that had been explored. It is estimated that five per cent of the adult population of the Miramichi attended one or more open-house sessions. These sessions provided the study-team a great opportunity to meet with area residents, share research information, seek views, and hear directly the concerns, thoughts and criticisms of potentially affected residents. These meetings took place over a full week, near the conclusion of the study. They were well publicized and well attended. Those attending were requested to respond to a questionnaire about the form of governance most appropriate for the Miramichi area. Those who expressed a preference stated overwhelmingly that an amalgamated community was the preferred option.

Attention provided by the media, both print and electronic, was extremely helpful throughout the process. While daily newspapers based outside the Miramichi community provided detailed coverage throughout the study, the local weekly newspaper provided an excellent forum for points of view. Editorially, the weekly newspaper, the *Miramichi Leader*, supported amalgamation, based on its view that unified local government would provide for the pooling of resources for the common good of the area and remove costly duplication evident throughout the Miramichi community. The *Miramichi Leader* had long-before established its reputation as an institution serving the entire Miramichi community. With a large following, and prepared to take an editorial position on any community issue, the newspaper had over the years exercised a strong unifying role. While very little liaison occurred between the study-team and the weekly newspaper, reporters and editorial staff considered the study its number-one story. All debate received coverage, as did relevant documents, research, decisions of municipal councils, and the views of residents wishing to venture a comment on the subject. As the final report *Miramichi City: Our Future – Strength Through Unity* was tabled, extensive coverage of the report was provided by the *Miramichi Leader*. With its high penetration into the Miramichi community, it helped most interested persons to become knowledgeable about the issues and debate surrounding the study and about the amalgamation issue.

PUBLIC DEBATE FOLLOWING THE REPORT

With the tabling of the report, both proponents and opponents of amalgamation very quickly offered opinions. While the report was generally received positively, a group in opposition to amalgamation generated considerable support through a petition calling on the provincial government to reject amalgamation. This group opposed amalgamation primarily based on the fear that the true financial costs had not been appropriately explored. They feared increases in taxes resulting from the loss of volunteer services, extension of services to currently unserviced areas, and uncertainty about the future. Underlying their opposition was the concern that the province was imposing its will and that residents of Miramichi would have to deal with problems that should rightfully be handled by the province and not by Miramichi residents through increased property taxes. In short, doubts were expressed regarding the financial impact of amalgamation. Such opposition brought about requests for more information from the study-team and led to a number of public meetings throughout the Miramichi area. These meetings presented an opportunity for elaboration on the recommendations contained in the report and provided an opportunity for public questions and for the continued expression of views, both for and against amalgamation. While public interest had been relatively strong throughout the study process, interest intensified as it became apparent that the creation of one local government for the entire urban community was approaching reality.

The provincial government had committed itself to a decision within a month of tabling the report. This time delay was provided to allow recommendations and suggestions directly to the minister of municipalities, culture and housing. Several interested parties took advantage of this opportunity, with amalgamation opponents calling for a plebiscite among potentially affected residents. This call for a plebiscite on amalgamation drew considerable attention. Supporters of the idea cited the right of potentially affected residents to determine their own form of government, as well as to decide on the basic question of amalgamation. The organizing group pushing for a plebiscite was identified as being motivated by partisanship in the provincial political context. Further, holding a plebescite was viewed as being an obstacle to amalgamation. As a result, the call for a plebiscite did not generate as widespread a support as might have been expected. This request was denied by the provincial government.

CONCLUSION

As one examines the study-process and the direct involvement by Miramichi residents, one must conclude that it was a highly transparent exercise. It was this very openness that brought about support for the process by municipal councils, community organizations, news media, community groups, and individuals. While the newly amalgamated community has had and will continue to have growing pains, the community involvement, participation and the leadership taken by individuals have given the new city a momentum, vitality and sense of optimism for the future.

What are the lessons to be learned from the experience leading to the creation of the City of Miramichi? First and foremost, the reality that people, not government, make a community, is very important. Miramichi residents were not willing or prepared to leave their future to any outside study-team. With the majority of study-team members from the area, as were all twenty-one members of the Community Advisory Committee, there was an acceptance of the reality that Miramichi people should and must determine and shape the future of their community. This was borne out by the fact that as the final recommendations were developed, they were accepted unanimously by all members of the Community Advisory Committee.

Public participation through invitations for submissions, letters, voice messages and verbal comment was important not only to the study-team but to those who sought a direct involvement in the process. The commitment by the study-team to meet with any individual or group provided an opportunity to share information. It also helped to develop an appropriate comfort level by residents, who learned that any and all who wished to share ideas and opinions would be heard.

The very active involvement by the news media and their willingness to devote a significant portion of their coverage to the amalgamation study became the best vehicle for communicating with the public. While three news conferences were held during the review process by the study-team, it was the in-depth reporting of research, comparative information, along with views and opinions of residents, that was so vital. Without such attention to comprehensive reporting and the public participation that it brought, there would not have been an informed public willing and prepared to take such a major leap of faith with their community.

Weaknesses and shortcomings also require identification. As previously mentioned, the Miramichi study-area comprised five incorporated communities, along with six unincorporated areas. Each of the incorporated communities was served by an elected council and supported by an appointed staff. Each of the unincorporated communities was served by a local advisory committee for the minister of municipalities, culture and housing. Minimal contact and discussion occurred between the study-team and appointed staff, other than with the more senior appointed officials. Such discussions and liaison occurred primarily with officials of the two larger towns. The various bargaining units made submissions expressing their views as to how any restructuring should occur. The study-team is of the opinion that greater liaison should have occurred with appointed staff of the municipalities. Municipal staff are important stakeholders in their existing communities, and their commitment to improving government for the area cannot be minimized. They must be informed, and their views should have been sought continuously. Had this been undertaken, some transition problems may have been avoided.

Among the members of the legislative assembly serving the Miramichi was former Premier Frank McKenna, who represented the constituency of Chatham. A dynamic and focused leader, Premier McKenna had served the community in many roles, prior to his election to the legislature, including that of president of the Miramichi chamber of commerce. A proponent of amalgamation of Miramichi communities both before and after his election, Premier McKenna was often seen as an invisible force on the amalgamation issue. While he clearly stated that as premier he would follow the recommendations of the study-team, his personal views were well known. While there was no reason to believe that the premier would impose his personal views on the matter, knowledge of his thinking served to some degree as a threat during the study.

After release of the study-team's report, there were public calls for a plebiscite on amalgamation. The provincial government responded negatively but gave no appropriate reason as to why one should not take place. Amalgamation is a major decision regarding government structure for a community. In this case, the failure to accommodate the request for a vote on the issue caused many to believe that the provincial government was unprepared to listen to public opinion. While it is likely that a plebiscite would have supported amalgamation, in this case the negative connotation that it was being forced against the will of the people seemed to detract from the positive thrust that had been demonstrated throughout the course of the study.

Finally, the new city came into existence on 1 January 1995. However, the decision of the provincial government to appoint the first Miramichi council, rather than provide for election by local residents, was disastrous. With province-wide municipal elections scheduled for the following May, the government thought that an interim appointed council would suffice, allowing for election of a council five months hence. The decision brought about a court challenge by two councillors from the Town of Newcastle, with the provincial government losing the case. This led to the appointment of an administrator to make required decisions until such time as a council could be elected. Needless to say, it was not a good start for the new city. Sadly, it detracted from the excitement, challenge and momentum that existed. It has taken some time to overcome the negative aspect of any imposed council.

Overall, the study into the feasibility of amalgamating eleven communities into the one City of Miramichi was a highly public exercise. While the amalgamation initiative already had momentum among Miramichi communities, the final decision to amalgamate is one of enormous magnitude. It is the product of public opinion led by the various institutions and community leaders throughout the area.

10

Local Governments On-Line: How are They Doing it and What Does it Mean?

Monica Gattinger

INTRODUCTION

New communications and information technologies are transforming society. Shopping electronically, banking electronically, and holding electronic conversations with many individuals simultaneously are just some of their potential uses. Local governments, too, are beginning to make use of the potential afforded by these technological developments. They are marketing themselves globally via electronic networks like City.Net and are beginning to communicate electronically with one another. One area of "on-line" activity that is particularly interesting is the effort by many local governments to forge an electronic connection with their constituents. This chapter explores that effort, drawing on the experiences of the Regional Municipality of Ottawa-Carleton and the City of Ottawa, two governments which have been in the forefront of this activity.

The experiences of these governments, complemented by a survey of local government experience nation-wide, will be analysed from two perspectives. The first is loosely termed a public administration perspective. Here, on-line activities are viewed through the public manager's looking-glass, focusing attention on the policy decision to go on-line, its implementation, and its advantages and disadvantages. The second analytical perspective is grounded more in political science. It seeks to answer the question: does a "wired" local government, accessible electronically by its constituents, represent a change in local governance? In answering this question, the nature of local government on-line activities is examined. The central question is whether local governments are simply using computer networks as another medium to disseminate information to their citizens or whether they are using them to empower their citizenry to participate in local decision-making.

THROUGH THE PUBLIC MANAGER'S LOOKING-GLASS

Across the country, local governments are "catching the wave" and establishing an electronic presence in their communities. From the City of Halifax to the City of Vancouver, local governments are on-line. Even smaller centres, like the District of Squamish, British Columbia, and the Town of Halton Hills, Ontario, are getting involved. Citizens in these towns and cities can access electronic copies of minutes of council meetings, can correspond electronically with their councillors, and can even peruse employment opportunities with their local government. To gain an appreciation of how this has come about, the experiences of the Regional Municipality of Ottawa-Carleton (RMOC) and the City of Ottawa are instructive.

The Decision to Go On-line

The idea to go on-line did not originate in either of these municipalities. In the National Capital Region, the impetus came from the external environment, by way of the National Capital FreeNet (NCF). The NCF is a non-profit community network, providing its users with free access to community information, electronic mail, electronic discussion groups, and a gateway to computer networks across the country and across the world. While there are currently several dozen freenets in Canada, the NCF was the second to sprout in this country (the Victoria FreeNet was the first). Shortly after it opened its virtual doors, it approached many community institutions, encouraging them to establish a presence on the network. It did this in order to nourish the growth of the fledgling network. New users would be attracted if more community institutions were involved (because there would be more information to access on the network), and the larger the user base, the more community institutions would be attracted. The NCF was also interested in community organizations as potential sponsors of phone lines. As a non-profit organization, sponsors are crucial to the NCF's continued existence.

The RMOC and the City of Ottawa were approached by the NCF in 1992. These first meetings were attended by city staff, who entered the gatherings as curious, freenet "ignoramuses" and emerged as converted freenet enthusiasts. At the City of Ottawa, two employees met with NCF representatives: one employee from economic development and another from engineering and works. The former attended because she worked for the department the NCF first contacted, and the latter went out of a personal interest in technology. These people championed their local government's participation in the NCF, not only by sharing their enthusiasm with others, but by investing time and effort in research to persuade council to buy into the idea. Without them, it is unlikely that the idea to go on-line would have taken hold. Their commitment to the concept ensured that the policy idea worked its way through the municipal administrative machinery.

The idea they were pitching was extremely attractive. The NCF assured them there were few financial strings attached; all that was required were several modems and a modest time commitment on the part of a few city staff. The NCF provided free training; services were free, and most of the information to be uploaded already existed in electronic format. The only direct cost was the eventual sponsoring of a couple of NCF phone lines by each government, at a cost of approximately $800.

In the RMOC, the scales tipped in favour of going on-line because of something more than just financial considerations. The director of public affairs remembered how the facsimile machine revolutionized public-relations work by replacing costly, time-consuming communications like courier and mail with instantaneous, inexpensive facsimile transmissions. He believed that computer-mediated communications – of which the NCF was only the beginning – would cause a similar transformation. Even though there were only three to four thousand NCF users at the time, the majority of whom were "techies," the director believed this number would skyrocket and that membership would become representative of the population at large. In his eyes, the NCF's offer was a low-cost opportunity for the region to experiment with computer-mediated communication and to share the knowledge it acquired with other municipalities. It was with this eye to the future that the RMOC got involved.

A similar line of thinking was followed at the City of Ottawa, where those involved believed the Information Highway was well established and that the NCF was just the beginning of a transformation in communications and service delivery. Also influencing the decision to go on-line was the city's position as the nation's capital, giving it a perceived responsibility to be at the forefront of new technology adoption. In addition, the city had previously identified a need to improve communication with the local population; the NCF's proposal dovetailed well with this need.

At both municipalities, councillors had next-to-no involvement in the decision to go on-line, despite the effect this decision has had on the manner in which their constituents can interact with the government. This was an initiative led by the administrative arm of government. In the RMOC, the decision to participate in the National Capital FreeNet was made in mid-1992 by the region's public affairs and information office. At the City of Ottawa, the decision to go on-line was made by the committee of department heads, in November 1992.

Implementation

The RMOC placed responsibility for implementation in the hands of an information clerk in the public affairs and information office. This individual set up the region's menu system (please see Appendix A for an "on-paper demonstration" of the system), held demonstrations for all of the region's departments, and encouraged them to provide her with information to upload onto the NCF.

In designing the region's system, she patterned it after local government involvement in American freenets in Cleveland (the first freenet established) and in Chicago. This seems to be typical of the design process: governments going on-line model their systems after existing systems. When it comes to going on-line, local governments do not attempt to reinvent the wheel.

Currently, when users enter the RMOC's menu system, they can select from a wide variety of information, ranging from general information on the region, to a directory of its services, to information on street closures, to accessing councillors. The region also created a section called "Questions and Comments," a popular interactive electronic bulletin board where citizens can post questions and comments, view the postings of other citizens, and view the region's response to these communications. Unlike other NCF bulletin boards, whose postings are deleted on a monthly basis, the region decided that postings on "Questions and Comments" would remain indefinitely. This would provide a permanent record of all questions ever asked and their answers, and would eliminate the need to answer the same question twice. Citizens can check if their question has already been posed or, conversely, if the region can refer citizens to a previous posting that answers their question.

The City of Ottawa's committee of department heads created an interdepartmental working group whose goal was to "develop a strategy for corporate participation on the National Capital FreeNet and determine an action plan for implementation."[1] Beginning in April 1993, this group met biweekly, and, by June 1993, the city opened its virtual doors, uploading information describing its political and administrative structures. It patterned its menu system after the region's, including its own "Questions and Comments" section. Throughout 1994, further information was uploaded to the system, including tax information, tenders, street closures, a directory of municipal services, and an area for councillors to post information and communicate with their constituents.

The interactive "Questions and Comments" area is administered centrally by each municipality's corporate communications division. At the RMOC, an information clerk regularly logs onto the NCF checking for new postings, while at the City of Ottawa, the senior information officer performs this task. A new entry is routed by these individuals to the appropriate department, where a staff member drafts a response. Departments use the same vetting and records-management procedures they use for telephone inquiries or letters. So, for instance, at the City of Ottawa's department of engineering and works, questions or comments are first received by the commissioner's desk, which "bounces" it to the section that can best respond. An employee then drafts a response, which is sent to his or her manager for approval. Once approved, one copy of the document is stored in departmental records, and a second is forwarded to the senior information officer for posting on the NCF.

For both governments, implementation has been characterized by flexibility, a willingness to learn, and responsiveness to citizen needs. They approached implementation as a learning process, welcoming change and new ideas. For instance, the two governments originally moderated their "Questions and Comments" sections. Messages that citizens wished to post would be screened by a city administrator before being posted to the electronic bulletin board. This practice was frowned upon by users, who tend to espouse an unwavering commitment to freedom of expression in electronic forums. Moderation was perceived as a form of censorship and an indication that the governments were not truly open in their desire to interact with citizens. Due to this reaction, both governments discontinued moderating the section, and, now, any message can be posted to this area.

Another instance of learning and flexibility is provided by the sorts of information that are available electronically. Where feasible, citizen requests for new types of information have been acted on. The City of Ottawa even formally requested (in its questions and comments section) input from users as to what other types of information the city should make available. Interestingly, the high level of client involvement has resulted in a sort of camaraderie between the senior information officer of the City of Ottawa and users. This officer has received private electronic mail from users, encouraging her and giving her positive feedback throughout implementation.

Advantages and Disadvantages

Going on-line has familiarized municipalities with the Information Highway and given them valuable experience to operate in the information and communications environment of the future. It has also increased the efficiency of local government administration. Not only is information disseminated more rapidly but the need to print paper copies of documents has declined. Time spent responding to the same questions is reduced, because the electronic inquiries made by citizens can be answered in a forum where *all* users can see the response. In addition, in contrast to telephone inquiries, staff attending to electronic queries can do so at their convenience.

This is not to say that all is "sweetness and light" in cyberspace. There are a number of significant obstacles for local governments on-line. Most of the problems are technological in nature. The first deals with language. As this is being written, the lingua franca of electronic networks is English. While the NCF is working on establishing a French version (Libertel), the wrinkles posed by French accents are still being ironed out. This difficulty is particularly problematic in the National Capital Region, given its high proportion of francophone residents. At the City of Ottawa, the senior information officer obtained special permission to break the city's bilingual policy and operate in English until Libertel is operational.

A second technical problem is the carrying capacity of the NCF. Demand for access to the system far outstrips its supply of telephone lines. To lessen this problem, the NCF imposed a one-hour time limit on user visits to the system, but the probability of getting a busy signal when trying to log-on far outweighs the probability of connecting to the system. This poses a dual problem for local governments. First, citizens may have difficulty accessing them electronically. And second, users, who, after repeated attempts to log-on are finally successful, may use that hour to undertake other activities such as sending electronic mail, participating in discussion groups, and accessing information from other community institutions. These other activities tend to be more popular with users. In the words of one of the NCF's founders, "We wouldn't need 169 [telephone] lines if only the region and city council were on the FreeNet."[2]

Access to the FreeNet is also problematic from three other standpoints. First, users outside the local dialling range of the FreeNet (which is located at Carleton University) incur long-distance charges to use the system. Local governments may not wish to go on-line if they or many of their residents are not located within the local dialling range of a freenet. Second, within the City of Ottawa and the RMOC, access for city workers is a problem. At the City of Ottawa, for example, there are only four computer lines. These are used not only for the FreeNet but for computer-mediated communication with the RMOC and the National Capital Commission as well. As NCF use by staff and politicians increases, competition over these lines will intensify. Finally, access has been raised as a problem because of the economic barriers to participating on the FreeNet. In order to participate, a user must own a computer and a modem – for those citizens of lower economic means, this could erect an insurmountable hurdle. This access issue should not be accorded too much weight, however, because there are numerous public-access terminals located throughout the region in public libraries, community centres, and at the City of Ottawa and the RMOC.[3] Furthermore, as discussed below, low income does not appear to prohibit FreeNet use.

Other problems that local governments have when they establish an electronic presence stem from sociological factors. First, the profile of FreeNet users is not representative of the region as a whole. The low participation rate of women is striking: a recent study of NCF users revealed that eighty-two per cent were men (compared to forty-nine per cent in the population at large).[4] Users also tend to be more educated than the general population of the region, with about half holding university degrees, compared to roughly twenty per cent for the region as a whole. The on-line population's age also does not reflect the general population's age distribution, with more FreeNet users falling into the fifteen-to-fifty-four age bracket, and fewer being over fifty-five. Surprisingly, the household income of FreeNet members is fairly representative of the region, except for a larger number of users earning over $70,000 and a larger number earning less than $9,000 (the latter statistic possibly refuting the belief that low income poses a barrier to freenet participation, although a portion of these low-income earners could be students).

Regional councillor Diane Holmes has remarked that the unrepresentativeness of the FreeNet decreases its utility, because she cannot reach a substantial portion of her constituents.[5] At the administrative level, unrepresentativeness was highlighted when the human resources department of the RMOC wished to upload information for single mothers. The department had to consider the utility of making this information available electronically when its potential to reach its target audience was questionable.

Far from being inaccessible for certain people, the FreeNet has actually *enabled* some people to participate and to access government more easily. This was highlighted when a disabled constituent thanked the RMOC for going on-line: the FreeNet is a lifeline for this individual who cannot visit government offices in person.

A second challenge for municipalities on-line relates to the expectations of FreeNet users. They tend to be more demanding, expecting answers to their questions far more promptly than users of traditional media like the telephone or mail. Perhaps because a message can be posted in seconds, a user expects an answer should be posted just as quickly. However, it can take a week or ten days – even longer, in some cases – for an answer to be posted, given that a question or comment is "bounced" around, first to the appropriate department (where it can change hands several times), then back to the corporate communications division. Neither the RMOC nor the City of Ottawa has accorded electronic requests any special treatment over other forms of communication, and this is made known to FreeNet users when they enter the "Question and Comments" section. In order to placate those who have posted messages, both the RMOC and the city send electronic mail messages to users as an assurance that their concerns are being addressed.

A curious disadvantage is the potential for negative publicity resulting from criticism of the "darker side" of the Internet. This was experienced by both the City of Ottawa and the RMOC, when a local newspaper tarred both governments with the same brush it used to tar the Internet. The incident involved DeathNet, a network created by the Right to Die Society of Canada. This network, accessible through the NCF, provides information on how to commit suicide. The newspaper linked local government use of the FreeNet to this story in what appeared to have been an attempt to create a negative image of local governments that go on-line.[6]

The aforementioned difficulties are likely to dissipate over time. The language barrier is being overcome and, as the FreeNet continues to increase in popularity, so likely will its financial support, enabling it to increase its carrying capacity. Similarly, local governments that currently are not located close to a freenet will likely find one coming to their area very shortly. The list of Canadian freenets is growing by leaps and bounds, with several dozen having been established during the last several years and many more in the works at the time of writing.[7] In addition, as the use of information and communication technologies expands, the demographics of users will increasingly represent the population at large. As Canadians' use and awareness of these technologies grow, the less likely objectionable activities on the Internet will be linked to the on-line activities of local governments.

A final difficulty bearing close examination is the political resistance to going on-line. While councillors have been supportive of FreeNet use by their civic administrators, they themselves – with a few exceptions – resist efforts that encourage them to establish an electronic presence. At the RMOC, only half of the eighteen-member council has FreeNet accounts and, of these, only five are active on-line. The others set up the menus by which their constituents can access them, but they do not upload information regularly, update it regularly, or respond to citizen postings. Even the regional chair and the mayor of Ottawa, despite their financial support of the FreeNet and their promotion of high-tech industry, have resisted the efforts of municipal administrators to get them on-line. Ottawa's mayor has previously stated that she has not gone on-line, because she believes that citizens have no difficulty accessing her by traditional means of communication and because she believes she would not have the time that participation would require.[8]

At the City of Ottawa, staff made a concerted effort to sell the idea to councillors. They highlighted the FreeNet's potential as a channel for information dissemination (e.g., notices could be posted about community meetings and events) and as an electronic forum, where they could discuss political issues with constituents, where they could advance their position on issues, and where they could probe constituents about their positions on issues. Administrators even recommended a menu that councillors could use. This menu included a legal description of the councillor's ward and its demographics and composition (to be uploaded by region staff), a section called "Who's your Councillor" (for biographical information, telephone number, facsimile number, etc.), a "Questions and Comments" section, and a section for ward events and meetings. Councillors were directed to check the "Questions and Comments" section twice a week and to ensure that queries were addressed. Despite this effort, Ottawa councillors (with a few exceptions) have been less than active on the FreeNet. As mentioned, some councillors do not attend to their "Questions and Comments" sections and fail to keep electronic information up to date. FreeNet users have posted complaints about councillor apathy to the main "Questions and Comments" section, but councillors have been slow to change.

The only time politicians at both the regional and city levels were participating more enthusiastically was during election campaigns. During the 1994 municipal elections, the NCF launched the Municipal Elections Project to provide "a forum for information and discussion, concerning candidates."[9] While background information on all candidates was uploaded, the highlight was an interactive, unmoderated electronic discussion, where citizens could post questions to candidates. As politicians realized that their competitors were on-line, they took a much greater interest in electronic communication. Even so, many did not get involved, and the interest that was sparked among many victorious candidates fizzled out after the elections.

Politicians point to the small percentage of the population on-line, a lack of time, or their limited access to the FreeNet as reasons for their resistance. Councillors raise a good point with regard to the first reason, because, as mentioned, FreeNet membership does not mirror the general population. In addition, the number of registered FreeNet users represents a small percentage of the area's population. The second reason that relates to apathy and to lack of time may be a weaker argument. Staff in both municipalities estimate that it would require several hours per week for a councillor's office to attend to this additional forum. While this may still represent an onerous time commitment for politicians whose schedules are already overflowing, it could translate into a time-savings if councillors are able to communicate with their constituents more effectively and more successfully (e.g., on-line announcements of upcoming events, a "Frequently Asked Questions" section, responding to citizen electronic inquiries at the councillor's convenience rather than through interruptive telephone calls, and informally bouncing policy ideas via the FreeNet). The third justification for not using the FreeNet – limited access – is also a weak argument, because councillors can overcome this problem inexpensively by using a very small portion of their discretionary office budget to upgrade their computer equipment.

These reasons for non-use conceal what is more likely at the heart of political dislike of electronic forums: technophobia and political rationality. A number of individuals interviewed in the course of this research suggested that technophobia is a significant barrier to political participation on the FreeNet. Councillors tend to perceive the technology as a tool they *have* to use rather than a tool they *want* to use. Many have minimal computer experience, and, even though the FreeNet is user-friendly, councillors don't feel confident enough to use it. This difficulty applies to their staff members as well and indicates that training is a necessary prerequisite for the successful launch of an on-line initiative at the political level.

But training is not enough. Even with technical training, councillors may still resist the new technology for political reasons. Some are reluctant to provide another avenue through which their constituents can access them. Councillors are already extremely busy, pulled in many different directions by a multitude of competing interests, and they do not want another medium through which more demands can be made on them. In addition, some councillors perceive the medium as too public – one councillor participating during the election campaign was flabbergasted to learn that he could not delete citizen postings portraying him unfavourably. Lacking the capacity to censor postings that could be read by all users, this politician was not eager to become involved again. The medium's openness may also cause resistance, because, unlike a telephone call where there are only two parties involved (councillor and constituent) and no record is made, electronic communications can be viewed by all constituents and, because they are text-based, leave a permanent record.

A POLITICAL SCIENCE PERSPECTIVE: IS GOING ON-LINE A CHANGE IN LOCAL GOVERNANCE?

Many have pointed out that the growing number of local governments that are on-line represents a move towards electronic democracy: "an emerging concept of using information and telecommunication technologies ... to enhance, strengthen, and enable [society] to carry out the functions of governance."[10] Based on the evidence in the previous section, one can certainly say this is true from the perspective of improved client service and increased efficiency of service delivery. However, service functions are not the only "functions of local governance." Another aspect of governance, arguably of greater importance, is the task of determining the way ahead, identifying those issues a community wants to confront, and arriving at socially acceptable, feasible and implementable solutions. In this "steering" function, computer-mediated communications can play a catalytic role. They offer a rich medium for citizen participation in the local governance process. This section explores this potential and examines to what extent local governments are seizing this opportunity.

Computer-mediated communications (CMC) as a medium of communication between governments and their citizens will grow dramatically in importance. Bruce Kirschner posits that this growth is fuelled by the decreasing cost of computer hardware, the growing number of homes owning computers with communications capabilities, the growth rate of computer literacy, and the limited time citizens have to interact with their governments.[11]

As CMC grows, it can alter the way in which citizens participate in the governance process. Those who lament the withering of democratic values often point to "[t]he absence ... of mechanisms and forums for the dissemination, sharing, and understanding of complex issues and diverse opinions."[12] Computer-mediated communications answers this cry by providing a "virtual" public forum to reinvigorate democratic debate, compromise and consensus. It overthrows the "one-to-many" paradigm of mass communication, where a single, centralized information provider sends a message to a wide, passive audience. It replaces this unidirectional, interactionless communication with a "many-to-many" model of communication, where power is distributed equally among all parties. With CMC, institutions and individuals can hold two-way conversations with a wide audience. Electronic mail, listservers, and newsgroups enable simultaneous communication between numerous individuals separated in both time and space. The opportunities that this holds for citizen participation in local government affairs are remarkable. Newsgroups could be used to discuss any community issue, local governments could float policy ideas in these forums, and citizens, through dialogue, could flag local issues meriting government attention.

In the City of Santa Monica, California, CMC has been used in precisely this way. Santa Monica established its own community network (one of the only government-operated community networks in the United

States), the Public Electronic Network (PEN). The network holds "conferences" on topics from planning and land-use to homelessness. One success story resulted from the communication between homeless citizens (who participated by using public-access terminals) and their better-off counterparts in the community. The increased awareness of the difficulties faced by homeless citizens led to the establishment of new facilities to meet the needs of these members of the community more effectively.

On-line cooperation to achieve common goals has also occurred closer to home. The Public Advisory Council on Information Highway Policy project was recently undertaken by Canadian citizens concerned about the lack of public input into the deliberations of the federal government's Information Highway Advisory Council (IHAC). These citizens started an on-line lobbying effort in the can.infohighway newsgroup. The project enjoyed considerable success, with bulletins outlining the participants' concerns being well received at monthly meetings of IHAC and with IHAC monitoring the newsgroup to gain a sense of public opinion on the policy issues with which it grapples.

With these positive stories in mind, this chapter surveys the on-line strategies of local governments in Canada (for a listing of freenets surveyed, see Appendix B). The pioneers of this sort of research in the American context are K. Kendall Guthrie and William H. Dutton. They highlight the importance of design when studying the nature of a local government's electronic presence: "one can view the adoption and design of a community information system as a process comparable to legislating public policy on citizen participation."[13] The architecture of the system determines *whether* citizens have the opportunity to participate in local government affairs and what the *scope* of this opportunity will be.

In comparing different systems, Guthrie and Dutton make a useful distinction between *broadcast* and *interactive* systems. The former refers to the use of the technology as a medium of mass communication, where a local government, as the centre of communication power, "broadcasts" information to citizens. Opportunity for public participation in this model is non-existent. The latter refers to a CMC model, where interaction between government and citizen, and between citizen and citizen, is emphasized. In this chapter, another distinction will be made. This is to further separate the interactive model into two components. The first is interaction of the "Questions and Comments" style, which is characterized by *bilateral communication* between a local government (either politicians or administrators) and its citizens; it is based mostly on citizen queries and comments. Citizens can participate, but the scope of participation (in terms of influencing policy outcomes) is limited – substantive policy issues are not addressed in a coherent, comprehensive or focused manner. The second component is *multidirectional interaction*, involving communication between local governments and citizens, and among citizens themselves, where the topics of discussion are substantive policy issues. In multidirectional interaction, the extent of participation ranges from consultation to sharing of decision-making power. The Santa Monica discussion group focusing on the homeless is an example of multidirectional interaction.

Table 1 outlines the activities of Canadian local governments in each of these categories (broadcasting and bilateral communication are further broken down into communication at the political or administrative level). As the table shows, the on-line activities of Canadian local governments do not bode well for the use of CMC as a tool to reinvigorate democracy and enhance public participation. One can readily observe that activities are dominated by broadcasting. While the provision of information is a useful and important function of local government, "[e]lectronic democracy means more than accessing data files. It should provide a new avenue to public participation in government – a sharing of information and ultimately a sharing of power."[14]

The work of Guthrie and Dutton sheds some light on the reasons why broadcasting dominates the local government on-line scene. They point out that an important determinant of a system's architecture is the goals of its designers. In the case of the City of Ottawa and the Regional Municipality of Ottawa-Carleton, these designers were predominantly corporate communications officers. Because of the public-relations environment in which they work, they may have been more inclined to develop a broadcast or bidirectional model of communications.

A further point, one that does not emerge from Table 1, relates to political involvement. While Table 1 suggests that politicians are generally active, this is a faulty conclusion. As was pointed out in the previous section, it is only *some* municipal politicians who are on-line. This is discouraging news. Guthrie and Dutton, Kirschner, and Costis Toregas believe that CMC initiatives *must* be led by the political level in order to live up to their potential as virtual public forums: "Our elected officials must become involved early on in all facets of this technology. If representation and connectivity to the resident are to be enhanced, they must be part of it and indeed lead the charge. If their representational function is undermined and confused, ominous and negative results are ensured."[15] This points to a potentially dismal future for computer-mediated public participation.

But local governments should not be given bad marks too hastily. The RMOC, for example, tried to involve citizens electronically in the review of its official plan. It established an unmoderated discussion area where

Table 1. *Nature of Local Government On-Line Presence*

Location*	Broadcasting		Bilateral communication		Multilateral communication
	Admin.	Political	Admin.	Political	
Bedford, N.S.	X				
City of Edmonton, Alta.	X	X			
City of Halifax, N.S.	X	X			
City of Ottawa, Ont.	X	X			
City of Prince George, B.C.	X	X	X		
City of Saskatoon, Sask.	X			X	
City of Toronto, Ont.	X	X			
City of Vancouver, B.C.	X	X			
Dartmouth, N.S.		X			
District of Squamish, B.C.		X		X	
Gloucester, Ont.	X	X			
Metro Authority, N.S.	X				
Metropolitan Toronto, Ont.	X	X			
Regional District of Fraser-Fort George, B.C.		X		X	
Regional Municipality of Ottawa-Carleton, Ont.	X	X	X	X	
Town of Halton Hills, Ont.	X	X			X
Winnipeg, Man.	X	X			

*Location names are listed as they appear on-line.

Other local governments who were in the midst of going on-line at the time of writing: City of Calgary, Fort Erie, Halifax County, Municipality of Rockyview, Niagara Falls, Niagara-on-the-Lake, Regina, Resort Municipality of Whistler, Squamish-Lillooet Regional District, St. Catharines, Village of Pemberton, and Welland.

citizens could communicate with one another about different components of the plan (e.g., transportation, water and waste-water) and, in so doing, opened a window for the region to see the issues as perceived by the electorate. The effort, however, enjoyed little success. Few citizens participated. The low participation rate stems from a characteristic of public-network users: they are highly sensitive to ownership issues. If they perceive that an electronic forum is dominated by its creator, it is not legitimate in their eyes. Domination can manifest itself in attempts to direct discussion, to dictate how discussion should proceed, or to limit the issues open to debate. Users abhor efforts to control them; they tend to be ardent believers in free speech and are mistrustful of those in positions of authority. In this case, the region tried to control users by telling them how discussions should proceed, and users rebelled. Users made a point of refusing to participate in the region's discussion area, abandoning it in favour of a forum they established for themselves. Interestingly, the region began monitoring this second area, and many of the ideas it contained found their way into regional documents. Learning did occur.

This case opens a new door for public participation: monitoring ongoing electronic discussions. Rather than structuring a formal arena or avenue for participation, local governments can readily survey the attitudes of interested members of the community by observing existing discussions. This provides a quick, cost-free and convenient sense of public opinion. It can also, however, be a parochial sampling of public opinion. In order to broaden the opinion base, local governments must simultaneously structure their own electronic participation forums. Because of sensitivities about ownership, this will be a difficult but necessary task if local governments are to capture the full potential of CMC.

Computer-mediated communications provide a participation forum unlike any other. First, citizens can interact with each other and with local governments at their convenience. Parties separated in both time and space can debate complex issues in a shared forum. Second, computer-mediated public participation widens the participant base. Those who would otherwise be physically unable to attend meetings can do so electronically, and those who are uncomfortable with speaking in public can communicate without fear. Third, CMC can increase the quality of citizen input. Participants can take time to organize their thoughts on paper before they post them and can take time to absorb others' postings, rather than giving knee-jerk reactions to statements with which they disagree. Finally, CMC leaves a written record of proceedings, obviating the need to invest time in compiling public input.

In order to overcome the ownership issue, governments must create on-line forums that are not control-oriented ("big 'O' ownership") but that are stripped down to bare administration. This "small 'o' ownership" means performing only those administrative tasks necessary to implement and maintain the discussion area, such as constructing the forum and responding to participant requests (e.g., writing and posting a "frequently asked questions," or FAQs, file; posting information users want to access). It is only through "small 'o' ownership" that computer-mediated public participation will stand a chance of success.

CONCLUDING REMARKS

Stronger embrace of on-line communication for administrative purposes rather than for policy discussion emerges from this review. It would be hasty, however, to conclude that the potential for improved public participation has been lost. The current state of affairs is better seen as a period of experimentation with these new technologies rather than as a trajectory that will leave computer-mediated public participation behind. The more CMC becomes ubiquitous in social relations, the more political resistance to this method of communication will be overcome – councillors will become more receptive to going on-line, as the number of their constituents on-line increases and as they learn more about these new technologies.

Whether greater citizen involvement in local governance by way of computers will come to pass is a question that can only be answered by time. Constructing credible computer-mediated public-participation initiatives will be challenging but worth the effort, given the advantages of this form of public input and the growing use of CMC. In the meantime, local governments can make gains in efficiency by using computer networks to distribute information and communicate bilaterally with their citizens.

This study suggests the following to local governments considering going on-line:

- *It is not necessary to reinvent the wheel.* Other local governments have paved the way for computer-mediated access to municipalities. Be aware, however, that much of the experience to date involves using local freenets as tools to broadcast the activities of local government and to respond to citizen inquiries. Community computer networks have not been used extensively as a medium for citizen empowerment. Regardless of the purpose or purposes for going on-line, the architecture of the system put in place will determine whether citizens have the opportunity to participate in local government affairs and what the scope of this opportunity will be.

- *Consider the implications of the technology.* There are issues related to access to computer networks, to the dominant language of communication (English), and to the tendency for users not to represent the population at large. It is equally important to be attentive to future developments, which will alter the nature of access and use.

- *Citizens who currently use freenets to interact with their local governments have certain expectations, some of which may be unrealistic.* These include the presumption that responses to citizen queries will be instantaneous and that the municipality will not insert itself as a moderator, selecting which queries and comments receive broad dissemination. Dealing with these and other expectations suggests the need for local governments to be careful in setting the "rules of the game" regarding computer-mediated communications, both by making rules explicit and by being open to changing them, as familiarization with this type of communication and technology evolves.

- *Different actors have different needs, within local government.* It is important to recognize the different needs and perspectives of politicians and staff regarding computer-mediated communication with citizens and public participation more generally.

Appendix A

A PAPER DEMONSTRATION OF THE RMOC ON-LINE

<<< The National Capital FreeNet – Main Menu >>>

1 About the National Capital FreeNet...
2 Administration...
3 Post Office...
4 Public Discussion...
5 Social Services, Health and Environment Centre...
6 Community Associations...
7 The Government Centre...
8 Science, Engineering and Technology Centre...
9 Schools, Colleges and Universities...
10 The Newsstand...
11 Libraries...
12 Special Interest Groups...
13 Communications Centre...
14 Professional Associations...

15 Help Desk...
16 Menu principal francais...
17 Make a donation to keep FreeNet free
---
h=Help, x=Exit FreeNet, p=previous, u=up, m=main
Your Choice ==> 7

<<< THE GOVERNMENT CENTRE >>>

1 About the Government Centre
2 The Regional Municipality of Ottawa-Carleton...
3 The City of Ottawa...
4 The City of Gloucester...
5 The Police...
6 Ontario East Municipalities/Community Profiles...
7 The Rideau Valley Conservation Authority...
8 Federal Government / le gouvernement federal...
9 Ontario Government Information Service...
10 Federal Politics...
11 Embassies of Other Countries...
12 Inter-Government Projects...
13 LobbyNet...
14 National Capital FreeNet Municipal Elections Project...
---
h=Help, x=Exit FreeNet, p=previous, u=up, m=main

Your Choice ==> 2

aa303
<<< THE REGIONAL MUNICIPALITY OF OTTAWA-CARLETON >>>
(go rmoc)

1 About the Regional Municipality of Ottawa-Carleton...
2 Service Directory (phone numbers)
3 Regional Council...
4 Regional Committees (Weekly Agendas, Motions and Decisions from meetings)
5 Regional Departments...
6 Information of Interest for Business (tender contracts)...
7 Public Meetings, Notices, Hearings, etc. ...
8 Press Releases...
9 Questions & Comments >>>

10 The Newsletters...
11 Events at Ottawa-Carleton Centre
12 Traffic Update
13 Regional Planning Initiatives...
14 Ottawa-Carleton Entrepreneurship Centre...
----
h=Help, x=Exit FreeNet, p=previous, u=up, m=main

Your Choice ==> 9

Welcome to the regional government of Ottawa-Carleton Questions and Comments section.

The Information and Public Affairs Office who coordinates FreeNet accesses the network on a daily basis to see if any questions or comments have been received. Upon receipt of a query or comment an acknowledgement and / or reply will be given. Should further consultation with the regional departments be required, the request will be forwarded to the appropriate department for response. As soon as a answer is received, the Information and Public Affairs Department will post/reply to the demand.

Si vous desirez posez des questions ou faire des commentaires en francais soyez assurer que nous vous repondra en francais.

   1 Questions and Comments (ncf.government.rmoc) >>>
----
h=Help, x=Exit FreeNet, p=previous, u=up, m=main

Your Choice ==> 1

The first article is #17, last article is #423.
**17. Refrigerator and refrigerant disposal   Sandy Shaw
   19. Freenet and Gloucester   Charles E. Hunt
   20. Bikeway Survey   Al Crosby
   21. Leitrim Road south of airport   Jules E. Lafrance
   22. Contracts/tenders   Mike Lynch
   23. Needle-exchange program   Jeff Godard
   24. Hunt Club extension   John R. Elliot
   26. Re: Contracts/tenders   Josee Michaud

27. Re: Needle-exchange program   Josee Michaud
28. Directory of high-tech companies   Jacques LeBoeuf
29. Homelands Multicultural festival   Walter Brown
30. Re: Hunt Club Extension   Josee Michaud
31. Re: Directory of high-tech companies   Josee Michaud
32. OMFAC address change   Walter Brown
33. Toxic Waste disposal   George Tillman
34. Re: Toxic Waste disposal   Josee Michaud
----
c=contribute a new article
n=read next unread article
s=read next unread article with same subject
h=help, list of additional commands
q=quit
Enter Command: 30

Article #30 (423 is last):
Newsgroups: ncf.government.rmoc
From: aa303@freenet.carleton.ca (Josee Michaud)
Subject: Re: Hunt Club Extension
Reply to: aa303@freenet.carleton.ca (Josee Michaud)
Date: Mon Jul 19 09:18:17 1993

In a previous article af990@freenet.carleton.ca (John R. Elliott):

> I would like to know when the portion of Hunt Club Rd. between
> Merivale and Woodroffe is to be complete.
>
> --
> John R. Elliott af990freenet.carleton.ca

The Construction of the Hunt Club Road extension between Merivale Road and Woodroffe Avenue, will begin in mid July 1993.

Due to the size and complexity of this project, not all the work will be completed before the winter arrives. However, weather permitting every effort will be made to open at least two lanes of the new roadway to through traffic by end of 1993. This will eliminate cut-through traffic through nearby residential communities, especially Tanglewood-Hillsdale.

Construction work will be completed by July 1994. The planting of trees according to the master landscaping plan, as approved by the National Capital Commission, will take place in the Spring of 1994, depending on construction progress and weather conditions.

If you have any questions about the project, please feel free to contact any of the individuals listed below.

Jamal Toeg, P. Eng., Projct Manager, 560-6011, ext. 1276

Brian Murray, Project Supervisor, 225-0856

Dan O'Keefe, Assistant Project Supervisor, 225-0856

The general contractor for this project is Wimpey Minerals Canada Ltd. of Nepean. The contractor's construction manager is M.J. (Mike) Larkin, 829-1770.

--
Josee Michaud, aa303
Information and Public Affairs, RMOC
Information et relations publiques, MROC

Appendix B

Freenets Visited

Calgary Free-Net

CIAO! (Trail, British Columbia)

Edmonton Free-Net

Free-Net de Montréal

Great Plains Free-Net (Regina, Saskatchewan)

Greater Kingston CommunityNet

Halton Community Network (Oakville, Ontario)

HOMEtown Community Network (London, Ontario)

Manitoba Blue Sky Freenet

Newfoundland Free-Net (including Cornerbrook FreeNet and St. John's InfoNET)

Niagara Peninsula Free-Net

Prince George Free-Net

Saskatoon Free-Net

Sea-to-Sky (Squamish and Whistler, British Columbia)

Chebucto Free-Net (Halifax, Nova Scotia)

Toronto Free-Net

Vancouver Regional Free-Net Association

Yarmouth FreeNet

NOTES

1. City of Ottawa interdepartmental correspondence to departments heads from the chief administrative officer, 10 May 1993.
2. Jay Weston. Interview, 14 March 1995.
3. The public-access terminal at the RMOC became so popular with a small group of citizens, that city staff began kindheartedly referring to these individuals as "FreeNuts."
4. A.S. Patrick, A. Black and T.E. Whalen, *Rich, Young, Male, Dissatisfied Computer Geeks? Demographics and Satisfaction From the National Capital FreeNet* (Ottawa: Communications Research Centre, Department of Industry, 1995).
5. Councillor Holmes made this statement at a presentation to a Master's-level class in urban and local government management at Carleton University's School of Public Administration, 30 January 1995.
6. It is also worth mentioning that the newspaper neglected to report that users of DeathNet must wait three months before receiving information on how to commit suicide and that this information is freely available from any local library.
7. Joe Clark, "Free-Nets aim to plug in anyone with yen to browse," *The Globe and Mail* 21 March 1995, p. C3.
8. Karyn Wichers, "Governments and Free-Nets: Implications for Democracy in the 21st Century," *Working Papers in Public Access Networks*, Carleton University.
9. National Capital FreeNet (file = government/munelect/about/about.txt).
10. Costis Toregas, "Electronic Democracy: Some Definitions and a Battle Cry," *Public Management* 71, no. 11 (November 1989), p. 2.

11 Bruce Kirschner, "Going On-Line: A Guide for Local Governments," *Public Management* 75, no. 1 (January 1993), pp. 12–15.
12 Henry Cisneros and John Parr, "Reinvigorating Democratic Values: Challenge and Necessity," *Public Management* 73, no. 2 (February 1991), p. 4.
13 K. Kendall Guthrie and William H. Dutton, "The Politics of Citizen Access Technology: The Development of Public Information Utilities in Four Cities," *Policy Studies Journal* 20, no. 4 (Winter 1992), pp. 574–97.
14 Judy Weiss, "Pasadena's Two-Tiered Technology," *Public Management* 71, no. 11 (November 1989), p. 11.
15 Toregas, "Electronic Democracy," *Public Management*, p. 3.

11

Conclusion: From Public Participation to Citizen Engagement

Susan D. Phillips and Katherine A. Graham

Public participation is undergoing a fundamental reappraisal by local governments. Ongoing innovations in the practices of participation are attempting to replace static and "thin" participation with more deliberative and "thick" means of engagement. As a sign of this transition, even our choice of language for how we describe the process of involving the public is changing – from "participation" to "engagement." In order to think about the future, we need to confront the basic question about citizen engagement and local government: Does citizen engagement matter? From an analytical perspective, this question has three issues:

- *Legitimacy*. We need to consider whether public engagement contributes to more informed decision-making in the activities of local government. We noted in Chapter 1 that the role of local government in Canada is changing. Does citizen engagement enhance public consensus about the responsibilities local government should undertake in this new environment and about how it should undertake them? A government with responsibilities but inadequate resources to carry them out lacks full legitimacy. What has the contribution of citizen engagement been towards ensuring that local governments have the necessary fiscal and human resources to carry out their mandate? We ask these questions in the context of the current fiscal challenges facing local government; the trend of other governments to download responsibilities to the local level or to vacate policy fields of keen local interest; and the fuller embrace of a co-production relationship between local governments and their citizens.

- *Capacity*. Does citizen engagement equip local governments to make better decisions than they would otherwise? "Better" is always in the eye of the beholder. It certainly does not always coincide with blindly following public opinion. We can consider, however, whether or not citizen engagement provides local decision-makers with information and views that they would not have otherwise. We can also take into account the extent to which citizen engagement enables decision-makers to develop solid rationales for the decisions they take. Governments' ability to justify policy judgements is not only a sign of capacity; it enhances the legitimacy of governments as well.

The other side of this question is community capacity. An important consideration in assessing whether public participation made a difference is whether it contributed to the development of social capital in both the short and longer term. For example, we can evaluate whether it encouraged the emergence of new leaders and organizations in the community.

- *Vitality.* Does citizen engagement enhance public debate and provide real opportunity for members of the public to influence the policy and planning process between local elections? Those who follow local government in Canada are well aware of the much lower voter turnout for local elections, compared with those at the federal or provincial levels. One of the standard reasons given for this is that local governments are relatively uninteresting and, therefore, are not commonly considered to be battlegrounds for hard-fought elections. This suggestion can be turned on its head, however. We should think about whether the role and responsibilities of local governments in our lives render them the subject of relatively continuous public fomentation and engagement. Perhaps people are more likely to participate in debates about the future of local community centres or the upkeep of local roads *between* local elections than to vote *in* them. These issues are immediate; people want specific and immediate action. Thus, the terrain of local politics is possibly more hotly contested between elections. Do the types of public participation discussed in our case studies enhance the vitality of these inter-election policy debates?

We have concluded that citizen engagement with local government can make a difference. We can learn both from the positive experiences presented in the preceding chapters and from those that are less positive. As citizen-engagement exercises come under increasing scrutiny, in terms of their cost and impact, we need to remember how they can make a difference to the legitimacy, capacity and vitality of local government.

This chapter is intended to reinforce what we have learned from the foregoing. First, this chapter offers some integrative conclusions, based

CONCLUSION: FROM PUBLIC PARTICIPATION TO CITIZEN ENGAGEMENT

on some of the central characteristics of public participation that were presented in Chapter 1. It then turns to two specific issues that emerged as being particularly important in making public engagement effective: who should participate; and how should effective connections be made, at a time when it is more apt to refer to "publics" than to a seemingly monolithic public. We conclude by suggesting, based on what we have learned, the principles and elements for a constructive citizen-engagement process.

THE BASICS REVISITED: CONCLUDING OBSERVATIONS

In Chapter 1, we discussed some of the basic characteristics of public participation. It is useful to return to these to determine the contribution of the case studies to our understanding of these basics.

- *Public participation involves citizens in processes other than those during municipal elections.* Public participation, as we have studied it, does, however, interact with the municipal election process and the casting of individual ballots. We have seen election campaigns put issues on the consultation agenda and serve as a time when incumbents and competitors vie for votes, based on the record of consultation between elections. In the Burlington case, we saw evidence of the interaction of consultation with elections in both ways. Council used citizen surveys to assess whether the positions of anti-tax groups, which were particularly vocal during the campaign, were shared by the general population. The success of the processes used in Burlington became a matter of pride among incumbent candidates at election time. If we look specifically at consultation via the Internet, we should take note of Monica Gattinger's assessment that local politicians are aware, but wary, of the impact of Internet communication on their electoral prospects. We also saw an example of how constructive public participation in the Miramichi case reversed the province's decision not to hold elections for the city's first council. The success of public participation in generating consensus for restructuring in the Miramichi made the province's initial decision to appoint the first council unpalatable for local residents.

- *At a minimum, public participation involves interaction and two-way communication, which entails some potential for influencing policy decisions and outcomes.* Most striking were the exercises that did not have this characteristic. It would be blunt to call the arbitration exercise in the London annexation a charade; but this is what it seems to have been. The public was being encouraged to make representations on matters that the provincial government wanted to decide internally. Related to land-use planning in Toronto and Vancouver, John Sewell described two consultation exercises that were elaborate but disconnected with the local policy process because politicians were not involved. In Edmonton, the various consultation processes seemed to have been more connected with senior administrative officials than with members of council. The intent seemed largely to educate senior staff, particularly the city manager, about the perspectives of various groups, and the general public on budget issues. Edward LeSage noted that Edmonton council took it upon itself to cancel one aspect of the initiative – the public forums – largely on the grounds that council members thought themselves to be adequately in touch with their grass roots.

The district councils in Quebec provide an obvious counterpoint. The Quebec case illustrated the potential influence on city council's policy agenda and decision-making when citizens are empowered to set their own agenda and undertake concrete actions.

– *Public participation involves individuals and groups, either ad hoc groups or more permanent stakeholders.* Come one, come all is a general theme emerging from the cases. This does not, however, imply that public participation will be carried off well or will have a salutary impact on policy if everyone is thrown together. This is such an important point that we will return to it, for more extended discussion, later in this chapter.

There is one final concluding observation about the characteristics of public participation. It is implicit in our earlier exploration of the concept.

– *Public participation is an art, not a science.* At the most fundamental level, the diversity of the cases and the approaches used to encourage participation bears this out. There are also some underlying factors that are worthy of note.

First, public participation in local government occurs in a political environment. Perhaps more than in the federal or provincial context, the ebb and flow of politics at the local level imparts an important dynamic to efforts to engage the public. The political milieu in most Canadian cities is rendered less predictable because of the absence of strong party politics and the strictures of cabinet secrecy and of party discipline generally associated with the British parliamentary system. Linking efforts to have the public engaged with the deliberations and political agendas of municipal councillors *between* elections can present quite a challenge and require artful adaptation. This was perhaps most evident in the Edmonton case.

CONCLUSION: FROM PUBLIC PARTICIPATION TO CITIZEN ENGAGEMENT

The intergovernmental context is also important. In almost half of the cases presented here – Edmonton's budget deliberations, planning in Ontario municipalities, London's annexation, and restructuring in the Miramichi – the operative decision-maker or catalyst for change was the provincial government, even though consultations occurred on a local basis. The potential of local and provincial officials holding different perceptions on the issues and policy prescriptions makes the process and content of public engagement more complex. These differences can be found within both the political and bureaucratic realms.

Techniques of survey research, use of focus groups, citizens committees, the technology of the Internet and town-hall meetings are among the important tools for soliciting public participation. Each of the preceding cases illustrates the use of different techniques. Each technique stands on its own and provides specific "lessons" for others. Ultimately, however, we must remember that the objective of all of these efforts is to inform the judgement of councillors and other decision-makers involved in local governance. As Sir Geoffrey Vickers keenly pointed out, judgement is an art, not a science. Judgement occurs in a context, formed as different individuals interpret "facts," which they see through their own lenses. Efforts to inform judgement or to influence it may involve presenting relatively objective facts and opinions, such as those which can be gleaned by using the techniques of social and administrative science, in the process of public participation. Coming to judgement, however, involves an alchemy that can be strongly influenced by the strategies and techniques associated with public participation but that can never be predetermined by them.[1]

In addition to these integrative conclusions, we can draw some more specific observations from the cases. These observations deal with issues related to the people involved in public participation and with the processes used. They raise some basic questions and strategic choices for local government officials, as they consider the prospect of citizen engagement in an increasingly critical and financially strained environment.

CITIZEN ENGAGEMENT: STRATEGIC CHOICES

If one were to play the traditional word-association game, the phrase "public participation" would probably conjure up the image of town-hall meetings and what Andrew Sancton termed a "joyfully participatory" experience, as in the case of the London annexation arbitration hearings. Our cases suggest a different practical reality. They demonstrate some important features of refining the question "who should participate?" They also illuminate some important and practical suggestions for making connections with the public and about the need to adapt to changing constellations of public interest in a particular issue over time. These "who" and "how" questions underlie the strategic choices to be made at the beginning of any process of citizen engagement and as the process evolves.

Who Should Participate?

One of the most consistent lessons arising from the cases is the importance of thinking very specifically about the different publics involved in an issue and how and when to best involve them. Large numbers of participants may count in some instances, but not always. John Sewell's discussion of the planning exercises in Vancouver and Toronto illustrates the expense and lack of value-added information for planners and the absence of real public engagement in planning issues when the basis on which public sentiment is gauged is too broad. To refine our approach, we offer two interrelated suggestions:

- focus on the nature of different audiences; and

- think specifically about what different audiences can and want to contribute.

Local government officials are often already quite attuned to thinking about differences within the population of their own particular city. Jeff Fielding and Gerry Couture, for example, have detailed the nuances of inner-city publics in Winnipeg. Michael Fenn described the need to gear the questions in Hamilton-Wentworth's citizen survey specifically to the residents living in Hamilton's city core, those living "on the mountain," and those living outside of the City of Hamilton. Jean Dionne and his colleagues point out the importance of different neighbourhood histories, demographics and conditions that influenced the priority issues and activities of the two pilot district councils in Quebec. These differences were reflected in the interaction between the district councils and the city's office of public consultation, as well as with city council. Patrick Smith looked at the different lenses through which diverse communities in the Vancouver region view economic development.

But we can also learn from the differences among the populations in various cities. The interests and availability of the public vis-à-vis local affairs may vary considerably from a commuter suburb to a central city.

Michael Fenn's piece illustrated the need for taking different approaches to engage the public when a large portion of that particular population works outside of the municipality. This speaks to both the need to focus on the nature of the public and the need to reflect on what different populations can and want to contribute.

Our final observations about the nature of participants concern sceptics and vested interests. Both the Winnipeg and Burlington cases showed the wisdom of not excluding the sceptics. In Winnipeg, the consultation processes associated with Plan Winnipeg were greeted with scepticism in some quarters, particularly within the city's business community. The demonstration effect of city officials engaging the business community in good faith earned its constructive participation in Plan Winnipeg, as it progressed. In Burlington, council's Citizens' Budget Advisory Committee intentionally included some of the municipality's sharpest critics. Their discernment was honed by the information and insights the committee gathered, as it worked. The result was well-founded criticism and recommendations that were grounded in the context of what the city would actually be able to achieve, in terms of budget reform. The same two cases illustrate the potentially disruptive role of cynics and sloganeers. Walk away from cynics is what Jeff Fielding and Gerry Couture suggest. Find out if the assertions of sloganeers are well founded, suggests Michael Fenn, who sees anti-tax groups as having played a major role in instigating Burlington's budget review and citizens-survey exercises.

It is equally important to understand the role of so-called "vested interests" in public-policy debates at the local level. In attempts to shape politicians' budget agendas in the Edmonton case, we saw evidence of the tension between efforts to build a "big tent" for public input and the efforts of interest groups representing the business community and a few well-established neighbourhood organizations. Self-described "progressive" councillors had a distaste for these established interests, which were perceived to be dominating budget forums.

Well-established interests will be present, and they will vigorously advocate, but it is important to avoid giving particular vested interests undue advantage. Giving the appearance of being hijacked by particular interests is equally damaging. Andrew Sancton discusses, for example, the in-camera meetings that the provincially appointed arbitrator in the London annexation dispute held with developers and other representatives of the business community. The arbitrator's ultimate admission that these meetings had a "50–50 impact" on his recommendations contributed to the erosion of confidence in a process that was flawed in many other ways. John Robison's discussion of amalgamation in the Miramichi suggests how a provincial government's sensitivity to vested partisan interests influenced its response to an apparently reasonable request for a plebiscite on the amalgamation issue. In this case, the leading proponents of a plebiscite were well-known Conservatives. They were appealing to a Liberal government.

Making Connections

It is one thing to be sensitive to the idea that different segments of the population may have different contributions to make to deliberations on local issues; it is another to actually make the right connections. Generally, our case studies suggest the importance of making contact and drawing in people by meeting them on the paths of their everyday lives. As Monica Gattinger and Edward LeSage suggest, the Internet may give local governments ready-access to regular browsers.

Some of the most important connections, however, were anything but hi-tech. Local media outlets can play a useful role, either as basic bulletin boards or as more engaged players in local debates. Burlington used information spots on the local radio station and media exposure by the mayor to promote participation in its citizens survey. Community cable television played an important role in the GVRD regional planning exercise. The contribution of a more independent role by local media outlets is evident in both the Miramichi and Edmonton cases. In both instances, local newspapers took it upon themselves to inform the public about their opportunity to participate and offered journalistic or editorial opinion on the issues and the public engagement process. John Robison credits the local newspaper in the Miramichi with exemplary initiative in this regard, indicating that the restructuring commission did not make any particular effort to encourage coverage but did benefit from the result. This raises the question of whether it might be useful to develop a specific strategy for media engagement, as part of a broader public-participation initiative. The Vancouver and Toronto cases suggest that mere advertising, while expensive, does not bring stellar results.

Aside from the media, other connections can be particularly important in making first contact and in building the relationship that encourages engagement. Winnipeg's use of public-health nurses to solicit participation by inner-city residents on economic development is particularly imaginative. It might foster other ideas about how to engage people on their own ground. Why not think about using city public transit as a venue for public education and engagement? Perhaps parents sitting in the stands of municipal ice rinks and swimming pools would like to spend part of that time thinking about issues affecting their local community.

CONCLUSION: FROM PUBLIC PARTICIPATION TO CITIZEN ENGAGEMENT

The cost and sparse results of blanketing the public with opportunities for participation suggest that other approaches may be more effective and may meet increasingly straitened municipal budgets. This raises the question of whether there is merit in focusing on "community leaders" as representatives of the public. This seems to have been accomplished quite successfully in the evolution of economic-development strategies in Vancouver and in the Miramichi. The clear requirement, as illustrated in both of these cases, is for a high degree of confidence that community leaders are actually representative of their particular communities and are connecting back to them, while playing their role in policy and planning debates. In the Vancouver context, this seems to have occurred as a matter of tradition, particularly as different ethnic and cultural groups took an interest in economic-development policy. In the Miramichi, the Miramichi Community Advisory Committee, which was fully engaged throughout the restructuring exercise, was selected from nominees provided by municipal councils and community groups in the area. Not only did these people have strong community origins, their nomination implied an obligation to remain active within their communities, as the restructuring process evolved.

If being specific about one's public(s) and engaging people when they are on comfortable ground is axiomatic, are the mass-media techniques of sounding public opinion and communication at all useful? The answer, it seems, is an unequivocal "yes." Again, the Burlington/Hamilton-Wentworth experience with citizen surveys indicates that well-conceived soundings of a relatively large population can be useful. Edward LeSage sees the potential for a similar approach, after evaluating Edmonton's experience with public participation in budget deliberations. Jeff Fielding and Gerry Couture also suggest the utility of a public survey on economic-development issues in Winnipeg as a source of preliminary information to inform further deliberations. It should be remembered, however, that the surveys were actually quite focused, both in terms of the groups sampled and in the nature of the information and opinions solicited.

Another standard tool associated with sounding public views is the focus group. Again, focus groups appear to have some utility, but, as LeSage points out, one must be sensitive to the fact that some segments of the population may be more prevalent among focus-group participants than others. Monica Gattinger also shows the importance of really understanding the demographics of users of a mass, interactive communication technology such as the Internet. For many segments of the population, the word "surf" may still be associated with a name-brand laundry detergent rather than with interactive communication.

231

ELEMENTS OF A CONSTRUCTIVE CITIZEN-ENGAGEMENT PROCESS

We have concluded that there are some basic elements that are inherent in constructive citizen engagement. They are internal to the process itself. It is important to understand, however, that one can have the best process in the world without effect. Certainly, for example, planners in Vancouver and Toronto were trying to mount the best process possible. We must also consider, then, what attributes of public engagement make it effective in a public-policy sense. As Edward LeSage put it, when and how can we make the connection between public engagement and better decision-making by local governments? A constructive citizen-engagement process would have the following components:

- *Purposes should be clearly set out*. The objectives of the process should be made explicit, for local governments and the public. It would be naïve to suggest that objectives will always be explicit or transparent. The multilateral character of many consultation processes and the temptation to obfuscate, particularly when tough decisions are looming, make this a difficult goal to achieve. Nonetheless, it remains important, particularly if we are to quell cynicism about and mistrust of government and politics.

- *Terms of reference should be established for all parties*. The London annexation case provides the starkest demonstration of the need for clear terms of reference for public engagement. Public perception of the role of the arbitrator, appointed to rule on the dispute was quite different from his real mandate and *modus operandi*. The Edmonton case also illustrates the consequences of a drifting process that involved various types of consultation but with little sense of how it was actually connected to the real stuff of budget-making.

  A citizen-engagement process, as we conceive it, involves real engagement, not therapy – it is not intended merely as an opportunity for the public to blow off steam. Furthermore, it is intended to commit local government to more than the token gesture of using participation as a forum for disseminating information to the public, a concern first identified by Sherry Arnstein in her now-classic ladder of participation.[2]

  The following are useful guidelines for thinking about terms of reference. As in a contract, all parties have obligations. It is important for local governments to think through what is expected of the public. This ranges from the amount of time involved, to when and how the public will actually be engaged. It is also important for local governments to be explicit about the limits of engagement. In many cases, criticism may come from those who think that "citizens" (in this context, a code word for their particular interest) should be in the driver's seat. Nonetheless, the preceding cases provide evidence that the public and local officials work together more constructively when there is a recognized prospect of closure and a context for the work that is being done, in terms of ultimate policy decisions. As the Winnipeg experience suggests, public engagement might benefit from fewer "round tables" and more "end tables."

Terms of reference should also deal with the commitment of local governments and of their elected and appointed officials. Specifically, the terms of reference should identify what the municipality will do and how. This relates both to the nature of the process that will be undertaken and to the use that will be made of the public's contribution. Commitment by local government to record and report what it has heard and learned is equally important. There is a real distinction between hearing and learning. Both are important in communicating with the public, if local governments are seeking more transparent policy processes. Local governments can hear views and reject them. In this circumstance, the important thing is to acknowledge diverse views and to make a sound argument for the position finally taken. Ultimately, this can strengthen the legitimacy of local governments' decisions.

– *Flexibility must be inherent.* In most cases, local governments need to be flexible and to adapt their public-engagement initiatives to changing circumstances. The impetus for adaptation can come from two sources. First, local governments may obtain new information as the process proceeds, which prompts them to conceive of the issues at hand in different ways. This can come from either the process of public engagement itself or – as in the two cases dealing with financial decision-making illustrated – from external developments, such as the retrenchment of other governments. In addition, new constellations of public interest may develop around an issue as the engagement process evolves. Changes in the locus of community interest in economic development in the Vancouver area illustrated this phenomenon. Again, flexibility in the engagement process is important to consider, should this occur. "Damn the torpedoes and full speed ahead" is not the best approach in either circumstance.

These are some of the basic elements that we have concluded will set citizen engagement at the local level on the right path. By themselves, however, they are insufficient to make the process effective. There are "big picture" issues in the design of the process that should be considered as we search for effectiveness.

TOWARDS AN EFFECTIVE PROCESS

In his case study, Edward LeSage explored the question of whether citizen engagement in Edmonton's budget deliberations led to better budget decisions. After exploring this question along several dimensions, he concluded that the quality of budget-making was not greatly enhanced by Edmonton's public-input initiative. Andrew Sancton characterized the public consultation in London's annexation bid as a side show. In contrast, Jean Dionne and his colleagues found that the newly established district councils in Quebec did have a salutory effect in shaping Quebec's council agenda and actions. The Miramichi, Burlington/Hamilton-Wentworth, Winnipeg, and Vancouver economic-development case studies also demonstrated a more positive connection between public engagement and outcomes, as did John Sewell in the case of the Ontario Planning Act Review.

There appear to be at least four elements that allow well-conceived engagement process to be plugged into real decision-making and to have the potential to improve the quality of local government decisions:

- *Timing is critical*. One might think that we are advocating the "Goldilocks" approach – not too early and not too late. To some degree, this is true. At least two of our cases showed the consequences of trying to engage the public prematurely. In Edmonton, the engagement process was specifically set at the first phase of the budget-deliberation process: direction-setting. The public was thus excluded from that part of the process when tangible choices were on the table. Similarly, "visioning" exercises accompanying major plan reviews in Toronto and Vancouver yielded little of real use to political decision-makers, because the public was not able to connect platitudinous visions (clean, green and safe) with the hard choices, which were the desired result of the plan reviews. In the Miramichi restructuring, the possibility that there might be final public judgement, in the form of a plebiscite on the amalgamation proposal, did not emerge until very late in the process. Regardless of the provincial government's reasons for rejecting the plebiscite idea, some prior thought should perhaps have been given to public expectations of involvement in the latter stages of the restructuring process.

  The problem of finding the elusive "just right," in terms of timing, is made more difficult by the fact that conditioning and knowledge prepare the public to make different kinds of judgements at different stages in public-policy debates. Daniel Yankelovich argues that there are seven stages, from the awakening of the public to an issue to the time the public can make responsible and informed policy choices.[3] In his view, each stage presents unique constraints and opportunities, in terms of government–public engagement. Many of our cases suggest that there is an interaction between public awareness of an issue and the potentially deepening and changing understanding of desirable policy choices with the learning process that local political and administrative officials are undergoing. This suggests the merits of thinking in terms of a public-engagement process oriented to the peak opportunities in the political decision-making process.

– *Involve the politicians throughout.* Citizen engagement is ultimately a part of politics in the broadest sense of the word. It is also inevitably entangled with the world of practising politicians. John Sewell argues strongly that politicians need to be involved throughout the process of citizen engagement. There are at least two reasons for this. First, is the interactive nature of the learning process, which we have discussed above. Second, is the fact that politicians need to feel a sense of ownership of the process and confidence in it.

The Edmonton case illustrates the consequences of disconnecting politicians from staff-led efforts at public engagement. Politicians rely on their traditional political antennae and can become downright suspicious, if not dismissive, of the engagement process. John Sewell's discussion of the Vancouver and Toronto plan reviews provides further illustration of the consequences of political disengagement.

In contrast, the Miramichi Community Advisory Committee of local politicians and community representatives, who assisted the restructuring team, provides an interesting example of how local politicians, with diverse starting positions, can be fruitfully engaged. The Quebec case is also worth considering in this context. The issue there was how to gain the confidence of city councillors in district councils, over which they had little political control. Building council confidence slowly, through the use of pilot projects, seems to have been effective. Finally, Patrick Smith's discussion of regional economic development in the GVRD points to the merits of considering whether new political forums might best link public views to political decisions. The "council of councils," which met to consider the region's growth strategy is a case in point.

– *Ensure that the politicians buy into the administrators' role.* This is the obverse of creating a political connection. Local government staff have an important function to play in citizen engagement. Their functions extend from developing approaches to engaging the public on specific issues, to being on the front line in the meetings, focus groups, call-in lines, shopping mall sites and home visits, which can emerge as the "arms and legs" of a citizen-engagement strategy.

We discussed the broadening of public participation beyond the land-use planning process in Chapter 1. The case studies attest to the increasing diversity of skills and seniority among municipal staff who are directly involved in designing and executing citizen engagement – from city managers to front-line public-health nurses. We view this as a positive trend that, depending on specific circumstances, will likely continue. Although we can offer no prescriptions on how to do so, we think it important that the respective roles and competencies of various kinds of municipal staff become well established. This may be borne out of experimentation and the demonstration effect. The end result, however, should be a working relationship surrounding public engagement that politicians perceive as efficient and that is effective in terms of the learning process of local politicians, their staff, and of the public, as it comes to judgement.

– *Avoid thinking of citizen engagement as push-button democracy.* It is evident that not all of our case studies illustrate fruitful results. This is true whether we think in terms of "better decisions" or some criterion related to public or political satisfaction with the process of engagement itself. It would, in fact, be quite surprising and somewhat suspicious if the cases were not as mixed as they are. In Chapter 1, we discussed the increasing pressures, from various quarters, for more public involvement in local issues. Nonetheless we speculate that there may be an additional factor, other than financial cost and the perceived weaknesses of past approaches, that might dampen enthusiasm for citizen engagement among local politicians and administrators. It is the pitfall of equating public engagement with erosion of the latitude for political or administrative judgement.

The purpose of citizen engagement is to contribute to better decision-making by local governments, not to reduce their capacity to govern. Even when public engagement involves survey techniques to garner public opinion, local governments are rarely bound by the results, in a legal sense. Furthermore, there may be particular factors that work their way into final decisions. These include the calculus of whether to make judgement on a short-, medium- or long-term basis; assessment of external factors, such as provincial policy or the changing economic outlook; and the sense of momentum and connection among issues that

CONCLUSION: FROM PUBLIC PARTICIPATION TO CITIZEN ENGAGEMENT

may build up between a local council and its senior staff over time. Michael Fenn alludes to the congruence of opinion on servicing issues among council and senior staff that contrasted with the views of rank-and-file staff and members of the public responding to the community survey in Burlington. In this particular case, council and senior staff reformulated their views, in light of the alternative perspective. Presumably, they had confidence in both the process of public engagement and its attendant results, which permitted them to reassess their position in light of everything else that they knew. But they were not bound to follow slavishly "the majority view." What they were bound to do was explain to the public the rationale for the direction they ultimately took. This speaks to the requisites of political representation and accountability. It is important to bear this in mind at a time when we see direct democracy associated with people pushing "yes" or "no" buttons, wired into sporadic "peoples' choice" shows in the electronic media.

– *Think about strategy and learning.* A learning perspective is crucial for a fruitful citizen-engagement process. There is a process of education and adaptation that should accompany the process for both local officials and the attentive public. This may seem trite; but we think it is important to make this explicit, especially in light of the accompanying prerequisites that citizen engagement be well planned and have a visible framework. These latter attributes can impart the quality of a forced march to public engagement, unless they rest on a social-learning foundation. The first thing to realize is that our perception of a problem will shape the process we design. As we proceed, our understanding of the problem may change. At that time, flexibility and adaptation of the citizen-engagement process and, possibly, revision of the planning and policy options being considered become the watchwords.

FROM PUBLIC PARTICIPATION TO CITIZEN ENGAGEMENT: FINAL THOUGHTS

In writing this conclusion, we have gradually and intentionally replaced the term "public participation" with the phrase "citizen engagement." We have done this for two reasons. First, we think that the term "public participation" has fallen into disrepute. It has become what Stephen Brooks has called one of the plastic words of democracy, words that have moral connotations and the effect of precluding open debate.[4] Beginning in Chapter 1, we saw the origins of cynicism and distrust in local government officials and the public surrounding efforts at public participation. In some of the case studies, most notably those dealing with the London annexation and Edmonton's budgeting process, we saw ample evidence to support this perspective. In most of the other cases, initial scepticism and distrust had to be overcome. Public participation conjures up the image of many players taking the field but few really playing the game.

More positively, we think that the term "citizen engagement" helps us to re-conceive the process as one that involves two-way obligations on the part of local governments and their citizens, which is an ongoing practice of how civic business is conducted. We suggested earlier the merits of considering the process of engagement and its end results in terms of a contract. Contracts are not fundamentally about litigation or rancour. They are intended to provide an identifiable foundation for trust and the regularization of relationships. Also, the parties to a contract actually have to do things – they have to get into the game. This is why the term "citizen engagement" is apt. It rids us of many of the negatives associated with the past and starts us thinking in terms of solid footings.

Principles for Citizen Engagement

Just as the case studies failed to reveal any cookie-cutter approach to constructive citizen engagement, we cannot offer one in the abstract. The basic contingencies of needing to understand the issues or context for engagement, the nature of the public(s) to be engaged, and constraints related to timing and finance are too powerful. In the spirit of "food for thought," however, we do suggest six principles that might inform development of citizen-engagement initiatives at the local level.

- *The process should be community-based.* The process should be conceived in terms of the communities involved. The conception of "community" need not conform to municipal or district boundaries or to the sometimes-standard distinction between business and resident interests. There are many other ways of conceiving community that may be relevant in particular cases.

- *Citizen engagement should be connected to the political process.* It should directly involve elected officials and be linked to the working agendas of council and senior staff. This will enhance the likelihood that city hall will really "buy into" the process and will use the results constructively.

- *Citizen engagement should also involve public education.* To put the process in context and to help the public come to judgement, the process needs to start with educating the public about the need for change. This will lay the groundwork for citizen engagement in the development and assessment of options.

- *The process should be open regarding the options considered and emphasized.* It sometimes seems like a standard operating procedure that governments display a fixed number of policy or planning options before the public. (Three is often the number of choices proffered.) Public input is then sought regarding "the best." This effectively stunts the capacity of citizens and local officials to break the mental binders associated with limiting choices in this way. At the same time, practicality suggests that citizens find it difficult to deal with a completely empty policy or planning horizon.

  What is needed is a process that first informs the public about the environment in which choices will be made. This is a central element of the public-education component identified above. But, it involves considerable work on the part of local governments. The challenge then is to harness public knowledge and energy in thinking about options and the best way ahead. Absorbing the information proffered and doing the hard intellectual work of thinking through options are important elements of the public's obligation to deliberate. The approach to doing this will vary significantly from process to process.

- *There is need for flexibility regarding methods of engagement and timing.* This principle speaks to the need for variation in the approaches used, depending on the particular circumstances of engagement. It also, however, alludes to the need to adapt the process, as it evolves. Citizen engagement does not imply a forced march. It does imply collaborative learning between local officials and the engaged public, which may modify and improve the process itself in mid-stream.

- *The process should be transparent.* Information about the nature of the engagement process and its progress should be promulgated from the start and emerge throughout. Any substantive conclusions should also be disseminated, along with information about why these are the conclusions that have emerged. There are a number of reasons for this. First, a transparent process will become more inclusive, as new or previously obscure communities of interest emerge and contribute to the deliberations. Second, it carries more weight, in terms of public and political legitimacy, when it reaches fruition. Finally, a transparent process will contribute to accumulated social learning about citizen engagement generally and will inform subsequent experience.

Much of this study-team's work focused on the specific cases that comprise most of this volume. We hope, however, that readers will not become case-bound and think that citizen engagement is "an event" or a tributary to the main flow of government activity. Instead, we argue that citizen engagement between elections has become one of the underpinnings of our democratic life. A principled approach to citizen engagement has the potential to improve the quality of our politics and public administration by encouraging a process whereby citizens, politicians and public servants educate each other and engage in constructive and purposeful dialogue. This will have a salutary effect on government decision-making and on the level of debate and the choices made, by citizens and politicians alike, both at election time and in between.

NOTES

1 Sir Geoffrey Vickers, *The Art of Judgement* (Thousand Oaks, Calif.: Sage Publications, 1993).
2 Sherry Arnstein, "A Ladder of Citizen Participation," *Journal of the American Institute of Planners* 35, no. 4 (July 1969), pp. 216–24.
3 Daniel Yankelovich, *Coming to Public Judgement: Making Democracy Work in a Complex World* (Syracuse, N.Y.: Syracuse University Press, 1991); also Daniel Yankelovich, "How Public Opinion Really Works," *Fortune* 5 October 1992, pp. 102–108.
4 Stephen Brooks, "How Ottawa Bends: Plastic Words and the Politics of Social Morality," in Susan D. Phillips, ed., *How Ottawa Spends 1994–95: Making Change*. Carleton Public Policy Series No. 16 (Ottawa: Carleton University Press, 1994), p. 73.

Contributors

Gerry Couture is coordinator of long-range planning for the City of Winnipeg. He also has recently completed his term as president of the Canadian Institute of Planners.

Jean Dionne est directeur du Bureau de consultation publique, Ville de Québec.

Céline Faucher est membre du personnel du Bureau de consultation publique, Ville de Québec.

Michael Fenn is chief administrative office, Regional Municipality of Hamilton-Wentworth

Jeff Fielding is manager of strategic planning for the City of Winnipeg.

Monica Gattinger is an alumna of the School of Public Administration, Carleton University.

Katherine Graham is a faculty member in the School of Public Administration, Carleton University.

Edward LeSage is director of public administration studies, Faculty of Extension at the University of Alberta.

André Martel est membre du personnel du Bureau de consultation publique, Ville de Québec.

Susan Phillips is a faculty member in the School of Public Administration, Carleton University.

CONTRIBUTORS

John Robison is city manager of the Town of Flamborough, Ontario, and former director of the Municipal Review Panel of the Government of New Brunswick.

Andrew Sancton is a faculty member in the Department of Political Science and director of the local government program at the University of Western Ontario.

John Sewell is a consultant and columnist on urban affairs in Toronto. He was mayor of Toronto from 1978 to 1980 and chair of Ontario's Commission on Planning and Development Reform.

Patrick Smith is a faculty member in the Institute of Governance Studies and the Department of Political Science at Simon Fraser University.

MONOGRAPHS ON CANADIAN PUBLIC ADMINISTRATION

MONOGRAPHIES SUR L'ADMINISTRATION
PUBLIQUE CANADIENNE

Iain Gow, Paul Pross
Co-directeurs / Co-editors

This monograph series is sponsored by the Institute of Public Administration of Canada as part of its continuing endeavour to stimulate and publish writing in the field of Canadian public administration. It is intended to be a complement to other publications sponsored by the Institute such as the Canadian Public Administration Series, the magazine *Public Sector Management*, the journal *Canadian Public Administration* and the Case Program in Canadian Public Administration, as well as the proceedings of its public policy seminars. By launching the monograph series for medium-length manuscripts and those of a more specialized nature, the Institute ensures that there is a wide variety of publication formats for authors in public administration. While the first titles were in the area of urban local government, the series is intended to cover the broad public administration field and is under the guidance of the co-editors and of the Research Committee of the Institute.

Cette collection de monographies est parrainée par l'Institut d'administration publique du Canada et témoigne de l'effort suivi de l'Institut pour promouvoir et publier des écrits dans le domaine de l'administration publique canadienne. Elle a été conçue comme un complément aux autres publications parrainées par l'Institut telles la Collection administration publique canadienne, le magazine *Management et secteur public*, la revue *Administration publique du Canada* et le Programme de cas en administration publique canadienne, de même que les comptes rendus de ses colloques sur des questions de politique publique. En lançant la collection de monographies pour les ouvrages de longueur moyenne et ceux de nature plus spécialisée, l'Institut s'assure que les auteurs dans le domaine de l'administration publique disposent d'une grande diversité de formats de publications. Bien que les premiers titres traitaient du gouvernement local urbain, la collection s'étend à l'ensemble du domaine de l'administration publique et est sous la direction des co-directeurs de même que du Comité de recherche de l'Institut.

IPAC
The Institute of
Public Administration of Canada

IAPC
L'Institut d'administration
publique du Canada

Monographs on Canadian Public Administration/
Monographies sur l'administration publique canadienne

1. *Shaping the Canadian City: Essays on Urban Politics and Policy, 1890–1920* – John C. Weaver
2. *Structural Changes in Local Government: Government for Urban Regions* – C.R. Tindal
3. *The Politics of Urban Development: Canadian Urban Expressway Disputes* – Christopher Leo
4. *Quebec's Health System: A Debate of Change, 1967–1977* – Sidney S. Lee
5. *An Approach to Manpower Planning and Management Development in Canadian Municipal Government* – Anne B. McAllister
6. *Le côté humain des systèmes d'information: une vue pratique* – Rolland Hurtubise et Pierre Voyer
7. *The Effects of Transition to Confederation on Public Administration in Newfoundland* – J.G. Channing, C.M.
8. *Coordination in Canadian Governments: A Case Study of Aging Policy* – Kenneth Kernaghan and Olivia Kuper
9. *Public Non-Profit Budgeting: The Evolution and Application of Zero-Base Budgeting* – James Cutt and Richard Ritter
10. *Institutions and Influence Groups in Canadian Farm and Food Policy* – J.D. Forbes
11. *Budgeting in the Provinces: Leadership and the Premiers* – Allan M. Maslove (editor)
12. *Getting the Pink Slip: Severances and Firings in the Senior Public Service* – W.A.W. Neilson (editor)
13. *City Management in Canada: The Role of the Chief Administrative Officer (CAO)* – T.J. Plunkett
14. *Taking Power: Managing Government Transitions/Prendre le pouvoir: La gestion des transitions gouvernementales* – Donald J. Savoie (editor / directeur)
15. *Agencies, Boards, and Commissions in Canadian Local Government* – Dale Richmond and David Siegel (editors)
16. *Learning from Others: Administrative Innovations Among Canadian Governments* – James Iain Gow
17. *Hard Choices or No Choices: Assessing Program Review / L'heure des choix difficiles: L'évaluation de l'Examen des programmes* – Amelita Armit and Jacques Bourgault (editors / directeurs)
18. *So-called Experts: How American Consultants Remade the Canadian Civil Service 1918–21* – Alasdair Roberts
19. *Genesis, Termination and Succession in the Life Cycle of Organizations: The Case of the Maritime Resource Management Service* – M. Paul Brown

20. *New Public Management and Public Administration in Canada/Nouveau management public et administration publique au Canada* – Mohamed Charih and Arthur Daniels (editors/directeurs)
21. *Value for Many: The Institute of Public Administration of Canada, 1947–1997/D'une grande valeur pour beaucoup : L'Institut d'administration publique du Canada, 1947–1997* – V. Seymour Wilson